# A SHORT HISTORY OF
# LAOS

**Short History of Asia Series**

*Series Editor: Milton Osborne*
Milton Osborne has had an association with the Asian region for over 40 years as an academic, public servant and independent writer. He is the author of eight books on Asian topics, including *Southeast Asia: An introductory history*, first published in 1979 and now in its eighth edition, and, most recently, *The Mekong: Turbulent past, uncertain future*, published in 2000.

# A SHORT HISTORY OF

# LAOS

## THE LAND IN BETWEEN

Grant Evans

ALLEN&UNWIN

First published in 2002

Copyright © Grant Evans 2002

Allen & Unwin
83 Alexander Street
Crows Nest NSW 2065
Australia
Phone: (61 2) 8425 0100
Fax:     (61 2) 9906 2218
Email:  info@allenandunwin.com
Web:   www.allenandunwin.com

National Library of Australia
Cataloguing-in-Publication entry:

Evans, Grant, 1948– .
   A short history of Laos : the land in between.

   Bibliography.
   Includes index.
   ISBN 1 86448 997 9.

   1. Laos—History. 2. Laos—Politics and government.
   3. Laos—Economic conditions. I. Title. (Series : Short
   histories of Asia).

959.4

Set in 11/14 pt Goudy by Midland Typesetters, Maryborough, Victoria
Printed by South Wind Production, Singapore

10 9 8 7 6 5 4 3 2 1

# CONTENTS

Laos. (US Central Intelligence Agency, Washington DC, 1993)

# Preface

Laos stands at the crossroads of mainland Southeast Asia. Surrounded by China, Vietnam, Cambodia, Thailand and Burma, this small country has been both a bridge and buffer between neighbours who, in glory days, provided a field of territorial expansion by Lao kings. Yet more often than not Laos has been an arena in which more powerful neighbours and their allies have interfered. In the 1950s Laos, newly independent from France, set out to build a modern society but was soon engulfed by the Vietnam War, which brought with it invading North Vietnamese troops and high-flying US bombers that wreaked havoc. Few states could have survived the enormous pressure the Royal Lao Government came under in those years and, not surprisingly, it was finally crushed. The harsh communist regime that came to power in 1975 drove perhaps one-tenth of the population into exile. Just how this came about is part of the story that follows.

Visitors to Laos are usually charmed by the people's grace and good humour, and are consequently prone to romanticise the country. Lao also traffic in romantic images of themselves, but the idea of an 'untouched' Southeast Asian idyll has its flipside: Laos is one of the least developed countries in the world. Thus, successive Lao governments have been committed to 'development', and millions upon millions of aid dollars have flowed into the country—too often straight into the pockets of its leaders, and too often creating a psychology of dependency. In the following pages I have tried to give some sense of the way Lao culture confronted and grappled with the dilemmas of social and political change. Unfortunately, the 'untouchedness' so beloved by tourists is often a consequence of failed development plans and enforced communist isolation for almost two decades. Young Lao today are impatient for real change.

This book is mainly intended for inquiring tourists, journalists, consultants, diplomats, businesspeople and students. But I have also written it with young Lao in mind, both those overseas who know little of their homeland, and for Lao inside Laos whose information on their past is limited. I sincerely hope that it will soon be translated into both Lao and Thai, for the Thai also need to understand their nearest neighbour.

Although I have not burdened the book with academic argument, its investigation of key events in new ways presents serious challenges to those who are familiar with Lao history. It offers new ideas and new information, accompanied by many photographs that have not been published before. Footnotes have been kept to a minimum and a list of selected further reading is provided at the end.

# Acknowledgments

Several people generously set aside time to read the text and helped me to clarify many points. I asked my old friend Stuart Macintyre, who is one of Australia's leading historians, to read it because he knew little about Laos and could draw my attention to things specialists take for granted. His renowned meticulousness has ensured that the following pages are clear to other novices. The response of Soren Ivarsson, one of a new generation of historians of Laos, made me feel easier about some of the readings of Lao history that I have advanced in the following pages. Thongrith Phoumirath, in exile in Australia, reassured me that the text spoke to Lao people, even if it doesn't always speak in terms that are familiar to them. Peter Koret kindly allowed me to reproduce part of his translation of the poem 'Leup Pha Sun' in the opening chapter. Others have helped in various ways, but especially through discussions and the sharing of information. They are George Dalley, Arthur Dommen, Chris Goscha, Joel Halpern, Pheuiphanh Ngaosyvathn, Phouvong Phimmasone (who sadly passed away during its composition) and Prince Mangkra Souvannaphouma. The librarians at the Kennedy Library, Boston, were especially helpful when I visited there. Rosemary de Dear's wizardry sharpened many of the photos. Finally, I would like to thank Milton Osborne for inviting me to write for the Short Histories of Asia series. I had never thought of writing an historical overview of Laos, but doing so has helped me clarify things about the country's past that have bothered me for years.

*Grant Evans,*
*Hong Kong*

# Note on transcription

Generally I have tried to follow the system laid down by the American National Standards Institute in their *System for the Romanization of Lao, Khmer, and Pali* published in 1979. However, all researchers on Laos are confounded both by the absence of any generally accepted system of transcription to date, and by convention. I have deviated from the above system to conform both to the spelling contained in the modern map used for this book, and to conventional spellings. Thus, most renderings of the letter 'S' for Lao words tend to use the French transcription 'X', and so what should in the American system be, for example, Lan Sang is rendered Lan Xang, or Siang Khoang as Xiang Khoang, while King Samsaenthai is rendered with an 'S' rather than an 'X' out of convention, and Chiang Mai is rendered with a 'Ch' rather than an 'X' to conform to recognised practice. Similarly with personal names, such as Phui, which is spelled by convention as Phoui, and Suvanna, which by convention is Souvanna.

# Note on 'Lao' or 'Laos'

Some confusion has emerged among visitors to Laos and foreigners working there about whether it is more correct to call the country 'Laos' or 'Lao' because the 's' is absent in the Lao language.

Historical sources suggest that the first writing of the term 'Laos' was in a Portuguese dictionary created by missionaries based in Macau. It is possible that the French and English borrowed from this source, but there is a reason why an 's' may be added to 'Lao', and that is to transform it into a noun. Thus, the term 'Lao' is an adjective; with the 's' added it becomes a noun. This is a logical solution to a linguistic problem within most European languages. Therefore I have opted in this book for the terms 'Laos' for the country and 'Lao' as an adjective. For the latter 'Laotian' is used by some writers. This is also correct, although I do not use it.

Laos with an 's' was one solution in English for the country's name. It could have been 'Lao', but it may well have been 'Lao-land', by literal translation from the Lao, *Muang Lao* or *Pathet Lao*. This of course happened with Thailand when *Prathet Thai* was translated as 'Thai-land'. Indeed, the latter has become so entrenched through tourist promotion and encounters with foreigners that one now often sees 'Thai-laen' written in Thai. But, for reasons that are obscure, *Pathet Lao* is not 'Lao-land', although it could quite easily have been.

In Lao the 's' is not necessary because 'Lao' is almost always assisted by another word, for example *khon* Lao for a Lao person, or *Muang* Lao for the country. Of course, many Lao when speaking English are likely to say 'Lao' instead of 'Laos', just as many Italians speaking English are probably tempted to say 'Italia' rather than 'Italy'. In other words, they assimilate the pronunciation to their own language's speech norms. Most of us have a tendency to do this when speaking a second language. It does not, however, make it correct.

As far as I am aware the Lao People's Democratic Republic has no official position on the usages of either 'Lao' or 'Laos' in English. The English language *Vientiane Times* newspaper uses Laos for the country, which perhaps makes this use semi-official.

# Glossary

| | |
|---|---|
| *ban* | village |
| *ban nok* | country bumpkin |
| *boun* | Buddhist merit |
| *chao khwaeng* | provincial governor |
| *chao muang* | lord of the muang |
| *kha* | designates subordinate status, applied generally to minorities in the traditional system |
| *khun* | aristocrat |
| *khwaeng* | province |
| *kiatong* | district head in Hmong areas under the French |
| *lak muang* | chao muang's protective spirit |
| *mandala* | model of the cosmos and the world |
| *muang* | district, and also a traditional concept of political space |
| *Neo Lao Hak Xat* | Lao Patriotic Front |
| *ouparat* | viceroy |
| *Pathet Lao* | popular name for the Neo Lao Hak Xat |
| *phi* | spirit, or ghost |
| *phi muang* | protective spirit of the muang |
| *phu mi boun* | man of exceptional merit |
| *phu nyai* | 'big man', powerful individual |
| *phu sao* | young unmarried woman |
| *phu viset* | man of supernatural power |
| *sakdi na* | traditional system of ranking developed in Ayudhya |
| *saksit* | magically potent |
| *Sangha* | the organisation of Buddhist monks |
| *tasseng* | sub-district |
| *than* | sir |
| *vat* | temple |
| *vinyan* | spirit |

# Acronyms

| | |
|---|---|
| ASEAN | Association of Southeast Asian Nations |
| CDNI | Committee for the Defence of the National Interest |
| CIA | Central Intelligence Agency (US) |
| DRV | Democratic Republic of Vietnam |
| IMF | International Monetary Fund |
| LPDR | Lao People's Democratic Republic |
| LPRP | Lao People's Revolutionary Party |
| NLHX | Lao Patriotic Front (Neo Lao Hak Xat) |
| NLSX | Lao Front for National Construction (Neo Lao Sang Xat) |
| NVA | North Vietnamese Army |
| PL | Pathet Lao |
| RLG | Royal Lao Government |
| USAID | United States Aid for International Development |

# 1
# BEFORE LAOS

At the end of the nineteenth century Laos emerged as a national entity. This was the culmination of a long and often chaotic historical process in which the traditional kingdoms of mainland Southeast Asia fought with each other and often absorbed one another. Disparate populations of ethnic Tai and other ethnic groups were slowly moulded by the influence of Theravada Buddhism, which gradually ensured a broad cultural continuity across the region. Nevertheless, local differences remained important. Although the Lao kingdom, Lan Xang, was a major regional player in the fifteenth century, it and subsequent Lao kingdoms were overshadowed by the kingdoms that emerged in what is today known as Thailand. Landlocked and distant from the economic and political changes brought to the region by European expansion, the inland kingdoms of the Lao almost disappeared in the nineteenth century while neighbouring states were consolidated. Only French colonial expansion averted, perhaps, the absorption of Laos by Thailand and Vietnam.

# The Tai

'Tai' is a general linguistic category that at one time may also have referred to a broadly shared culture. The Tai people are believed to have originated in the region of southern Kwangsi, China, and under pressure from an expanding Chinese empire began to march south-west sometime in the first millennium CE (common era). Today the Tai are spread across the whole of mainland Southeast Asia. They are found along the southern borderlands of China, in northern Vietnam and Burma, in northeastern India and, of course, form the majority in Laos and Thailand. The Tai who remain in the high mountain valleys of northern Laos and Vietnam have been called 'tribal' because they never formed states. The Tai who descended to the plains and formed states, however, crossed both a cultural and a political watershed.

It would be centuries, however, before the units we know today as Laos or Thailand emerged from a complex regional history in which Tai people were key actors. Indeed, prior to the nineteenth century it makes little sense to use the ethnic terms 'Lao' or 'Thai', although it is common for national histories to project such entities into the distant past. I believe that this kind of nationalist historiography distorts our under-standing of how the modern world came into being, hence I have called the period covered in this opening chapter 'before Laos'. But equally it is 'before Thailand, Cambodia, Burma, Vietnam or China', to name just the states which encircle modern Laos. It sometimes becomes difficult to avoid using these names, however, and out of convenience I have used them from time to time. But if we really wish to understand the pre-modern period in Southeast Asia then we must try to enter a world which thought of itself in very different terms from our own.

A key physical feature of the landlocked area that would become modern Laos is the Central Vietnamese Cordillera that runs from north to south, along which the country's eastern border is located.

There are other secondary ranges, and to the north of the capital Vientiane is found the highest peak, Phu Bia, 2818 metres. It is out of these ranges that all the main rivers flow, running from east to west into the Mekong River, and it is along the rivers that one finds the alluvial flood plains suitable for rice paddy fields. There are no other lowland plains of any note. While upland soils are not in general very fertile, there are two important upland plains areas: one in the north in Xiang Khoang Province, the rolling grasslands of the Plain of Jars, and the other the Boloven Plateau in Champasak Province in the south, with fertile soil supporting increasing numbers of coffee plantations. Most of the country, however, is rugged and mountainous and covered by monsoon forests that contain a relatively rich wildlife. The whole country lies in a tropical monsoon climatic region.

Mainland Southeast Asia at the time the Tai began their migrations was covered in forest and inhabited by ethnically diverse peoples who spoke languages belonging to the Austronesian and Mon-Khmer families. In the Laos of today these peoples form part of the country's complex ethnic mosaic and live mainly in the mountain ranges. The Tai who moved into the upland valleys of Indochina long ago were led by warrior chiefs, 'men of prowess' who were acknowledged by their deeds to have unusual amounts of powerful 'soul stuff'. It was this sense of innate differences between individuals, found across the region, that would later enable the rapid absorption of Hindu ideas from India, with elaborate ideologies of caste difference and state building. The warrior Tai moved steadily along the mountain valleys, conquering the indigenous groups they found in their path, who became subordinate members of Tai villages and polities. The conquered peoples were called *kha*, a modern translation of which is 'slave'. This rendering, however, fails to capture the peculiarities of a stratified society in which conquered peoples were tied to overlords, and through a process of intermarriage assimilated to the culture of the Tai. Indeed, this process of miscegenation was fundamental to Tai expansion.

## Tai social organisation

Besides answering the ecological imperatives of an expanding population, conquest was a way of continually confirming the prowess of the warrior chieftains. They developed notions of aristocratic lineages that in turn gave rise to myths of origin, a variation of which is the Lao myth of *Khun Bulom*, shared widely among the northern Tai. In this myth three aristocrats (*khun*) intercede between earth and heaven after a great flood. Among the gifts they receive from the gods is a buffalo which, after it dies several years later, produces a vine out of its nostril from which grows a gourd. Upon hearing voices from within the gourd the *khun* pierce it. Thereupon: 'All those who, born in the gourds, came out through the hole cut with the chisel were Tai, while those who came out through the hole burned [by the hot iron] were Kha. Both were servants and subjects of the three *khun*.'[1] The charcoal from their burns marked the darker Kha as inferior. The Tai were arms-bearing commoners, while the descendants of the *khun* were the overlords of all.

In those days, looking down from the mountains on to the Tai habitat in the upland valleys, one would see compact established villages with sturdy thatched houses raised on stilts. Running through the valleys are rivers, a swift means of transport for the Tai and an important source of food. Among the houses some stand out as large longhouses. These belong to the chiefly lineages. Around the village are fields for growing wet rice, sometimes in terraces, which are owned in common by the villagers. Parcels of these fields are redistributed annually according to need. On the slopes of the surrounding hills patches of forest have been burnt away to plant fields of dry rice, and also cotton and maize. If the village was new, the slopes would be covered with such slash-and-burn fields and the houses would be more like bush huts.

At the core of the villages of new settlers would be a band of Tai warriors sent to conquer new land and any people holding it.

Politically these warriors remained attached to their original village, and in this way several villages formed themselves into a *muang* (district) headed by a paramount chief. The *muang* has remained a central feature of Tai cultures and societies, the key aspect of which is the hierarchical encompassment of smaller units. Villages make up a small *muang*, and several small *muang* can make up a large *muang*, and the latter at times could become a *muang* confederation. This structure of similar segments could be galvanised into action in times of war, or might disintegrate quickly as new alliances formed.

Parallel to this sociopolitical structure ran a hierarchy of territorial spirits. House spirits were encompassed by the village tutelary spirit, just as the latter was subordinate to the spirits of the *muang*, the *phi muang*; these higher level spirits would be called together once a year or for major events. The *chao muang*, the paramount chief, had his own protective spirit, a *lak muang*, embodied in a wooden post often placed outside his house, to which offerings were also made. When he died or was killed the post would be removed by his successor, who would have his own magically powerful *lak*. In a sense, the old chief's 'soul stuff' died with him. Many of these features of Tai social structure would persist after the momentous changes that overtook the Tai when they reached the plains of mainland Southeast Asia.

## Contact with lowland states

The Tai who remained in the mountains of southern China and northern Vietnam were influenced by these two civilisations over the centuries. They adopted aspects of Sinitic belief; their aristocrats in particular were incorporated into these states as vassals and began to adopt their dress styles. It was probably through this lengthy encounter with the Viet states that the upland Tai acquired the classifications of Black, White and Red Tai by which they are known in Laos and Vietnam today.

The Tai who marched further southwest came into contact with very different civilisations, the Buddhist culture of Dvaravati, usually associated with the Mon people, and the empire of Angkor. On their way the Tai may also have encountered a Mon-Khmer chieftainship on the Plain of Jars. Still to be seen in places on the plain are large megalithic funerary jars used for the burial of nobles, characteristic of a culture that grew up around trade routes crossing the plain on their way to the Khorat Plateau or to Yunnan. The culture collapsed when this trade was disrupted, perhaps helped along by the expansionist and warlike Tai.

Dvaravati culture also sprang up along trade routes, in this case strung out along the rim of the Central Plain of Thailand between Angkor and Burma and beyond. Buddha images connected to this culture have been found by archaeologists in Laos, in both northern Vientiane province and the Luang Phrabang area. While little is known of the Dvaravati, archaeological remains show that it was an extensive and prosperous Buddhist civilisation. It was this culture that some groups of Tai would have first encountered as they descended from the mountain valleys and through it exposed for the first time to Buddhism.

The Dvaravati were overwhelmed not by the Tai, however, but by the rapid expansion of the Angkor empire in the ninth century, westwards and northwards over large swathes of modern Thailand and Laos. This Hinduised kingdom led by its Siva-like 'God Kings' was the regional pioneer of what has come to be known as the 'mandala' state model. Mandalas, often represented in Buddhist or Hindu art as circles, model an idea of the cosmos that includes the human body and the state. In relation to the state, the mandala represented a geopolitical idea used to discuss the spatial configuration and fluctuation of friendly and enemy states, from the point of view of a particular kingdom, a model that the later Tai states would adopt from Angkor. These mandala states were focused on sacred centres ruled by a king who had direct access to divine power and used that power to create worldly order. The magnificent Angkor temple complex stands as a monument to this world view and as a material statement of the king's worldly power. Mandalas at their extremities waxed and waned, shading off into vassal states and peoples. During expansionary phases of a mandala, smaller states were drawn directly into its realm; when it contracted they regained their autonomy or perhaps became attached to an adjacent mandala. Sacred centres, and not sacred territories and boundaries, were the preoccupation of these polities, which were made up of personalised networks focused on the king rather than territorial units. The king's innate spiritual power attracted followers, and had to be shown to attract even greater numbers of followers, as expansion in the known world demonstrated prowess and spiritual potency. This spiritual prowess was not automatically transmitted to sons, however, thus the death of a king threatened to unravel the structure of personal loyalties making up any particular mandala.

At the centre of the Angkor mandala the population was made up mainly of Khmer peoples. While it is highly unlikely that the majority then saw themselves in ethnic terms, ethnicity is a favourite trope of historians of the region. Of course, as one moved further from the empire's centre so the populations ruled by it became more diverse culturally, and on its northern fringes these included the Tai. Macro-ethnic categories for these groups lay in the future; then they would have seen themselves as simply the people from a particular village or local area who had been drawn into a hierarchically organised cultural and political system. Xai Fong, which lies just outside Vientiane, was an important centre of this empire, as were the Khmer temple ruins, or *vat phu*, in Champasak in the south of Laos. The Tai who were drawn into this system, their chiefs as local officials, the rest as commoners, began to assimilate many elements of Hinduised Khmer culture.

## The spread of Buddhism

The Buddhism spread in the region by the Dvaravati had continued as localised cultural custom under Angkor rule, and Tai groups who moved down onto the northern lowland plains began to adopt Buddhist practices from their neighbours. Various ethnic groups intermixed, especially Mon and Tai communities, with the suppression of internecine warfare by the Angkor state facilitating cultural exchange. In the late twelfth century, the Khmer King Jayavarman VII (r.1181–1201) introduced Mahayana Buddhist practices into his state-craft. The thirteenth century witnessed momentous changes across the region. After Jayavarman VII died, Angkor went into rapid decline. Mongol armies crippled the kingdoms of Dali in the far north (in southern China) and Pagan (Burma) to the west. As these regional powers waned, warrior confederations and statelets were able to emerge, and soon flourished as the first Tai states. The most important was Lan Na, under King Mangrai (r.1259–1317) who built his capital at Chiang Mai. Lan Na encompassed *muang* from regions which now lie inside modern Burma, southern China and northern Laos. The Kingdom of Sukhothai, to the south of Lan Na, emerged soon after, listing among its vassals states the region of Luang Phrabang. By this time Theravada Buddhism from Sri Lanka had spread from the south and conquered the hearts and minds of the peoples of Angkor, Lan Na and Sukhothai. While Brahmanic ritual continued to surround these Buddhist kings, they were not god kings, but more like incarnate Buddhas or bodhisattvas, whose power derived from their accumulated merit (*boun*), which they used to create a righteous world order. While these are recognised as the first Tai kingdoms it is important to remember that they ruled over polyethnic populations, including remnant Khmers.

The Tai had diversified culturally during their migrations, acquiring rituals and habits from the peoples they conquered or coexisted with, and they invented new cultural practices combining elements from these groups. When cultural differences among the Tai were recorded much later, especially by Europeans, macro-categories such as 'Tai Lue' or 'Shan' were applied to them, whereas the ordinary people saw themselves in localised terms as people from a particular village or region. Anthropological studies of Tai even in the late twentieth century have demonstrated the continuing importance of this parochialism, and we can be certain that it was even more pronounced in the thirteenth and fourteenth centuries. While Buddhism easily encompassed the pre-existing diverse cultural practices of the Tai, most importantly it provided a framework for conceptualising the Tai beyond their localised practices. Henceforth a fundamental marker of lowland Tai identity would be Buddhism.

# The Lan Xang kingdom

It was the foundation of the kingdom of Ayudhya in 1351 (north of modern day Bangkok) and its military competition with Sukhothai to its north that provided the space for the formation of the kingdom of Lan Xang in Luang Phrabang. At the time Luang Phrabang was a vassal *muang* on the edge of the Lan Na and Sukhothai mandalas. The founder of Lan Xang, Fa Ngum, had been exiled to Angkor along with his father after the latter had seduced one of the minor wives of the *chao muang*, the lord, of Luang Phrabang. The locale of his exile was indicative of the continuing political sway of Angkor in the region. There seems little doubt that Fa Ngum himself was a vassal of Angkor, and it is possible that he was of Khmer descent.

In these mandala polities where ties of personal loyalty were paramount, the offering of royal daughters as wives to the leaders of subordinate *muang* was a key stratagem of statecraft, and indeed Fa Ngum married a Khmer princess, Keo Keng Nya. In late 1351, as Angkor came under pressure from an ascendant Ayudhya, Fa Ngum was dispatched at the head of a mainly Khmer army in an attempt to reimpose Angkor's control over the northern Khorat Plateau. His conquests augmented his army and he began a march north to capture *muang* Sua (Luang Phrabang). He was unable to subdue the reigning lord at Vientiane, but an exiled aristocrat from *muang* Phuan on the Plain of Jars assisted his conquest there, from where he could conquer *muang* Sua. His uncle, who was on the throne, committed suicide and in 1353 Fa Ngum became lord of *muang* Sua. His success in warfare had built up his prowess and gathered around him lords of other *muang* as personal vassals. From this base he began the construction of the kingdom of Lan Xang. Angkor could not rein in this rogue vassal, challenged as the kingdom was by the forces of Ayudhya and Sukhothai, and the latter were too preoccupied with each other and Angkor to notice the burgeoning new Tai kingdom.

Fa Ngum sent his forces north to draw the various *muang* there into his mandala, until they came up against the power of Lan Na. Then Fa Ngum marched his armies south to subdue the lord of Vientiane and other *muang* down along the Mekong River as far as Nakhon Phanom. Upon returning to his capital, now called Xiang Dong Xiang Thong, he announced the foundation of the Kingdom of Lan Xang Hom Khao, 'a million elephants under a white parasol', symbols that proclaimed military might and kingship. While Lan Xang was a Buddhist kingdom like those of Ayudhya and Sukhothai, its cultural roots lay closer to the tribal Tai than did theirs. This is most apparent in the centrality of ritual sacrifices made to the territorial spirits of *muang* Lan Xang, in which the *phi* and *chao* of subordinate *muang* would gather in the capital for grand sacrifices. Furthermore, the laws associated with this state, the *kotmai thammasat Khun Bulom*, are unsystematic and show little influence of Buddhism, as later *kotmai thammasat* would. While later chronicles credit Fa Ngum with introducing Buddhism to the Lao, we have seen that Buddhism was already widespread in the region; Lan Xang was simply the first Buddhist kingdom based in Luang Phrabang.

## Buddhism and society

The importance of Buddhism was that it provided a universal ideology able to draw disparate peoples into a common cultural framework. Furthermore, for a leader of a mandala the Buddhist *Sangha*, the organisation of monks as a church, of which the king was the supreme protector, provided a rival source of metaphysical power to the territorially based

*During the New Year in Luang Phrabang the masks of the tutelary spirits of the muang, Phu Nyoe, Nya Nyoe and the lion king Sing Keo Sing Kham (centre), are activated by their mediums before they parade through the streets during purification ceremonies.*
*(Courtesy EFEO)*

spirits embodied in the *lak muang*, and therefore was a means of weakening the power of these local spirits and the metaphysical power of local lords. Buddhism encompassed these spirits, often quite literally behind the walls of its temples. The *lak muang* of Vientiane, for instance, is

11

completely encased within Vat Simuang. Similarly, with the Buddhisation of ethnic groups, the temple replaced the central men's houses or, among the Tai, displaced the longhouses of the aristocrats. In the past most temples were made of wood and thatch, with their Buddha images also carved out of wood, and hardly stood out architecturally as they do today, being often the only mortar and cement building in a rural village. It was only in the main centres of power that large, sturdy temple structures were built, with large Buddha images either cast in metal or carved out of stone.

As the temples became established as the main ritual centres for the communities, so *sing saksit*, magical objects, gravitated towards them and were encompassed. These could be something as simple as a rock or a peculiarly shaped piece of wood. Outside the temple precincts local magical places, trees or maybe caves, were incorporated into the Buddhist ethos as Buddha images whose power could mediate between the local spirits and a larger religious world were placed there. Many western historians, especially from monotheistic Christian backgrounds, find this syncretism (blending) puzzling or inconsistent. But except in the most austere textually oriented religious sects, syncretism of this kind is common the world over. Buddhism as a pure theology provides little practical guidance for the everyday uncertainties of love, fertility and death, and hence humans seek clues to the future and solicit assistance through magical objects or places, or people such as spirit mediums. Protective amulets, whether of penises or Buddha images, are almost universal in the religious repertoire. Wherever Buddhism spread it absorbed local beliefs and practices, giving rise to forms that varied slightly from place to place.

While Buddhism was instrumental in creating a unified kingdom, Lan Xang faced serious material constraints to its ability to rival the other Tai kingdoms, especially the one emerging in Ayudhya. In the valley plains of the north, the peasantry continued to combine paddy and dry rice cultivation, producing small surpluses and supporting populations much less dense than was possible on the larger

Vientiane plain to the south where the peasantry engaged only in paddy cultivation. For this reason, as the kingdom grew, its centre of power gravitated towards Vientiane and eventually the capital was relocated there. Oddly, there is little evidence that the state ever sponsored irrigation as a way of augmenting its economic surplus. The construction of dams and irrigation networks was left to local communities. The relatively small surpluses restricted the taxes and *corvée* (labour) that could be levied on the peasantry and thus the scale of public works that could be carried out, whether it be building roads or major temple complexes and cities.

The other main source of revenue for Lan Xang was trade in forest products such as sticklac, cardamom and beeswax, which were supplied primarily by minorities who remained in the mountains, some still as hunter-gatherers. This economic connection underpinned the ritual relationship between the Lan Xang court and the surrounding minorities, the *kha*. Indicative of the relative weakness of the king's power was that, unlike the King of Ayudhya, Fa Ngum could not monopolise trade in these goods. Another source of revenue, of course, was war and plunder, and the capture of slaves augmented the population under the kingdom's control. While each new addition to the kingdom added to the tribute sent to the central court, the flows were not great by comparison with neighbouring kingdoms.

## Crises of succession

Fa Ngum was deposed around 1374 and sent into exile in *muang* Nan for abusing his power, especially for asserting seignorial rights over women of the leading families. Some have suggested that the balance of power shifted against Fa Ngum and the Khmer lords who had followed him from Angkor following the death of his Khmer wife several years earlier. He was replaced by his eldest son Unhoen, better known as Samsaenthai, who had grown up in a Tai milieu and was perhaps more attuned to the cultural ways of the emerging mandala. He took wives from the kingdoms of Ayudhya, Lan Na and Xiang Hung in the north, assuring his kingdom a period of peaceful consolidation, and also from local families and lords, thus treading a well established path for cementing alliances or acknowledging tributary status. The fragility of political structures built on personal connections that only last for an individual's lifetime was dramatised some years later following the short reign of Samsaenthai's son, Lan Kham Deng, whose death plunged Lan Xang into a prolonged succession crisis.

Crises of succession were endemic to all the Tai polities at the time. The king attracted followers by his prowess, which he manifested by sponsoring the building of temples and reliquaries all over his kingdom, and by waging war. A key way of cementing alliances throughout the kingdom was through marriage—both the taking of wives and the offering of daughters. A king's various wives gave their respective families and relatives access to power, and around such families factions would form. These families would make alliances with the families of other key figures associated with the court. As far as we know, there was no established order for a son's succession and therefore if a faction in favour of one particular son was not clearly dominant upon the death of the king, murderous disputes could break out among the rival claimants to the throne. An ambitious son backed by a powerful faction could depose, and indeed murder, his father. Few loyalties, it seems, were sacrosanct and factional alliances were in continual flux. Their volatility was fed by a deep-seated competitive concern with status and prestige, with slights and perceived loss of face a sufficient reason to move one's allegiances.

After more than twenty years and the rapid ascent and overthrow of several claimants to the throne, King Xaiyna Chakhaphat (r.1442–79) imposed his will and secured the kingdom by appointing his six sons and other close relatives to key administrative positions in the realm. His capital was Luang Phrabang. The long succession crisis had weakened Lan Xang, yet Xaiyna Chakhaphat would make little change to the personalised structure of rule, instead bolstering the role of Buddhism in the kingdom. His rule was brought undone by the rise of the powerful Le dynasty in Vietnam, which declared its suzerainty over the Plain of Jars, and when it encountered opposition invaded Luang Phrabang. The king's son, with support from the principality of Nan, dispersed the Le forces and retook the capital of Lan Xang and its devastated territories. He became the new king, Suvanna Banlang, ruling briefly, and was succeeded on his death first by his younger brother La Saen Thai (r.1486–96), then his son Somphu (r.1496–1501) and then Vixun (r.1501–20), also a younger brother. Challenged by the powerful Sinitic civilisation to its east, these kings quickly established close relations with Ayudhya, now the most powerful Tai state in the region, and political, cultural and commercial influences flowed from there into the re-emergent kingdom of Lan Xang.

# Rise and fall of Lan Xang

The sixteenth century saw the rise of Lan Xang to the height of its power, although even at its height it remained in the shadow of Ayudhya, the other major Tai kingdom in the region. In the previous century Ayudhya had begun a crucial process of bureaucratic central-isation, which accelerated in the sixteenth century. Ayudhya's centre of gravity had moved south as it began to incorporate the Malay penin-sula into its mandala, which enabled it to capitalise on the rapid expansion in international trade that was taking place in the fifteenth and sixteenth centuries. Through his increasingly centralised state the king was able to monopolise international trade and further strengthen both the crown's power vis-à-vis rival noble houses and regional elites, and the kingdom's power vis-à-vis the interior states of Lan Na and Lan Xang, which could not participate directly in this maritime trade.

The reigns of the kings Vixun (1501–20), Phothisarat (1520–47) and Sethathirat (1548–71), while together constituting a glorious period for Lan Xang, did not initiate any fundamental structural changes to the kingdom. Their reigns saw the increasing elaboration of the regalia of Buddhist kingship; Vixun is best remembered for installing the Phra Bang as the palladium (protector) of the Lan Xang kings. This Buddha image from Sri Lanka had made its way as far as Vientiane, in the company of Buddhist missionaries from Angkor, in the time of Fa Ngum. Legend has it that the Buddha refused to proceed to the northern capital because of premonitions of the latter's fall from grace. Finally called north by a righteous monarch, the image was installed in Vat Vixun. Before it the lords would swear loyalty to their king, and hereafter the capital would be recognised as Luang Phrabang, 'the place of the Buddha Phra Bang'.

The construction of temples and the installation of sacred Buddha images made the centre of a mandala its most sacred and therefore most powerful place, yet linked to all other sacred places in the state. Kings would sponsor the construction of stupas and temples in outer regions as physical expressions of this sacred power and link them through ceremonial to the rituals of the centre. Thus King Phothisarat, for example, erected new monastic buildings around That Phanom at the southern limits of Lan Xang and provided slaves for its upkeep. Ritual centralisation was pursued most strenuously by Phothisarat. He issued a decree in 1527 that appears to have been primarily directed against the worship associated with *lak muang* and other regional spirits, which was controlled by local lords, and led to the destruction of major shrines. While Phothisarat's endeavour to establish royal control over politico-regligious ritual was generally successful, the continued worship at *ho phi* (spirit shrines) by aristocratic families well into the twentieth century shows that these practices were never obliterated.

Political control of the kingdom, however, remained structured along personal lines. Although relations between mandalas continued to be cemented by marriages, strains between factions at court or between regional lords could easily erupt, as demonstrated in a revolt by *muang* Phuan on the Plain of Jars in 1532. Phothisarat's principal queen was the daughter of the king of Lan Na. When Lan Na fell into

*The royal palladium, the Phra Bang, is brought to the royal temple, Vat Mai, in Luang Phrabang during New Year for purification rites. (Courtesy EFEO)*

one of the perennial succession disputes that plagued the Tai world, the forces of Ayudhya, taking advantage of the disarray, marched on Chiang Mai and were only repulsed when Lan Xang came to Lan Na's rescue. This led to the installation in 1546 of Phothisarat's son Sethathirat, and his queen from Chiang Mai, on the throne of Lan Na, thus making Lan Na a vassal state and vastly extending the domain of

Lan Xang. This would only last a short time—within thirteen months Phothisarat died and Sethathirat was forced to rush back home to thwart his younger brothers' attempts to take the throne, probably backed by regional families in Vientiane from where Phothisarat had conducted most of his rule. Sethathirat established himself in Luang Phrabang with his noble allies there. His wife, who had been left in Chiang Mai as a symbol of his rule, soon fell victim to a resurgent local nobility and Sethathirat was unable to reassert Lan Xang's control over Lan Na. The inevitable succession crisis invited outside intervention from the west and Lan Na soon became a vassal state of Pegu (Burma), and would remain so for the next two centuries. Members of the Lan Na elite, many of whom were connected to Sethathirat by marriage, fled to Lan Xang, bringing with them a sudden infusion of Lan Na cultural influence to Luang Phrabang and Vientiane.

The threat from the kingdom of Pegu forced Sethathirat to relocate his capital to Vientiane. He brought with him the palladium he had acquired in Chiang Mai, the now fabled Phra Keo, the Emerald Buddha, which he installed in the Vat Phra Keo, a majestic new temple built on the banks of the Mekong. The Phra Bang remained in the northern capital, where Sethathirat also built a fabulous new royal temple as a symbol of his kingship, the Vat Xieng Thong, a marvel of northern Tai architecture. But perhaps the most powerful symbol of his kingship was the That Luang, the massive stupa he ordered built in Vientiane as the symbolic centre of his kingdom. The more populous plains of Vientiane and the northern Khorat Plateau made available the labour and wealth required for this spurt in Buddhist monument building, which established Lan Xang as a truly grand Tai kingdom.

But Lan Xang could not stand alone against the power of Pegu. Sethathirat now sought a close relationship with Ayudhya, and in 1560 he and King Chakrapat erected a memorial stupa to their alliance at Danxai (now in Thailand's Loei Province) on the watershed between the Chao Phraya and Mekong river systems. This was not a

*The That Luang, or Grand Stupa, in Vientiane, c.1953. Built by King Sethathirat in the mid-sixteenth century, the That Luang has become the central symbol of Laos. (Courtesy EFEO)*

modern border marker, as some later writers would like to imagine, only a symbol of the balance between two powerful sovereigns. The alliance was soon at war with Pegu, whose army repulsed them and marched on Lan Xang, carrying off members of the royal family and booty. Lan Xang and Ayudhya rallied and regained some of the northern reaches of Ayudhya. The king of Pegu then amassed a huge army and marched again on Ayudhya in 1568, sacking the kingdom in the following year. The army of Pegu then occupied Vientiane, but soon withdrew. Thereafter, briefly, Sethathirat was in charge of the only substantial Tai kingdom in the region. He died mysteriously in 1571

19

while campaigning in the southern reaches of the kingdom. A succession dispute invited renewed intervention by Pegu, who installed as their vassal a younger brother of Sethathirat who had been carried off in the years previous. For the next 30 years Lan Xang was a vassal state of Pegu, although towards the end of this period the latter's power was waning. During that time bloody succession disputes ravaged the ruling families in Vientiane, and only in 1638 did a clear leader emerge who was crowned King Surinyavongsa (r.1638–95), ending almost 70 years of political crisis for Lan Xang.

## Lang Xang and the wider world

Interestingly, it is from Surinyavongsa's reign that we have one of the first European descriptions of events in the kingdom of Lan Xang. A mission headed by a Dutch merchant, Gerrit van Wuystoff, reached Vientiane in November 1641 at the height of the That Luang Festival and, as the merchant recorded in his journal in a fascinating account of the pomp at the court of Lan Xang, they were taken to the environs of the stupa to be received by the king:

> Round about us on every side the noblemen had pitched their tents and prepared camps for their soldiers, their elephants and their horses; there was so much noise and bustle that you could have thought yourself with the army of the Prince of Orange [in Holland]. They kept us waiting during an hour. Then, seated on a white elephant, the King arrived from the town and passed in front of our tents: we did as the others were doing, and knelt down on the path; he is a man of around twenty-three. About three hundred soldiers marched in front of him with lances and rifles; behind him, a few elephants with armed men followed behind several musicians. After that came another two thousand soldiers who were followed by sixteen elephants carrying the King's five wives.[2]

The arrival of the Dutch merchant signalled the arrival of the larger maritime trading world in Vientiane, some 100 years after the Portuguese had first made contact with Ayudhya. This time-lag in itself demonstrated the relative insularity of the Lan Xang kingdom. The outside world had been known by hearsay, especially from travellers who had been to Ayudhya, and the products of this world had made their impression on warfare in the region in the form of musketry and cannon. Products from Lan Xang had also reached the wider world via the trading monopolies of Siam. Ayudhya had long been a cosmopolitan kingdom with agents from all over Asia and Europe, and in the coming years it would develop into one of Asia's major trading cities. Such economic development and sophistication, however, would elude Lan Xang.

It is around this time that we begin to see the formation of macro-ethnic categories for the Tai. Chinese navigators had named what is now called the Gulf of Siam, Hs'iem, and it was towards the end of the thirteenth century that Chinese sources began to refer to the Tai of Sukhothai by the same name. No doubt in trading circles this blossomed into 'Siamese' for the people and 'Siam' for the land. The term 'Tai' first appears in written form during the Sukhothai period. But here it appears to retain its primary meaning as 'person', a usage still found in Lao where one may use *Tai ban* to mean a person of the village, *Tai Vientiane* to mean a person of Vientiane city, *Tai Sam Neua* to refer to a person from a region, or indeed, *Tai Lao* for a Lao person or persons.

The most important distinction in the Tai world at that time was between Buddhists and non-Buddhists. These kingdoms were organised as hierarchical societies in which classifications of people implied hierarchy. Even the highest lord of the kingdom was *kha* in relation to the king. Upland non-Buddhists were *kha* to all Buddhists. *Kha* might occasionally be given a particular name, such as the Kha-kassak surrounding Luang Phrabang, but these were *kha* who were encompassed by a *muang* and tied to it by ritual relations, among others. Those beyond the *muang* were *khon pa*, 'wild forest dwellers', beyond the pale of civilisation. Tribal Tai, being non-Buddhist, were on the margin, and no doubt an important motivation for conversion to Buddhism among these Tai was to escape categorisation as *kha*.

All the Tai states were polyethnic, made up of Khmer, Mon, highlanders, 'sea gypsies', among others. There was no expectation of a uniform language in everyday discourse, although Buddhism provided a universal ritual language, *pali*. Of course, physical differences and differences of everyday practice were observed and curiously noted, even among the Buddhists themselves, but they seemed to give rise to few ethnic generalisations. The appearance of Europeans in this world simply added another group to be incorporated into the status structure of the society.

Hierarchies of merit and spiritual power in Buddhist polities did not require that the elite think of themselves as being made of the same stuff as their subjects. Nevertheless, kingdoms such as that of Ayudhya were increasingly encountering merchants and missionaries from across the seas who trafficked in general categories, such as Siamese or Chinese, and in this contrastive way they began to see themselves as such. They too would acquire general names for others, such as *farang* for the Europeans; this came from the Malay kingdoms to the south where the traders were known as *feringgi*, a word derived from *franks*, an old Arab term for the Crusaders. These encounters demanded general descriptions for those who lived beyond Ayudhya, and it would seem that it was in this context that the term 'Lao' came to be used. Although its precise origins remain obscure, the Vietnamese, who had had continuous contact with Tai groups for centuries, referred to those people on the opposite side of the cordillera as *Ai-Lao*, and the Vietnamese could be the source of the designation. These designations were primarily for elite usage; there is little evidence that most 'Lao' or 'Siamese' thought of themselves in those terms.

The sacred spaces and places being constructed across the region began to feature as part of Tai social memory, as part of the background and subject matter of literature and song, including the indigenisation of Indian epics such as the *Ramayana*. Literature was associated primarily with the courts, especially in Ayudhya where a substantial court literature developed. The smaller and less wealthy courts like Lan Xang had a less-developed literature and tended to imitate the more sophisticated courts of the region. Parallel to court literature were the popular stories that emerged from the literate tradition maintained by the temples. This was the stuff out of which an ethnic consciousness could be formed, but that still lay in the future. Dynastic chronicles were composed, but what is most striking about them to a modern reader is that individual motivation and more general causality is suffused with magic and miracles. Thus political developments are preceded by portentous happenings, bolts of lighting and unusual natural events, just as unusual features in a person, such as Fa Ngum who was supposedly born with 33 teeth, mark them as *saksit*, 'magically potent'. Spiritually powerful monks or warriors can repel or subdue whole armies. Clearly this style of thinking played a major role in the way people perceived what was occurring around them, and was more important than fantasies of ethnic superiority or ethnic hatred, as a modern reader might imagine.

## Political stagnation

While some foreign traders made their way to Lan Xang during Surinyavongsa's long reign in the seventeenth century, the economic base of the kingdom remained much as it had been in previous centuries. In other words, wealth was not available for building up a more powerful centralised state. Within the kingdom administrative positions were apportioned and ranked, but the relative power accruing to any position fluctuated according to the alliances that formed and dissolved around the court, but even at its height Lan Xang did not develop a *sakdi na* (incorrectly glossed as 'feudal' by twentieth-century writers) system of administration. In this Lan Xang did not follow Ayudhya, where as early as the fourteenth century the kings and their advisers, who had learned their lessons from the Angkor administration, had implemented a system of bureaucratic control over manpower, at least in its core provinces. Officers appointed by the king would organise the *corvée* of six months that peasants were required to render each year, which could be deployed on public works or military service. This broke the direct link between the peasants and their overlords that continued to exist in Lan Xang, for example. The growing power of the Ayudhya state allowed even further centralisation in the late fifteenth century under King Trailok. In the burgeoning state there was growing functional diversification and the state issued laws outlining in detail the hierarchy. They assigned to everyone units of *sakdi na*, literally 'field power', a typically agrarian-state way of symbolising power. For example, slaves were ranked at 5 units, freemen 25, petty officials from 50 to 400, and above that began the nobility. While this system weakened the power of the locally based nobility, factionalism continued to be an important dynamic in the mandala's politics.

The stability of Surinyavongsa's reign was a result of a finely balanced division of power between Phaya Saen Muang, a powerful noble in the north, and Phaya Chan, who was responsible for the southern parts of the kingdom. When Surinyavongsa died in 1695 this personal arrangement, which had been focused on the king, fell apart, and yet another long and bloody succession struggle ensued. Lan Xang within two decades had dissolved into three, sometimes four, separate small kingdoms. They were centred on Luang Phrabang, Vientiane and intermittently the Plain of Jars, while a new kingdom named Champasak came into being in the far south, led partly by aristocratic refugees from the strife in Vientiane. The division between Luang Phrabang and Vientiane, imposed by the intervention of the King of Ayudhya, reduced them to petty vassal states on the periphery of the Ayudhya's mandala.

Although Ayudhya was destroyed by the army of the King of Ava (Burma) in 1767, with the royal family being either killed or carried off, the resilience of the social and political structures that had been created in the Siamese region was demonstrated by the speed with which one of the Ayudhyan generals, Taksin, could rally the mandala's forces and reconquer within a few years what had been lost. He quickly went on to expand Siamese power to the north and to the east, bringing the various peripheral principalities firmly under Siamese suzerainty. Rival factions within and between the principalities of Luang Phrabang, Vientiane and Champasak resorted to the manoeuvre common in such political systems of seeking powerful outside support. The Burmese had been excluded as allies by Taksin's success, and the Vietnamese were at that time steeped in internecine warfare, thus the factions could only appeal to Taksin. Through factional alliances, Champasak was brought firmly within the Siamese mandala in 1778; Taksin's army then marched on Vientiane and easily conquered it the following year with the assistance of their northern vassal state, Luang Phrabang. Members of the royal family were taken as hostages, along with their palladiums the Phra Keo and the Phra Bang (which had been moved to Vientiane in 1705), while thousands of families were relocated to Saraburi, 120 kilometres northeast of Bangkok, as royal *kha*. By the time of the establishment of the Chakri dynasty in Bangkok in 1782, the Siamese kingdom was the undisputed major power in the region and Lan Xang had disappeared.

## The last of the warrior kings

The uprising of Chao Anou, King of Vientiane, against his Chakri overlords in 1827 has become a legend central to modern Lao nationalism. The story is surrounded by intense emotions and protected by an almost sacred untouchability that resists attempts to place Chao Anou's actions in historical perspective. Casting Chao Anou as some kind of proto-nationalist, however, is a typical case of misrecognition. Nationalism belongs to the modern state system that was still to come; Chao Anou's revolt was the last gasp of a dying pre-modern mandala state system.

Chao Anou served at the court in Bangkok for sixteen years, taken there with his family in the wake of Taksin's sacking of Vientiane. There he loyally served the court and distinguished himself in battle against the kingdom of Ava. His older brother Nanthasaen, placed on the throne of Vientiane by Bangkok in 1782, had carried the Phra Bang back with him as his palladium because the new Chakri king, Rama I, felt it brought bad luck to Bangkok. In 1792 Nanthasaen marched on Luang Phrabang, claiming the latter was conspiring with Ava, and after sending its rulers to Bangkok asserted control over Luang Phrabang and its vassals, *muang* Phuan and Houaphan. This success perhaps encouraged dreams of grandeur, and he was removed by Bangkok on suspicion of conspiring with the ruler they had appointed to Nakhon Phanom. In 1795 his brother Inthavong took his place, with Anou as his *ouparat*, or viceroy. On Inthavong's death in 1804 Anou became King of Vientiane.

The Siamese mandala at that time included a number of small states on its periphery which paid it tribute, but also paid tribute to other states, as Luang Phrabang did to China. Vientiane, however, along with Chiang Mai and Champasak, was more closely tied to Bangkok, both by lines of marriage, larger tribute, the provision of manpower for warfare and its dependence on Bangkok's goodwill at times of succession. On the Khorat Plateau, where the power of Bangkok had expanded rapidly at the end of the century, there were some 20 *muang*, from Nakhon Phanom in the north to Buriram in the south, whose leaders were ranked as governors. Many of them were members of local nobility. The inner core of the kingdom was made up of provinces directly ruled by appointees from the capital.

The *sakdi na* administrative system pioneered by Ayudhya was taken over by the Chakri dynasty and strengthened. The major preoccupation of the new central king was to centralise power, which meant segmenting the power of his ruling nobility so that they could not challenge him. Besides state control of the all-important international trade, this meant ensuring that no aristocrats or vassal kings on the periphery would be able to muster sufficient manpower to challenge the centre. To make it clear which freemen in the kingdom were bound to provide royal service as *corvée*, Rama I ordered that they be tattooed. At the same time he made the conditions of this service by the *phrai luang*, the 'king's men', less onerous. This clear assertion of control over manpower disgruntled some of the aristocrats.

The mandala of Siam thus combined, uneasily, elements of a newly emerging absolutist state system and an older system in which power had been more dispersed and had allowed for the emergence of new men of prowess. Clearly this diversive dynamic was at work in Chao Anou, who not long after his elevation to the throne of Vientiane began to use the manpower at his disposal to build new Buddhist monuments and to wrap around himself the mantle of a Buddhist king. He nevertheless appeared to remain a faithful vassal of Bangkok, and in 1819 intervened in Champasak at Bangkok's request after the local ruler, Chao Manoy, was unable to quell an uprising led by a man called Sa, a *phu viset*, a 'man of supernatural power', who had gained a large following among the upland minorities there. The revolt was partly fuelled by the growing disruption of these societies by the slave trade to the lowlands. Significantly, this *phu viset* was the son of a family that had been relocated to Saraburi after the fall of Vientiane in 1789. Chao Anou quelled the revolt, and in return asked that his son be installed in Champasak. Bangkok was clearly worried that this would expand Chao Anou's influence, but at the same time was deeply concerned about the expansion of the Hue emperor's power in neighbouring Cambodia and therefore wished to have a strong ruler in Champasak. This latter concern won the day, at the urging of Krommamun Chetsadabodin (the future King Rama III), and Chao Anou got his wish.

By this time Chao Anou began to dream of re-establishing the kingdom of Lan Xang. This would happen only if he could bring Luang Phrabang into line and gather under his sovereignty more people. However, given his brother Nanthasaen's earlier attack on

Luang Phrabang, there was little sympathy there for Anou, and when he began his march across the Khorat Plateau in 1827 Luang Phrabang tried to stay neutral. The uprising was given support by some of the nobility in the northeast, but others stayed loyal to Bangkok. Anou's forces took Nakhon Ratchasima by using the subterfuge that they were marching south to help Bangkok resist a British invasion. They were stopped only when they reached Saraburi, by a large army quickly assembled by Bangkok, which pushed them back. Anou's retreating army compelled as many people as they could to march with them to the north, and slaughtered those who resisted. The uprising, however, ended in a fiasco. His son was soon captured, and Anou himself fled to Hue in Vietnam. Siamese forces entered Vientiane and began to destroy the city. The Siamese commander Phrarajwang Bovon reported to Rama III:

> The people of Vientiane have fled to Muang Lakorn, Muang Chiang Mai, Muang Lamphun, Muang Phrae, Muang Nan and Muang Luang Phrabang in great number. To round them up would lead us to use brutal force which would be unpopular. The number of physically fit males in Vientiane and the cities under its jurisdiction is estimated to amount to about 20,000 men. When peace has returned and the area is settled, it is believed that over eight to nine thousand men can be recruited for our army . . . I shall proceed to the round up of about 10,000 men and their families which shall total about 50,000 in all . . . With regard to cannons and guns we have thus far captured, they are of the most obsolete types and are not worth the effort to carry them to our capital . . .[3]

The commander left a small contingent in Vientiane 'to run the affairs and to prevent any possible dispute among the various princedoms'. Rama III, he who had supported Chao Anou's son for the position in

*Ruins of the Vat Phra Keo, the temple of the Emerald Buddha, some 70 years after the sacking of Vientiane by Siam in 1827. It was restored in the 1930s under the direction of Prince Souvanna Phouma. (Courtesy EFEO)*

Champasak, was furious that Anou had not been captured and ordered the destruction of Vientiane and the depopulation of the city. In 1828, Anou was captured and brought to Bangkok in a cage, where he was paraded and humiliated and soon died.

The savagery of the Siamese response was driven by Bangkok's own concerns for security. It had witnessed the subduing of its old rival Burma at the hands of the British, and was under growing pressure from an expansionist Europe. To the east, Vietnamese power had grown in Cambodia. The death of Anou gave notice that centralisation of power in Bangkok would be stepped up and that no internal challenges to this power would be tolerated.

# The 'Lao-isation' of the Khorat Plateau

Following the revolt of Anou, the Khorat Plateau underwent a crucial transformation as the Siamese state set out to colonise it definitively with people forcibly relocated from the eastern bank of the Mekong. For hundreds of years this vast plateau had remained forested and relatively unpopulated. The forests no doubt contained hunters and gatherers not unlike the Mlabri, the last remnants of whom can be found today in the forested border regions of Nan and Xaignabouri provinces. Contrary to maps produced by the French in the nineteenth century, or by Lao nationalists in the twentieth century, Lan Xang at its height ruled only over *muang* along the Mekong River on the plateau's northern rim. Definitive Tai dominance in the area of Champasak occurred only at the beginning of the eighteenth century. Ayudhya also had little interest in the region, and only in the mid-seventeenth century did it establish the fortified outpost Nakhon Ratchasima on the ruins of two old Khmer towns. The region between this city and the northern towns associated with Lan Xang was largely a no-man's land. Khmer settlers remained scattered across the plateau, but were mostly gathered on its southern rim. Small groups of Tai had been migrating into the region for hundreds of years, some of them fleeing wars and dynastic disputes in Lan Xang, and their contact with the Khmer in the region would inflect their cultural development in a distinctive way. Other groups migrated across the Mekong to mix with the Khmer and other peoples indigenous to the region. The scattered groups of Suai or So in the northeast of Thailand today point to a complex ethnic history which remains largely unexamined, but the region was not uniformly 'Lao'. Most of these people lived on the extreme margins of the states in the region and evolved strongly rooted local traditions. The actual 'Lao-isation' of the plateau only really came in the wake of Chao Anou's revolt, which prompted the Siamese state to engage in a systematic policy of relocating tens of thousands of people from the east bank of the Mekong into a region it indisputably controlled. The ensuing political stability provided by an ever more powerful Bangkok ensured rapid population growth, and over the coming century more ethnic Lao would come to be found on the Khorat Plateau than in Laos itself.

Inevitably, the tightening control over local rulers undermined their traditional prerogatives, and the uprooting of people from their native villages produced a deep and pervasive sense of cultural insecurity across the Lao areas and caused occasional outbursts of millennial fervour. Such movements have been seen all over the world where a modernising state extends its rule into its hinterland, or capitalism begins to disrupt traditional economies, and they have often been a response to colonialism. Usually these movements draw on traditional religious and political beliefs to assert that an ideal society is coming into being, as predicted by their prophet, that will wipe away the bad world of the present. These sentiments can be seen in the deeply mystical set of poems 'Leup Pha Sun' ('To Extinguish the Brilliance of the Sun'), written sometime in the nineteenth century after the defeat of Chao Anou. Using the metaphorical language of love and religion, the poems paint a picture of time-out-of-joint which will be set right by a righteous Buddhist king:

> Mountains are destroyed; they have collapsed and are
> strewn about
> The edge of the land is pulverized,
> There is great turmoil in the villages, which are dark with
> smoke; the earth is on fire
> A shadow covers the brilliance (of the moon) which
> disappears in the clouds
> The universe is overturned and broken; the land is
> unbalanced; it quakes and trembles.[4]

'Leup Pha Sun' can also be read as a cultural statement of Lao against Siamese identity, and it was adopted as such by Lao nationalist intellectuals later in the twentieth century. 'Vientiane' is mentioned in this poem, but it serves as a metaphor for an ideal state presided over by the Buddha, rather than the real place. 'Vientiane' also featured as an ideal place for revolts led by *phu mi bun*, 'men of (exceptional) merit', in the Thai northeast at the turn of the century.

## Luang Phrabang in the nineteenth century

In the late nineteenth century, the north of Laos was ravaged by the backwash of the massive millenarian revolts of the Taiping and the Panthay in southern China. Remnants of their once massive armies marched south under their yellow, black or striped banners, through the mountainous border regions as far as Vientiane. Wreaking havoc as they went, they came to be feared by the Lao as the dreaded Haw.

In Luang Phrabang the outcome of Chao Anou's revolt had meant closer control by the Siamese of their tributary states. The action that led to the capture of Chao Anou in *muang* Phuan by the Siamese army was launched from Luang Phrabang, where Siamese soldiers would be stationed until the coming of the French. A major concern of Siam at this time was the Kingdom of Hue's encroachments on the Khmer kingdom and on the Lao principalities. Anou's flight to Hue had underlined the latter's role in the affairs of its neighbour. The rulers of *muang* Phuan were considered tributary rulers of the emperor in Hue, and they were removed and executed in Hue for their role in handing Anou over to the Siamese troops. *Muang* Phuan polarised into a faction that wished to place itself under Luang Phrabang and one which leaned towards Hue. Bangkok's alarm at this can be seen in an edict of the Interior Ministry in 1836:

> Vietnamese are sending men to inspect and demand taxes
> from Phuan officials and from households in every village.
> Those Vietnamese have made the Phuan of Chiang Kham

and Mo, who live close to Annam, dress and wear their hair in Vietnamese fashion, seeking thereby to garner the Phuan definitively into the Vietnamese fold.[5]

Bangkok's response was the same as it had been in the southern provinces—population relocation into territory it clearly controlled. Thus thousands of Phuan families were compelled to move on to the Khorat Plateau and beyond, and the plains around Xiang Khoang township were almost deserted for more than a decade. In areas bordering Vietnam a commissioner from Hue governed directly.

Ever since the early Tai migrations, the northern mountains between Vietnam and Laos had contained smaller Tai *muang*. The nineteenth century saw the emergence of an important confederation of Tai chieftains called the Sip Song Chu Tai, which covered much of the modern province of Houaphan. These Tai remained non-Buddhists, and their leaders were tributary rulers for the lowland Viet states, which conferred titles on them and whose mandarin dress they imitated. This style of rule followed the Chinese frontier model of *tu si*, a kind of indirect rule. While these Tai were occasionally drawn into a tributary relationship with Luang Phrabang, their relationship was stronger with kingdoms to the east. The Tai Phuan on the Plain of Jars, however, had been converted to Buddhism during the rise of Lan Xang and had established a small principality in the region which was tied by tributary relations to the lowland states. It also paid tribute to Hue, which asserted its right to a role in Phuan affairs. In the mandala era such overlapping, pulsating and ill-defined jurisdictions were normal, and factions at court would use them to their own advantage. In the second half of the nineteenth century, however, a new form of statecraft was introduced to the region in the form of European colonialism, which demanded an exclusive sovereignty over territory rather than over people or political units. Rulers in Bangkok, Hue and indeed Beijing had to respond to this new reality. The Taiping rebellion and its aftermath was one product of the dislocations induced in the old order by the new.

## The Haw raiders

The Haw remnants of these disturbances lived by marauding and swept south as far as Vientiane, where they ransacked the That Luang stupa looking for jewellery and gold. James McCarthy, a British surveyor in the service of King Chulalongkorn who travelled through the Phuan region in 1884, wrote of how 'the wats had been wantonly destroyed, and piles of palm-leaf records lay heaped together, which, unless soon looked at, would be lost forever'. In the Phuan capital Xiang Khoang:

> the pagoda [stupa] on the hill, the finest in the region, had not escaped. From a distance it looked perfect, but on a near approach rents were found in three sides, almost from pinnacle to the foundation. It was wonderful that the spire, 60 feet high, had not fallen in. The Haw are said to have obtained as much as 7,000 rupees weight in gold from this pagoda. Fragments of urns, which had contained offerings, lay strewn about, and still showed elegance of form.[6]

At times the Haw worked in concert with soldiers from the Sip Song Chu Tai.

Luang Phrabang was powerless against these marauders. The picture of Luang Phrabang drawn in mid-century by the French explorer Henri Mouhot gives some idea of its dimensions. He described it as 'a delightful little town, covering a square mile of ground, and containing a population . . . of 7,000 or 8,000 only'. The picture he gives in his memoirs of 'the princes who govern this little state, and who bear the title of kings' is of two men, the king and his *ouparat*, elevated on a raised platform, their subjects prostrated around them, speaking to the seated explorer. It displays little majesty and power, and clearly the kingdom now stood barely above the chiefdoms of the Sip Song Chu Tai. The lawlessness brought by the Haw weakened Luang Phrabang's control over the various chiefdoms that were

*Henri Mouhot, a mid-nineteenth century French explorer, and the King and Viceroy of Luang Phrabang. (From M. Henri Mouhot, Travels in the central parts of Indo-China (Siam), Cambodia and Laos, during the years 1858, 1859 and 1860, London, 1864)*

its vassals. Thus in 1875 it was faced with a Kha uprising whose leader Nhi, a Khamu, formed a group of marauders that was only disbanded on his death at the hands of a Siamese–Lao force later that year.

Siamese attempts to rein in lawlessness in its peripheral tributaries by traditional means during the 1870s, that is, by sending commanders at the head of hastily gathered bands of peasant soldiers, were ineffective. Furthermore, the policy of relocation practised in the Phuan areas alienated the traditional elites because, rather than trying to work through them, it undermined their base of power. Thus the latter turned to the Vietnamese for protection, because at least they did not have a policy of population relocation, and the region remained unstable. Haw attacks on Luang Phrabang led to the stationing of a Siamese garrison there in 1882.

The disturbances on the frontier, however, were now increasingly linked to political struggles and administrative changes in Bangkok, where King Chulalongkorn was replacing the old guard and forming new ministries. A Committee of Princes was formed in 1883 to formulate new frontier policies in response to the growing challenge from France, which was now laying claim to Hue's tributaries and talking the as-yet unintelligible language of modern mapping. This was why McCarthy had been on a mapping tour of the Phuan region in 1884, in the employ of Bangkok. As a result of his report, Bangkok laid its claims to the regions along the watershed, including much of the Sip Song Chu Tai. In an attempt to strengthen their claims, the Siamese issued regalia to the leaders of the towns in Houaphan, presented at an investiture in Luang Phrabang in 1886. But many of the leaders also kept their Vietnamese titles, which they used when dealing with mandarins and the French. The Siamese tried both bribery and coercion to bring the local elite into its fold. In 1887, however, they made the mistake of carrying off to Bangkok the sons of Deo Van Tri, the leader of the Sip Song Chu Tai. The latter retaliated by marching on Luang Phrabang with his Haw allies and sacking the city. The ignominious flight of the Siamese commissioner and his garrison demonstrated the relative weakness of Siamese power in the region. The aged king of Luang Phrabang fled alongside the French vice-consul, Auguste Pavie, bearer of a new form of overarching order and protection. The struggle for influence in the region, and more specifically in the northern mountains, was finally settled by gunboat diplomacy when, in July 1893, two French battleships sailed up the Chao Phraya River to Bangkok. An ultimatum was issued, and negotiations quickly ceded the whole of the east bank of the Mekong to French colonial control.

## Lao and Siamese

The cultural differentiation of 'Lao' and 'Siamese' was a product of the differential spatial and temporal integration of these societies into the modern world system. International trade and intercourse also traded in macro conceptions of peoples, such as Lao and Siamese, among those at the Ayudhyan court and at the pinnacles of commerce. For most ordinary people, however, these designations were irrelevant until the twentieth century. The cosmopolitan culture that grew up in Ayudhya, and the cultural and ritual elaborations that a wealthy state could afford, including cultural borrowings from outside, were among the first self-conscious cultural markers to emerge between Lao and Siamese. The Lao courts copied to some extent the style of the court in Ayudhya and later Bangkok, just as the latter copied the style of the courts of Europe. The collapse of Lan Xang exaggerated the difference between the increasingly worldly and sophisticated Siamese and the increasingly parochial Lao courts.

All across the Tai world in the early nineteenth century however, a broader sense of change was reflected in a sudden spurt of 'library-building' inside temples and the compilation of histories. A stronger sense of a Tai world versus a Vietnamese or Burmese world was reflected in these chronicles, but the Tai world remained undifferentiated. The modernisation projects launched in Bangkok by King Mongkut, and in particular by King Chulalongkorn, accelerated the differences between the centre and the periphery, or at least emphasised the centre's consciousness of its differences with the periphery, which it saw as increasingly *ban nok* or 'country bumpkin', uncivilised and steeped in superstitions unfitting to a modern age. This came to apply especially to the northeast and its poor peasantry, the 'Lao', and by extension to the rest of Laos. Thus it was modernisation that produced a more widespread consciousness of being Lao or Siamese.

The ethnic makeup of the peasantry, no matter whether in the Chao Phraya River basin or the northeast of the country on the Khorat Plateau, reveals extraordinary diversity. Indeed, the provinces immediately surrounding Bangkok were peopled in the nineteenth century by peasants from all across the region, and most importantly they were increasingly joined by immigrant Chinese. In Laos too, there was diversity. Tai Lue moved down from the north into Luang Phra-bang, Tai Phuan moved down to Vientiane, and there was ongoing cultural and social interaction between all Tai groups and upland peoples. Only occasionally were strong cultural differences encountered, and only occasionally did they inhibit interaction.

One cultural marker of 'Lao-ness', used by Lao themselves and others, is the eating of 'sticky rice', a variety especially adapted to the uplands. Sticky rice eaters abound in the areas identified as Lao today, although it is also eaten by most other ethnic groups in this area. Sticky rice travelled with the Tai to the lowlands, where they encountered long grain varieties grown by both the Mon and the Khmer, and farms with mixed varieties evolved. It was only the beginning of rice exports in Ayudhya, and then the later nineteenth-century boom in rice exports from the Chao Phraya plain, that led to a decisive shift away from sticky rice varieties, even in people who had traditionally eaten it. Thus it was in the nineteenth century that 'Lao', who did not participate in the rice export boom, were identified as sticky rice eaters and sticky rice became a symbolic marker of 'Lao-ness'.

The next major shift in Siamese–Lao differentiation came with the nationalist projects launched by Chulalongkorn and by all subsequent Siamese kings and governments to promote the idea of a unified and homogenous Siamese culture, including the standardisation of a central Thai language. Something similar would only begin to happen to the Lao later, under the French.

# 2
# LE LAOS FRANÇAIS

Nationalism in Laos grew slowly over the first half of the twentieth century. Laos remained a colonial backwater within the French empire of Indochina, experiencing little economic, social or political change. Opium, which became a major source of revenue for the colonial government, caused rifts in the highlands and revolts by Chinese traders and Hmong people. But overall the country was calm, and Laos was for many French considered a kind of 'Shangri-la'. Colonial society was racist and sexist, but only mildly so. The challenge of a strident Thai nationalism in the 1930s, and war in the 1940s, prompted the growth of a small Lao nationalist movement which, in 1945, sought unsuccessfully to expel the French. France tried to hold onto its Indochinese colonies, and the Royal Lao Government was established in 1947 within the French Union. But by 1954 French colonialism in Indochina had collapsed.

# Laos mapped

The French in the nineteenth century were the first to map Laos and to give it its current cartography. In particular this was the mission of Vice-Consul Auguste Pavie. As we have already seen, the confrontation of Siam and France in the Lao territories was also a confrontation of different world views about how states are organised. In the mandala system overlapping suzerainty over smaller principalities, known as *song fai fa* (two overlords) or *sam fai fa* (three overlords), was normal. In these terms Siam conceptualised the status of the tributary states on its periphery, such as Luang Phrabang, which acted as a kind of buffer between themselves and the next powerful mandala. Siam was well aware that these states sent tribute in several directions.

The nationalist concept of the state that the French colonialists brought with them, however, recognised no such intermediate spaces and insisted on territorial border lines. Initially puzzled by this new idea, the Siamese learned quickly and were soon employing Europeans to help them lay territorial claims. The Lao played little role in this manoeuvring, apart from supplying documentation to Pavie so that he could make claims on behalf of the French. The French claimed Laos as a tributary of Vietnam and in 1887 commissioned one Captain Luce to scour the archives of Hue to pursue their claim. All he could find were the ill-defined claims of a tributary world. These were quite unsatisfactory from the point of view of modern mapping, especially for making claims on the east bank of the Mekong, which was what Pavie was seeking. Pavie objected to using the Mekong River as a 'natural' frontier, and in a sense, quite rightly as it was a line of demarcation 'natural' to no one. In the buffer regions any boundary would end up being arbitrary and thus demarcation would ultimately be settled by force. Pavie wrote in 1893 that if the Siamese gave trouble, France should make a show of strength and, 'A protectorate over Siam will be our compensation'. To which he added: 'If we neglect such an opportunity now, will we ever again be offered another to round off our Indochinese empire?'

The agreement forced on Bangkok by France's gunboat diplomacy of 1893 secured a Mekong border along which, on the western side, the French insisted on a 25 kilometre demilitarised zone. This was a source of considerable anxiety for the Siamese. This zone, along with French extraterritorial claims over 'French subjects' (people born inside what was now French colonial space, such as Lao deported to Siam), ensured continued instability and provided pretexts for larger French claims. Indeed, a telegramme to colonial officials in 1899 from the Governor General of Indochina, Paul Doumer, repeated French claims to all of Siam:

> We must manage to ensure that Siam, which for some years has been moving towards British control, turns to France and links herself increasingly to Indochina. All the main irritants—protégés, the neutral zone, etc.— are of no significance in themselves. They only have importance as political weapons. We must achieve the occupation of Battambang and above all of Khorat. This would lead in time, by force of circumstance, to our achieving a protectorate over the whole of Siam.[7]

That none of this was achieved was primarily because of counter-pressure from the British and skilful diplomacy by Bangkok. In 1903 France's treaty with Siam was renegotiated, however, and the western bank territory of Luang Phrabang was restored to Laos, as territory on the western bank was to Champasak in the south. In Champasak, however, the capital, Bassac, lay on the west bank of the river and was aligned with Bangkok, and the local ruler was referred to as the 'pseudo roi de Champasak' by one French governor. Most of Champasak's royal family fled to Bangkok, apart from Chao Nhouy who was made governor, with its new capital in Paksé (after 1908), but his small kingdom was not restored. In 1907 a final Franco-Siamese agreement conceded a small amount of territory in southern Luang Phrabang, down to Danxai, to Siam. The French renounced their right to 'protect' French 'Asiatic' subjects in Siam, in exchange for the 'lost' provinces in Cambodia (Siem Reap and Battambang). The trope of the 'lost provinces' lived on in Bangkok, however, and it would reclaim them in 1940. It would also remain a nationalist trope among the Lao, who had their own 'lost provinces' in northeastern Siam. All such claims, however, were equally valid and equally spurious.

## La mission civilatrice

The late nineteenth century scramble for colonial possessions by European powers in retrospect is puzzling. Recent historiography has come to appreciate the complexity of colonialism as both a cultural and social phenomenon as well as a political and economic one. Contrary to Marxist-inspired arguments, colonial possessions like Laos were an economic burden on France and its motives for being there need to be sought elsewhere. French imperialism is best understood as an outgrowth of French nationalism.

The nineteenth century was a long process of turning peasants into Frenchmen—still incomplete when France took control of Laos in 1893. At that time the population of France was predominantly rural, and there was an enormous cultural gap between urban Parisian society and the countryside. For many, Paris was France, a sophisticated urban milieu that gave the nation an appearance of being more developed and 'civilised' than it really was. Members of this urban elite were often shocked to encounter peasants in rural areas who refused to speak French, who did not see themselves as Frenchmen, and who clung to local customs and 'superstitions'. S.P. Nginn, one of the first Lao students to study in France, on his arrival in 1906 observed of one region in the south:

These people have different customs, their temperament is gentle and they are very welcoming to us. Their local speech consists of many languages which are not French, and people use their local languages to talk to one another.[8]

This diversity did not seem surprising to him, coming as he did from the diversity that was Laos.

During the nineteenth century many writers drew parallels between rural France and conditions they found in the colonies. In the forests of the Pyrenees peasants took up arms against newcomers to the region, such as police and administrators, who were ignorant of the local situation. As late as 1900 the French state still faced rebellions in these mountains. (More or less at the same time, France was facing similar revolts in the Lao highlands.) While over the course of the nineteenth century most people in France had come to understand they were French subjects, they only came to identify themselves as 'French' following their integration into the wider national community through the development of roads, markets, schools, military service and other things that slowly broke down their exclusive identification with local communities. This process had only just begun in Siam at the end of the century, and not at all in Laos.

The 'loss' of the territory of Alsace-Lorraine in the Franco-German war of 1870, was a pivotal event in the spread of French nationalism, as well as a blow to national pride. The notion of the 'lost provinces' was transferred to Indochina where in order to advance their colonial aims the French began to speak of the provinces of Battambang and Siem Reap in Cambodia, and the Khorat Plateau in the case of Laos, as 'lost' to Siam. It was an idea that was later adopted by Lao, Khmer and Thai nationalists.

Colonialism presented an opportunity for national aggrandisement. Ardent nationalists, among the most active promoters of colonial expansion, justified their attitude in terms of the glory it would bring to La France. Many were driven by a desire to outshine the other European powers, especially England. Since one crucial dynamic of colonialism was the desire to deprive rivals of potential colonies, there was a scramble which left every colonial power with a part of their empire that quite quickly became a burden on them. The French had an additional burden, bequeathed to them by the 1789 Revolution, and that was their moral duty to spread the assumed universal values of the revolution—*liberté, egalité, fraternité*—around the globe. This unique *mission civilatrice* bound together administrators, adventurers, settlers, investors, soldiers and sailors, despite their often divergent immediate interests. The colonial explorers of Laos, such as Henri Mouhot and Francis Garnier in the 1860s, and Auguste Pavie in the 1880s, who initially harboured fantasies of finding great wealth in the hinterlands, continued with their endeavours even when such hopes were dashed, driven forward by their desire to achieve glory for France and to spread its civilisation.

Republican ideals of equality and citizenship pitted the French colonisers against the old 'feudal' classes and rationalised their overthrow. In its early days French colonialism was committed to the idea of turning colonial peoples into 'Frenchmen'—but they had to be 'civilised' before they could reap republicanism's rewards. The subject peoples' loss of political rights, however, produced contradictions in republican nationalist ideology and inevitably spawned racist ideas to justify the absence of rights. The central contradiction of colonialism in the twentieth century was its spreading of nationalist and democratic ideas to the colonies. Colonial racism in the early twentieth century would produce a modification of the early assimilationist goal into one of association in which 'native traditions' would be respected and colonies would evolve in their own way towards modernity.

The most ardent proponent of French colonial expansion into Laos was Auguste Pavie. He was supported by the *Parti Colonial* in Paris, whose fortunes waxed and waned with the ups and downs of French domestic politics. Pavie and his supporters were primarily concerned with British expansion from Burma into Siam and were determined to annex the latter, at least as far as the Chao Praya River that runs through Thailand's central plains and Bangkok.

## The colonial administration

In 1893 Laos was incorporated as one of the five associated regions of Indochina, along with Cambodia and Tonkin, Annam and Cochinchina in Vietnam. In the north of Laos the Kingdom of Luang Phrabang was incorporated as a protectorate. This meant a form of

*King Zacharine and his Viceroy, Boun Khong, as featured on a French postcard at the turn of the twentieth century.*

indirect rule in the north while the centre and the south were ruled together directly as a colony until 1899, when Laos became a single administrative unit.

Auguste Pavie was the first French governor of Laos (1893–95), but apart from replacing the ailing King Ounkham with his son (who took the name Zacharine) and proclaiming, 'I confirm the princes in their current positions in Laos, now become a French possession', he did relatively little. In 1899 Laos, now seen as a single administrative unit of Indochina, was headed by a Résident Supérieur based at Savannakhet. He moved to Vientiane the following year. In December 1895 Bulloche, the Résident in the north, drew up an agreement with the King which left him in charge of the day-to-day running of the kingdom through its traditional structure. The main concern was revenue, raised in a variety of ways. For the Lao, a head tax for males from 19–60 years was imposed, fixed at 2 piastres per year, plus 20 days of corvée, five of which were to be served close to home. For the Kha it was 1 piastre and 10 days of corvée. Most important was the *Régie de l'opium*, over which a member of the King's council maintained day-to-day operations. The 'receipts from the taxes and the benefits of the sale of opium will be shared 50/50 between the French treasury and the Royal treasury', so the agreement ran—but this was impossible to police, and in 1914 the budgetary independence of the kingdom was abolished and integrated into the overall colonial budget. A report the previous year had complained that 'the Royal Budget, inasmuch as it exists, constitutes in effect a marvellous and convenient facade which masks inadmissible financial practices'. It pointed to the weak control of the young King Sisavangvong over his budget: 'As for receipts, H.R.H. Sisavang can only close his eyes to the traditional abuses of his indigenous functionaries, and he has no means to oppose their expenditures . . . The result is that in the rest of Laos receipts have been increasing, in Luang Phrabang they have for several years been going down.' The King was now allowed a personal budget of 30 000 piastres, and his leading officials were also given a stipend. To assure

Sisavangvong that the French supported his monarchy, a new palace was constructed in Luang Phrabang in 1914.

Many Lao in the kingdom saw little difference between life under the French and the old *song fai fa* days. But times were changing, and one can see the loss of fiscal independence as part of the long road to constitutional monarchy. A new overall agreement was reached between the Luang Phrabang monarchy and the Governor of Indochina in 1917, under which all traditional ('feudal') privileges and services still existing, given that the French had abolished slavery in the 1890s, were abolished and the King's forestry rights delimited. Concern for the status of the leading aristocrats, however, was maintained. So, for example, the number of personal guards allowed were '60 soldiers for the king, 15 for the *Chao-Maha-Ouparat*, 12 for the *Chao-Latsavong*, 12 for the *Chao-Latsabout*'. The next important change that would come to Luang Phrabang was in 1931 when its protectorate status was confirmed by France; in 1933 the province of Houaphan was attached to the kingdom.

Virginia Thompson wrote in *French Indochina*, published in 1937, that the administration of Laos 'was an immense success because it floated gently on top of the old native administration, giving an appearance of modernization to what had already existed and with which it did not interfere'. The very top was peopled by French, but the colonial bureaucracy immediately below them was mainly staffed by educated Vietnamese (which partly accounted for their numbers in the cities in that part of Laos under direct rule). For the French-educated Lao intelligentsia such as Prince Phetsarath, interpreter and adviser to the Résident Supérieur in Vientiane, this Vietnamese predominance was unacceptable, but not until 1928 was a school for training Lao administrators established. In 1937 Vietnamese still held 46 per cent of the senior indigenous positions in the colonial bureaucracy (but not in the Luang Phrabang kingdom). In October 1937 the Résident Supérieur, M. Eutrope, lamented the low educational level of Lao entering L'Ecole de Droit et d'Administration, saying, 'It is indispensable that a Lao elite is formed in the schools because it is this elite who must, in the diverse employments as heads of a field, of medicine or teaching, under our aegis lead the youth of the country towards progress and well being.'

Provincial advisory councils were set up in 1920, comprising the head of each *muang* and two notables. In Vientiane three Vietnamese notables were also added to the advisory council. In 1923 an Indigenous Consultative Assembly was formed, composed principally of members of the provincial councils, but including a number of Lao with higher education. While the role of the latter was only advisory it had the important effect of bringing together Lao from all over the country, and thus advanced the formation of a modern national consciousness.

Initially the French paid little attention to that other great transformer of consciousness, state-run education. As in other countries,

*The French colonial system continued to use the temples and monks for schooling as a way of minimising colonial expenditures. (Courtesy EFEO)*

members of the aristrocracy, particularly from Luang Phrabang, were the first to be provided with higher education, either in Vietnam or France, but for most of Laos it was Vietnamese who provided educated staff, with the colonial state simply buttressing the traditional temple schools which gave Buddhist education to men, and thus rudimentary literacy in Lao. By the 1920s textbooks in Lao had been produced for primary schools, and in 1921 the first junior secondary school, the École Pavie, was established. By the 1930s aristocratic women had also acquired higher education and had begun staffing schools in both Luang Phrabang and in Vientiane. The powerful personality of Princess Sourichan had an important impact on the minds of young women at that time. By 1932 there were 7035 students (of whom 976 were girls) in the *écoles franco-indigènes* (state school system). Some came from ethnic minorities, including 110 Thai Neua, 65 Kha, 43 Méo, 35 Phu Noi, 33 Phu Thai, and 7 Red Thai, but a significant number were Vietnamese. Eutrope complained in his 1937 speech that one of the main obstacles to the diffusion of education was the failure of Lao parents to 'understand the absolute necessity in modern conditions of giving their children a solid education, at least to primary level. It is up to Lao families to use all their influence to send their children to our schools to follow the instruction there assiduously'. True as this cultural obstacle may have been, only in the 1940s did funds become freely available for education—when Lao could legitimately complain that it was too little too late. In 1945 Prince Phetsarath would write in one of his denunciations of the French colonial record: 'To tell the truth, the Lao have never ceased to look on with an envious eye at the progress education has achieved among their free brothers on the right bank of the Mekong [Thailand].'

## A rudimentary economy

Despite early fantasies of finding great wealth, the economic development of French Laos was a failure. A summary of the economic situation in 1932, nearly. 40 years after the French had taken control, would conclude: 'the political situation is good; the economic situation is bad'. There was still no industry, except for two relatively small French-owned mines near Thakhek worked by around 3000 Vietnamese. In Thakhek, Savannakhet and Bassac, only 300 hectares of land was being used by French planters for commercial crops, primarily coffee in the latter, and tobacco. Smallholder trade in cardamom by the Kha on the Boloven Plateau continued, as did the collecting of sticklac (an insect secretion used in polishing agents) and benzoin (a tree resin used in perfumes and ointments) in the north. Forestry provided some revenue. Agriculture generally was self-sufficient, with rice from 470 000 hectares under cultivation yielding 340 000 tonnes in 1932. The rice harvest fluctuated from year to year, however, and in some years severe regional shortages occurred. Small river transport companies plied the Mekong and its tributaries, carrying passengers and commercial traders. State-subsidised transport companies attempted to maintain the fiction that Laos was integrated into the rest of the economy of Indochina, when in fact the poor east–west roads through the mountains ensured that transport through Thailand was always cheaper, and that the Chinese merchants who used this route could easily outdo the French.

From the beginning the colonial government in Laos failed to pay its way—just the first of the modern states in Laos to experience a perennial fiscal crisis. It raised just enough money to pay its officials and no more. There was nothing for development, road building, schools, hospitals, or any of the other fruits of the *mission civilatrice*. Colonial governors never failed to remind the assembled *chao muang* of the Indigenous Consultative Assembly of the necessity to improve revenue collection, just as they never failed to point out the beneficence of the subsidy received each year from the central Indochina budget. This subsidy may have been illusory, as we shall see, but it was good fiscal propaganda.

As set out in the agreement with the King of Luang Phrabang in 1895, and applied to the rest of Laos, Lao and Kha were liable for tax and corvée—but to organise these properly required an effective administrative system, which did not exist. The grassroots structure relied on the traditional administrative system, which was a patron–client system, not a rule-governed bureaucracy that in theory applied itself evenly and impersonally everywhere. Among the Lao personal relationships had to be maintained and finessed at every level from the *ban* (village) to the *tasseng* (collection of several villages) up to the *muang*. This alone ensured that practice would not be uniform. Moreover, although the French had allowed that one-tenth of what was collected could be retained by lower level officials, the traditional notion of *kin muang* (literally, 'eating the *muang*') ensured that much higher levels would at times be retained. Similarly, corvée obligations could also be abused. What struck the French as abuse and corruption was in fact the workings of the system they relied upon, and their insistence on the application of the law uniformly was an irritant. However, as these long-standing abuses were now conducted in the name of the colonial administration, the French were now accorded a share of any resentment on the part of rural Lao. The colonial state also tried to use its power to tax people such as the various minorities who had settled beyond the boundaries of the state. Not only did these people resent the new impositions, they were particularly subject to abuse by Lao intermediaries. Corvée requirements could be commuted into cash, and indeed the state calculated that a significant proportion would be, as most people resented corvée labour. Cash-short peasants, we can be certain, resented cash payments only marginally less. The system staggered on. In 1930 Résident Supérieur Bosc optimistically assured the gathered Indigenous Consultative Assembly that 'the time is not far away when the misreporting of taxable persons and of tax fraud will be no more than isolated and exceptional cases'—but the deficit was still there ten years later.

Much has been written, at least in communist tracts, about the iniquities of the colonial corvée system. There is one particular photo, taken by the French, of a line of labourers pounding a road, which is reproduced again and again to illustrate claims made about the oppressiveness of colonialism. But while it is true that there were several cases of horrendous abuse and loss of life in Vietnam, there are no similar cases for Laos. Consistent with the ramshackle administrative system, the corvée seems to have touched the bulk of the population unevenly and lightly. In villages unlucky enough to be near a planned *route coloniale* they might have found themselves particularly burdened. Desertion rates from corvée gangs were high, however, and the simple inefficiency of the system finally began to give way to paid labour in the 1930s. Compared to the pre-colonial indigenous states, whose armies could sweep away peasants for months at a time as porters or for state-sponsored works, the French imposition was relatively benign. But then, unlike the French, the pre-colonial kings did not claim to be ruling in the name of *liberté et egalité*.

## The opium monopoly

One of the main sources of finance for the colonial regime in Indochina was opium. In 1937 Virginia Thompson remarked on the hypocrisy of the fact that a person could be jailed for the possession of opium in France while its colonial possessions in the Far East thrived on its sale. The French argued that to suppress opium in the region would entail a major military campaign, something they could not afford. The sale of opium formed one of several monopolies, which never contributed less than half of the central budget's revenues. In 1914 sales of opium in Laos contributed $265 000 to the central budget, out of which the subsidies to local budget in Laos were paid. Perhaps Laos did pay its way more than is thought. Most of the opium handled by the French opium monopoly came from India and Burma, but growers among the Hmong in both Laos and northern Vietnam, who were already engaged in opium production and sales to Haw traders from Yunnan, were encouraged by the colonial state. By the late 1930s opium production and sale was booming in northern Laos and silver flooded the mountains. With Laos cut off from the rest of the world during World War II, the central budget relied even more on locally produced opium, and everyone tried to get their cut, including the royal houses of Luang Phrabang and Xiang Khoang. It also made some Hmong rich and powerful. A confidential report written by Eric Pietrantoni in 1943 reflecting on the general political and economic problems of Laos, faced as it was by a more assertive Thailand, argued for the importance of opium to the Lao economy: 'We estimate that the organization of the production of opium is the only thing which will allow Laos to live within its means . . . Economically and fiscally, the control and the extension of opium cultivation is for Laos a vital necessity.' It noted that although King Sisavangvong was strongly opposed to opium use by his subjects, the local administration had become conscious of how much opium revenue they were losing to the central Indochinese budget. The question of opium revenues would be revived in the early years of the Royal Lao Government in the late 1940s.

# Revolts

Generally, Laos has been seen as the most docile of France's Indo-chinese colonies. Colonial rule brought a peacefulness and stability to Laos that it had not experienced for two centuries. This not only allowed the consolidation of the Lao traditional elite, but also meant the re-establishment of stable peasant villages in many regions. What-ever peasant disgruntlement with French impositions in the form of taxes or corvée, or the elite's complaints about the usurping of some of their traditional prerogatives, overall French control was supported rather than opposed.

Nonetheless, there was opposition. A revolt broke out in south-ern Laos as early as the end of the nineteenth century. The main groups involved were the upland minorities of the Alak, Nya Heun and Loven of the Boloven Plateau, and the Sedang of the Kontum Plateau in Vietnam. Their prophet was an Alak called Bac My or Ong

Keo. Interestingly, he drew on Buddhist cosmology, which probably explains the spread of the movement to some Lao villages. His military commander, Ong Luang, claimed to be a descendant of the kings of Vientiane. They were joined by the Loven chiefs Khommaseng and Khommadam (whose son, fifty years later, would join with the communist Pathet Lao). The causes of the revolt had been brewing for some time. Champasak had long been an important centre for trade in forest products with Ubon, Khorat and Bangkok, but it was also an important centre for the slave trade. The demand for slaves in the lowland states had caused the stronger upland groups, notably the Sedang, Ta Oi, Loven and Jarai, to prey upon weaker groups. They also captured Vietnamese from the eastern plains and traded them across the mountains. The slave trade had started to go into decline following King Chulalongkorn's 1874 decree on the progressive elimination of slavery, but when the French attempted to stamp it out completely and assert administrative control in the highlands, they met with several years of revolt. In April 1902 a 'horde' gathered outside the French Commissariat in Savannakhet, apparently convinced of their invulnerability in the face of French bullets that would turn into frangipani flowers. One hundred and fifty died when the French opened fire. The fleeing rebels themselves carried out their own massacre, of 40 Loven people at Ban Nong Bok Keo in 1905. Their leaders were finally hunted down and killed by the French. Like the revolt of Chao Anou, this outbreak drew on a vision of an old world which was passing rather than the one which was coming into being. These rebels were not proto-nationalists, as has been claimed by later nationalist historians. They were demanding the restoration of the old order, including slave trading.

An uprising in the north in 1914 was inspired by an emergent Chinese, not Lao, nationalism. The collapse of the Qing Dynasty in 1911 and the rise of republicanism had triggered many revolts against the old order in China, many of them anarchic. In late 1914 a band of Haw Chinese riding in from Yunnan sacked a French post in Sam

Neua in Laos and made off with a large amount of money and weapons; they repeated their success in Sonla, Vietnam. The rebels paraded flags of the Chinese Republic and their own banners, and succeeded in swelling their ranks from the local population, among them some local notables who had been displaced by the French. The Chinese rebels were remarkably well informed about events in the world outside, such as the war then raging in Europe. They issued a proclamation: 'All the soothsayers have predicted the annihilation of the French people. Even Paris has been crushed by the German army. It is no use counting on France. Drive out the French and the country will commence a happy and prosperous era and will enjoy entire religious freedom.' The willingness of Chinese across the northern region to participate in the revolt was a result of their opposition to the French opium monopoly, which was attempting to assert control over Haw opium smuggling in northern Laos and Vietnam. After the revolt was crushed by soldiers sent from Hanoi, and to protect itself from ongoing turbulence in China, the French established Military Region 5 in northern Laos, and Military Region 4 in northwestern Vietnam.

In 1914 the French were also faced with a traditionalist revolt among the Tai Lue of Muang Sing, a *muang* which in 1904 had been severed from the neighbouring Tai mandala of Sip Song Pan Na in southern Yunnan. The French had won over the reigning prince, but his succession in 1907 by one of his sons, Phra Ong Kham, set off a protracted struggle for power among the aristocrats of the *muang*. The undermining of his traditional seignorial rights by the French finally led to revolt by Ong Kham; he fled into Sip Song Pan Na and for two years led sporadic fighting against the French from there, to no avail.

## The Hmong uprising

The next major revolt faced by the French was not confined exclusively, or even mainly to Laos. This was a revolt among Méo (Hmong) highlanders over 1918–21, known among some French administrators as the *guerre de fou* because of the important role played in it by shamans. The

Miao, as they are known in China, had come under increasing pressure from the Han in the eighteenth century, with failed revolts in Kweichou forcing many of them to migrate south and southwest into southern China and northern Indochina. Beginning early in the nineteenth century, Miao began to occupy the high mountain ranges of northern Laos where, among other things, they continued to grow opium, one of their most important cash crops. The various Tai adopted a deformation of the Chinese name, Méo, to designate these people, who in their own dialects usually referred to themselves as Hmong. Méo for the Tai had similar connotations to *kha*, that is, subordinate to the Tai. The important difference was that the Méo never saw themselves, nor ever were, in a *kha*-like position vis-à-vis the Tai. They had experienced the full bureaucratic might of the Qing imperial system, and the Tai nobles must have seemed puny by comparison. In the mountains around the Plain of Jars they established relations with the enfeebled Tai Phuan princes, who quickly realised the importance of opium.

A small revolt among the Hmong in 1896 led to the appointment by the French of a representative, a *kiatong*, for the Moua clan in one *tasseng*. This attempt at administrative incorporation, however, high-lighted an important social difference between the Hmong and the Tai. They were not organised by *muang* (or sub-units thereof, such as *tasseng* or *ban*), but by lineages and clans, which facilitated their per-petual movement in search of new fields for their poppies. Like Tai *muang*, these lineages or clans could come together to form temporary confederations under a powerful leader, but equally, villages made up even of the same lineage could divide when a decision to move was made. Settled villages that were part of a larger political structure were the exception rather than the rule among the Hmong, and this rela-tive 'anarchy' has made them a headache for state-builders to this day.

In 1917, in the region of Dien Bien Phu in Vietnam, a Hmong named Pachay told his father: 'Father, I have been possessed and shaken, I have had visions from Houa Tai, the messiah whom we all serve, who has ordered me to lead the Hmong people against the

*Hmong people began to migrate from China into the northern highlands of Vietnam and Laos from the eighteenth century onwards, causing a realignment of ethnic politics in the mountains. Here, a man leads his wives in ancestor worship.*

corrupt Tai who oppress us all.' Soon he and a small band had repulsed their first French patrol and burnt several Tai hamlets to the ground. Pursued by French forces, Pachay and his supporters eluded them by moving through rugged mountain terrain to Laos, then back into Vietnam, raising the Hmong, and also the Yao, by his messianic message that a *chao fa*, a 'heavenly king', was coming to establish a Hmong kingdom. They did not hesitate to use force to win supporters. The pursuing French forces slowly fragmented Pachay's support, and various Hmong leaders made their peace directly with the French over the head of the Tai. Pachay himself was finally hunted down and killed by pro-French Kha, the latter having been treated no better by the Hmong than by the Tai.

The Pachay rebellion was part of a larger phenomenon that had begun in southern Yunnan and spread to the mountains in northern Vietnam. It was a product of the growing weight of the Hmong population in these mountain regions, which directly challenged what had been the relatively undisputed power of the Tai mandarins in the Sip Song Chu Tai, and of the Tai Phuan princes. The revolt was an attempt to redistribute power in the mountains. The Tai had tried to exploit the Hmong in the same way they had exploited the Kha, using the new administrative power brought by the French to not only exact taxes from them for the French administration, but to also assert traditional prerogatives, especially over the lucrative opium trade. The revolt showed that the newcomers had had enough. While some French saw the whole revolt as 'madness' those closer to the scene understood clearly what the problems were. Colonel H. Roux who was involved in the campaign to suppress the revolt, in his report soon after wrote:

> There are small local chiefs, lazy and often rapacious, for whom the Méo [Hmong] represent a milk cow which they can treat without mercy. Sometimes the warrior temperament of the Méo reveals itself and for good reason: crushing taxes, heavy impositions on opium, horses requisitioned without being paid for. Yet always, these petty chiefs brandish before the unfortunate Méo the scarecrow of the French.[9]

Barthélemy, as administrator of the Civil Service in Indochina, in his report on the events made an even more profound observation: 'Laos appears to be administratively organized as if it was inhabited only by Laotians. The [law] codes are Laotian, the mandarins who apply them are too and the provincial council, embryo of our future consultative council, does not have a single representative of the mountain races.'[10] He added that reliance on the pagoda schools meant that minorities fell outside the system and therefore could not understand the language of the state. Catholic priest Savina in his account written shortly after, one which remained secret for many years, asked: 'Seeing that the Méo detest the Tai and the Tai detest the Méo, I ask why? . . . Seeing that the Tais possess the land and are governed by chiefs of their own race, while the Méo cannot do the same, I ask why?' In fact, the Hmong had primarily revolted against Tai and Lao control over them and wished to be directly connected to the French administration. This wish was granted in the Nong Het district in Xiang Khoang to Lo Blia Yao, who had collaborated with the French for some years already and had been responsible for hunting down and killing one of Pachay's main supporters. His eldest son Song Tou was appointed *kiatong*. Such Hmong appeals to forces beyond the confines of Laos would become a pattern for the future.

## Colonial society

Unlike Vietnam, Laos never had a substantial group of *colons* (white settlers), and this made for a different kind of colonial society. White settler societies, founded as they were on the denial of basic political rights to the indigenous population whose land they had usurped, were notoriously racist—and racism seemed to burn most fiercely in the hearts of the colonists when they were resisted by their subjects, as they were in Vietnam. The census of 1907 listed only 189 French in Laos, of whom seventeen were women. The census also counted *métis* (those of mixed race), of whom there were already 49, some fourteen years after the French took control. The total population of Laos was counted as 585 285, though the accuracy of this figure has to be treated liberally. At its height the French population in Laos was hardly more than several hundred, most working for the colonial state in one capacity or another and most were concentrated in the main administrative centres. Some provinces were overseen by only a handful of French.

There were some dreams of settlers establishing themselves in the cooler climes of Xiang Khoang and ranching on the plains, but it came to nothing. Some became involved in coffee plantations in the south on the Boloven Plateau, but these were never substantial. The few French who settled in Laos either practised petty commerce or retired there, especially if they had taken a Lao wife. Louis-Charles Royer paints a typical picture of colonial society in his 1935 novel *Kham, la laotienne*:

> Some waited for their leave like ordinary soldiers; they thought only of that and were hardly interested in the colony they deemed to run; others truly loved Laos; but it was they who had been 'colonized'.
>
> They had been contaminated by the local indolence; they just let their life go; all they asked for was a clear sky, tasty fruit, fresh drinks and easy women.
>
> The first lot conserved, with their false collars, their French habits; the second, walked around in canvas shoes—at home in bare feet . . . Some smoked opium, to chase away the gloom of the worst nights; they entered into a voluptuous torpor from which they refused to emerge and it was like this that they stayed in Laos . . .[11]

Colonial society in Laos was inevitably affected by the racist notions that circulated throughout the French empire and beyond, but these views were always tempered by republican ideals. French colonial society was divided by different racial attitudes and by class. What was galling for the French-educated indigenous Lao elite, many of whom were also aristocrats, was to experience attitudes of racial superiority held by lower-class Frenchmen. Prince Phetsarath, who was one of the country's modernising leaders, would refer to them in his memoirs as 'the colonial riffraff'. Because colonial society was exaggeratedly *bourgeois*, especially among those who came with their wives, poor whites were an embarrassment as they contradicted the assumed superiority of their race. French society in Laos was small and inward looking, living on gossip which was driven partly by the ambitions of wives for their husbands, though Laos was usually considered a dead-end colonial posting. Appearances, however, had to be maintained. Katay Don Sasorith, later one of Laos's most colourful politicians, provides a

*A French colonial official in 1930 with his Lao assistants.*
*S.P. Nginn is standing immediately to his left.*

61

lovely picture of these pretensions in his *Souvenirs d'un Ancien Écolier de Paksé*:

> Despite their small number, they bickered and they quar-reled (not over political questions, but over the eternal questions of jealousy . . .); and quite often they even came to blows much to the amusement of the Laotians . . . It all ended, however, with reconciliation, at least for appear-ances. Some days, after an incident, all the French colony would walk arm in arm along the streets of the city, no doubt to show to the population that the French attach little importance to these small accidents of life.[12]

In his memoir Katay paints an interesting picture of his easy relations with young French boys who spoke Lao 'even better than their mother tongue'. Indeed, when he was older, Katay would savour the fact that he knew French better than the boys of small officials who were stuck in these provincial towns. From the vantage point of his father's restaurant in Paksé, Katay came to see the French in all their human frailty and failed to be intimidated by their assumed superiority.

## France as a model of modernity

At the same time, France was for many Lao the fount of civilisation, and indeed a central impulse of republican colonialism was the spread of French culture. The young S.P. Nginn was overwhelmed on his arrival in France in 1906: 'To see Marseilles was like going to heaven because I had never ever seen such a large and beautiful city', he wrote in his memoirs. In 1943, more than 30 years later, Nginn recalled in the article 'Comment j'ai vu la France?' in *Kinnary*, one of the first magazines to appear in both Lao and French:

> In Paris I was overjoyed on seeing other marvels. I remember like yesterday the Luxembourg Gardens which

were just in front of the Ecole Coloniale where I lived with fifteen other comrades from Indochina. A garden with its rectilinear paths peopled with statues, and from the window of my room in the evenings I could see the crowds of elegant men and women promenading there.

How can I paint for you the Eiffel Tower, the monuments, the modern art museum, the museums of paintings and of sculpture? . . . A visit to these museums gives in a few minutes more useful knowledge than one receives in several months at school.

What to say about the Theatres and the Cinemas with their magnificent decors? . . .

The excitement and activity of the city was a striking contrast with the calm of our Lao cities . . .[13]

Nginn's thrill at seeing 'real civilisation' was deep and genuine. Imperial Paris was designed to impress visitors, and indeed it still does. Nginn's father was Auguste Pavie's Cambodian guide and interpreter; he settled in Luang Phrabang with his Lao wife and embodied his love for France in his son by also giving him the name Pierre. Like father like son—Somchine Pierre Nginn concluded 'Comment j'ai vu la France?' with the paean: 'France is a powerful and generous Nation. We love her because she is our country of adoption, because she has given us support from her wealth and the benefits of her civilization.' In our jaded post-colonial era, such sentiments may seem strange, but many students who travelled to France found it a life-transforming experience.

The relationship between Lao students and Frenchmen who had been in Laos could be relatively warm and intimate, and Lao appreciated the propriety of the French middle-class people they met. The now-legendary Auguste Pavie who in colonial mythology had 'conquered the hearts' of the Lao, and saved them from the Siamese, also received Lao students at his home in Paris, among them Nginn and his brother. Prince

Phetsarath, who studied in Paris at the same time as Nginn, during World War I offered to raise a contingent of Lao troops to fight for *la Patrie*. This offer was declined as his services were needed in Laos. Even on Lao who did not make the journey to France, French ways of acting and thinking left an indelible impression. Phoui Sananikhone, a future prime minister, wrote in his 1967 memoirs about the things he appreciated, such as the French insistence on punctuality, the formal rules of dress for officials, the absence of corruption among high officials, the relative fairness of the judicial process, and so on. He may also have been reflecting on how things had evolved since independence.

King Sisavangvong, one of the first Lao to study at the École Coloniale, also found his sojourn life-transforming, and in the French archives colonial officials report again and again on his fidelity to France. It was something beyond the political debt that the Luang Phrabang monarchy owed to France, and was clearly felt personally. In 1927 King Sisavangvong wrote to Pavie's widow after she had written to congratulate him on receiving the Grand Croix de la Légion d'Honneur:

> I hold always a profound and grateful respect for the memory of your husband who was, as all the world knows, a great and close friend of my grandfather, His Majesty King Ounkham.
>
> Having had a very sincere love for my kingdom, which he knew in all respects from his study on the ground, with the consent of my grandfather he put it under the protection of Greatest France.[14]

In 1932 statues of Pavie were erected simultaneously in his hometown of Dinan in Brittany and in Vientiane, and the following year in Luang Phrabang. In 1939 King Sisavangvong conferred on Pavie's widow the Croix de Chevalier de l'Ordre du Million d'Elephants. The myth of Pavie and his *Conquête des Coeurs* in Laos remained powerful and plausible until the façade of French protection crumbled in World War II.

## Racism and sexuality

Racism in the colonial context was inextricably linked with sexuality, both in ideology and in reality. As colonialism wore on, colonial society became less, not more tolerant of sexual liaisons between French men and Lao women. Marriage was out of the question. Given the overwhelming preponderance of single men among the colonialists it was inevitable that such liaisons occurred, especially among men posted to the provinces. The term used in Vietnam for the women in these relationships, *congaï*, 'mistress', was applied across Indochina. By 1912, when Starbach and Baudenne published their novel *Sao Tiampa, épouse laotienne*, disdain for these relationships was rife in respectable colonial society. The central character in the novel, Vébaud, has brought his Lao wife from up-country with him to a party at the Résidence Supérieur in Vientiane, where he overhears two compatriots gossiping:

'See that *congaï*: do you know her? No doubt some European's woman.'
'Where are you from, my dear, that you don't know Sao Tiampa, the gracious tyrant of young Vébaud?'
'Truly? That's her, the *phu sao terrible* who leads him around by the nose? It is amusing the way she has driven him crazy. The Mekong resounds with her exploits.'
'She's not bad . . . if it's the heart you're speaking about, for several dollars . . .'
'It's cheaper than our boys and secretaries!'
'Oh! pardon, don't mistake me; this is a case of real love . . .'[15]

Stung, the naive Vébaud grabs Sao Tiampa and rushes out in shame and rage. Gossip, of course, did not stop interracial liaisons—it simply policed the racial barrier—and other Frenchmen exercised greater cynicism than Vébaud. In *Kham, la laotienne*, the inspector of the *garde indigène* instructs newcomers to Luang Phrabang on how he procures

SAO-SI. - Buste

'Sao Si—Petite Chanteuse de Khong (Bas Laos)', *as she was described on another postcard. Here, the focus is on her exposed breast.*

his women: 'I don't buy them, I rent them. I say to the parents: I will give you 20 piastres each month and your daughter will come to my hovel everyday to *faire la sieste*.'

Historians of both Cambodia and Vietnam have remarked on the feminisation of the colonial subjects there, and about how in colonial literature and imagery women came to represent the languid and sexual feminine subject who is conquered by the masculine, adventurous Frenchman. The much less abundant literature on Laos exhibits all of these features too, and one is struck by the almost obsessive references by French writers to Lao *phu sao*, 'unmarried young women'. Indeed, in *Kham, la laotienne*, there is an odd self-referential complaint about how colonial functionaries come from all over Indochina to '*chercher les filles de Luang Phrabang*'. The author continues: 'It is the fault of your novels which have promoted the beauty and the . . . temperament of Lao women.' Poems were also penned, such as André Escoffier's 1942 'Les Filles de Luang-Prabang', part of which reads:

> In each house where shines their smile,
> Is the *Cour d'Amour* of their soft empire,
> Whose participants are the young men
> Which all have one wish for their sovereigns,
> > By the rhythm of the khenes,
> > They sing their songs.[16]

By 1907 there was already a group of *métis* in the colony, a problematic category which confused racial boundaries. This is dramatised in *Sao Tiampa, épouse laotienne* when Tiampa becomes pregnant; this presents the hero, Vébaud, with yet another problem, a *métis* child. He ponders the child's fate in the racial idiom of the day: 'What, in the milieu of our civilization, will become of this *métèque* in whom sleeps *instincts sauvages*, this *déraciné* who will respond to insistent atavistic demands?' In some contexts *métis* could assume superior status, thus Katay notes in his memoirs how they would look down on the Lao, and Nginn also observes that they were given higher positions than Lao in the colonial bureaucracy, at least in the early days. In turn, they were often looked down on by the French because they were *déraciné*, 'impure'. In a milieu obsessed by racial purity, to be pure Lao was superior to being *métis*. This sentiment found an echo among the Lao themselves. A famous early liaison between a Lao aristocrat, Prince Souvanna Phouma, the future long-running Prime Minister of Laos, and a *métisse* woman scandalised court society in Luang Phrabang. Souvanna already had a Luang Phrabang princess as a wife, but she refused to follow him to Vientiane where he had taken up work as a government engineer after his studies in France. So Souvanna married the Xiang Khoang *métisse*, Aline Allard, in August 1933.

The ideology of association in late French colonialism was a paradoxical concession to racial ideas, in that it no longer argued that the colonies could or should develop along the same lines as France. They would, it was said, evolve according to the demands of their own 'race' or culture (for most people at this time race and culture were interchangeable concepts). In the face of the aggressive disdain for indigenous cultures by *colons*, or indifference by embourgeoisified administrators, the interest taken in the exploration and revival of indigenous culture by the École Français d'Extreme Orient, established in Hanoi 1898, was salutary. Its scholars sometimes went to the other extreme, 'orientalising' the people they studied as somehow utterly Other, but in the higher levels of the administration and in France it produced a new respect for the cultures of Cambodia or Laos. It led to the refurbishing of ancient monuments, such as the That Luang, and to greater support and reliance on indigenous monarchies. The leading colonial trope, of having saved both Cambodia and Laos from disappearing before the march of aggressive neighbours, is replayed by these scholars who see themselves as saving the culture. Archaeologist Jeanne Cuisinier, in a 1928 article, mourned the fact that any new pagodas in Laos were being built by Vietnamese masons, causing changes in style. Surveying the crumbling temples in Vientiane

Cuisinier 'felt a great pity for the Buddhas of Laos. They are being left to die: the Lao are forgetting their traditions while the French are ignorant of them . . .'[17]

## Colonial urbanisation

Vientiane became the French administrative capital as part of a calculated ploy to draw on the prestige of the ancient capital. Raquez, in his intriguing *Pages Laotiennes* published in 1902, writes about how the French had sought out the location of Chao Anou's palace, and of the Résident Supérior's plan to build his residence there. The contemporary residence, however, was humble: 'Built 4 years earlier by the first administrator of Vientiane, M. Morin, [it] is a spacious wooden house on piles and covered with a thatched roof.' Morin had been instrumental in attempting the first restoration of That Luang, the religious centre of Vientiane. At Vat Sisakhet, also built by Anou, the French had already begun the practice of *le serment de fidélité* (oath of allegiance) by Lao notables, who would recite:

> We Paya Si Savana Lavoutsa, Kromakan of Vientiane which is guarded by eight dragon heads and the spirit of Paya Si Kot Ta Bong on his elephant, as well as the Tiao Muong and the Kromakan who administer the territory of Vientiane;
>
> Our Sons, our servants, our satellites, our police, the soldiers who protect us and our forts and palaces, the Tasseng, the Pho Ban, the guardians of the pagodas, all have come to take the oath of allegiance to the Government of the French Republic represented in Vientiane by the Commissioner, M. Pierre Morin . . .[18]

Previously such oaths were given before the King, a practice that continued in Luang Phrabang with the addition of the oath of fidelity to France.

Laos was too poor to afford the extravagant recreations of French-style buildings that were once found in Saigon and Hanoi and, on a smaller scale, in Phnom Penh. Perhaps the palace in Luang Phrabang, built by the French for King Sisavangvong in 1914 is the one memorable, monumental piece of architecture that survives today. As Vientiane in particular grew, and the other urban administrative centres (Luang Phrabang, Thakhek, Savannakhet, and Paksé), a certain urban pattern appeared. The colonial administrators lived in two-storey concrete villas set in large gardens; there was a commercial centre, inhabited by Vietnamese and Chinese, made of bricks and cement, but in much more modest proportions; a Lao quarter, in which the houses were typically made of wood, raised on stilts, and surrounded by garden and coconut trees; and finally a quarter for poor Vietnamese coolies of huts made of bamboo and straw. As the Lao elite enriched themselves, they began to copy the higher status French villas, to which were added Lao decorative frills; examples of these houses are best seen today in Luang Phrabang.

The urban centres were relatively small, and except in Luang Phrabang their populations were predominantly Vietnamese. The table following gives some idea of the dimensions and composition of the urban areas in 1930 and 1943.

The 1930s saw the Vietnamese population almost double as a result of political and social unrest in Vietnam, and because there were no barriers to their migration to Laos. It caused much of the urban growth between 1930 and 1943, and as such alarmed the small Lao elite. Anti-Vietnamese sentiment was central to the Lao nationalism that stirred in the 1940s.

# Nationalism

When the French took over Laos there was no sense of a Lao nation among the population that fell within the boundaries that they

| Urban area | Lao | % | Vietnamese | % | Chinese | % | Others | % | Total 1943 | Total 1930 |
|---|---|---|---|---|---|---|---|---|---|---|
| Vientiane | 9 570 | 41.5 | 12 400 | 53 | 900 | 4 | 330 | 1.5 | 23 200 | 15 800 |
| Luang Phrabang | 3 000 | 61 | 1 400 | 28 | 480 | 10 | 70 | 1 | 4 950 | 5 400 |
| Thakhek | 800 | 10 | 6 900 | 85 | 300 | 4 | 100 | 1 | 8 100 | 3 400 |
| Savannakhet | 850 | 16 | 4 000 | 72.5 | 450 | 8 | 200 | 3.5 | 5 500 | 4 500 |
| Paksé | 1 000 | 14 | 4 500 | 62 | 1 700 | 23 | 100 | 1 | 7 300 | 3 400 |
| Xiang Khoang | 240 | 11 | 1 500 | 72 | 300 | 15 | 60 | 3 | 2 100 | 1 400 |
| TOTAL | 15 460 | 30 | 30 700 | 60 | 4 130 | 8 | 860 | 2 | 51 150 | 33 900 |

*Adapted from Eric Pietrantoni, 'La population du Laos en 1943 dans son milieu géographique'*, Bulletin de la Société des Études Indochinoises *(Saigon)*, N.S., Tome XXXII, No 3, 3ᵉ trim, 1957, pp. 7–8.

mapped. Even for the French, Laos was, at that time, more a carto-graphic reality than a social or historical one. But it was the French who brought the idea of the modern nation to Laos, and this idea would grow slowly among the population over the following 50 years.

State-sponsored education has always been a crucial vehicle for spreading the idea of nationhood, but in Laos French efforts in this respect were minimal. Reliance on the pagoda schools up until the 1930s had the effect of largely excluding non-Buddhist minorities from education; in addition, Buddhist education related to a religious space, a space traced by pilgrimages, which did not conform to the newly boundaried space of Laos, overlapping into Siam in particular. During the reign of Rama VI (1910–25) a powerful ideology of royalist nation-alism which linked the monarchy, Buddhism and the state was elaborated in Siam, and this would reverberate inside Laos. The need to nationalise Lao Buddhism received its first expression in the resur-rection of Vat Sisaket as a centre for Lao Buddhist ceremonial, or, in the words of the Résident Supérieur, as 'the Buddhist cathedral of Laos'. In the late 1920s a reform of the Sangha attempted to give it a more national character by making its rules of organisation uniform. In 1931, in a deliberate attempt by the French to redirect Buddhist learning away from Siam, a Buddhist Institute was established in Vientiane, and another in 1932 in the Kingdom of Luang Phrabang. (The establishment of two institutes, however, was indicative of the continuing fragmentation of national space.) The first institute of this type had been set up in Phnom Penh in 1930 and monks from Laos encouraged to go there; monks from Cambodia played an important role in the establishment of the institutes in Laos. In this way the French turned the eyes of both of their Theravada Buddhist colonies away from Siam and towards each other.

This turning of Lao eyes away from Siam had already found expression in the first Lao-language basic history textbooks written at the instigation of the French and published in the early 1920s. What is striking about these textbooks for a modern reader is that they begin with a discussion of the southern Mon-Khmer minorities in Laos and of their connection to the ancient civilisation of Champa. This subtly de-emphasises Lao roots in a wider Tai world to the west and attempts to connect it to a history of 'Indochina'. The first schoolbooks written in Lao were produced in 1918, and S.P. Nginn helped write the first text for the study of the Lao language the following year. The importance of these texts is that for the first time a conventional national history appears, presenting a sequence of pre-modern states and their kings as the natural precursors of Laos in the twentieth century. This message, even though it was in Lao, was received by very few people within the country. The next important step in this creation of a Lao national history was Paul Le Boulanger's comprehensive *Histoire du Laos Français* (1931), the prototype for all subsequent nationalist histories of Laos. In his preface Le Boulanger acknowledged the help of Prince Phetsarath, who was acutely aware of the national histories that had already come into vogue in neighbouring Siam. It was also in the schools that pupils were first introduced to potential national symbols, such as the map of Laos and the idea of a national flag.

It was the Lao elite, most of them aristocrats, who first received an education in French, and higher education in Hanoi, Saigon or in France. While this education taught them little about Laos, French schooling at that time was steeped in a celebratory French nationalism. Students from its colonies learned about the idea of nation second-hand, but it did not take a lot of imagination to transfer such a concept to their homelands. In the Lao context, however, the message that remained powerful and convincing up until the 1940s was that the French had saved the Lao nation from disappearing, and on this was based their special affinity. But given the racialist ideas in circulation at the time, there was always a tension in this claim, and literate Lao were becoming increasingly aware, through newspapers in particular, of nationalism in neighbouring Siam, which led to the renaming of the country as Thailand in 1939. A key issue facing Lao in the 1930s as they pondered the problems of a Lao nationalism was the standard-isation of the Lao language, a problem the Thai had confronted well before them. When Sila Viravong wrote his *Lao Grammar* in 1935, to counter the situation where religious texts in Laos were written in the 'alphabet of a foreign nation', he used Thai grammar texts as his model.

The importance of the Indigenous Consultative Assembly as a vehicle for national consciousness among the elite has already been remarked upon. However, this elite was very small, and at the lower levels of administration many Lao remained illiterate and ill-informed. Under pressure from increasingly nationalist-inclined administrators like Prince Phetsarath, from Thai nationalism and an increasingly aggressive Vietnamese nationalism, the French became conscious of the weakness of the Lao elite. At the first whiff of communist stirrings in Indochina Résident-Supérieur Bosc warned a probably bewildered Indigenous Consultative Assembly in 1930 against people who 'belong neither to your country or your race', the Vietnamese. This French fear of Vietnamese agitation, along with French claims of having saved Laos from disappearing, would always hold at bay the demands of some French in the 1930s to send 'energetic' Vietnamese settlers to accelerate economic development in Laos. The French, however, also began to see the need for Lao who were willing to save themselves.

Complex and important changes were taking place in France over these years as well. Laos was well represented, along with Cambodia and Vietnam, at the gargantuan Colonial Exhibition in Paris in 1931. Eight million people saw the exhibition, which created a tide of metropolitan opinion favourable to empire. But the images presented were ones that conformed to European ideas of national cultures, ideas that also found their way into tour guides as tourism to Indochina became increasingly important during these years. The increased effort the French put into the restoration of Lao 'national monuments' in the 1930s, such as the Vat Phra Keo in Vientiane, has to be seen partly in this context. The election of the reformist Popular Front government in France in May 1936 was a watershed event, not because it was explicitly anti-colonial, but because it wanted to 'humanise' colonialism, thus liberal administrators were appointed throughout the empire. Eutrope's 1937 appeal for the growth of a Lao elite capable of leading its youth grew out of this context. But in the end the Popular Front only highlighted the contradictions of republican colonialism, because it raised hopes in the colonies of a new era it could not deliver. In countries like Vietnam, with an already developed nationalist movement, this eroded any trust they might have placed in France. The fall of France to Germany in August 1940 and the subordination of the Indochinese colonies to Japanese power dealt a fatal blow to the grandeur of empire.

## The Thai challenge and WW II

Just before the outbreak of World War II, however, another challenge loomed for the French in Laos when Siam changed its name to Thailand as part of a bid to unite all Tai-speaking peoples. This was primarily a propaganda appeal to Tai living under the British and the French, and there was no suggestion that it would be carried out by

*The Governor-General of Indochina and King Sisavangvong during a*
*visit of the Governor to Luang Phrabang in 1935.*

armed force. Nevertheless, the French and the Thai fought a brief war
in December 1940–January 1941 after border negotiations that had
been going on for years broke down. The Thai, assured of the backing
of their new allies the Japanese, attempted to take back the territories
on the west bank of the Mekong that they felt had been unfairly taken
from them in 1904. Japanese arbitration of the dispute claimed the
Mekong was the 'natural' frontier and thus Bassac in the south and
Xaignabouri in the north were reoccupied by Thailand. This was an
enormous blow to French prestige in Indochina.

Nowhere was this felt more than in the Kingdom of Luang Phrabang which, while still loyal to France, had over the years under its
tutelage strengthened and come to better understand its position in
the context of Laos and Indochina. King Sisavangvong's son, Prince

Savang Vatthana, after studying politics and law in France, had returned to take up his position as Crown Prince and adviser to the King. Deeply impressed by his sojourn in France, he understood the modern world of politics and knew how to negotiate with the French. The bitterness of the King at the loss of Xaignabouri Province was thus played to its advantage by the court in Luang Phrabang which, in compensation, demanded sovereignty over the whole of Laos. While a confidential French report in March 1941 recognised this as 'a latent aspiration in the hearts of most Laotians' they felt they could not agree, primarily because they feared for the loyalty of the royal house of Champasak in the south which, if it was going to be subordinated to any other royal house, might have chosen Bangkok. The loss of Bassac had already made the French hold in the south tenuous. Thus, on 21 August 1941 in Vientiane, Prince Savang Vatthana and the Résident-Supérieur, M. Roques, signed an accord which attached the provinces of Xiang Khoang and Vientiane to the Kingdom of Luang Phrabang, and placed the protectorate on the same footing as Cambodia and Annam (northern Vietnam). The French also let it be known that they had no objection to the extension south of the Kingdom after the new arrangement had consolidated itself. The change was accompanied by a significant modernisation of the administration of the Kingdom, with the abolition of the King's council and its replacement with a ministerial system. Prince Phetsarath, who came originally from Luang Phrabang, and through his many years in Vientiane had become the highest ranking Lao in the French administration, became Prime Minister. His cousin, Prince Souvannarath, became Economics Minister, while Prince Setha, a brother of the King, became Minister of the Interior. Phoui, a member of the nobility, became Minister of Justice, while a commoner and former provincial governor of Khammouan Province, Outhong Souvannavong, became Finance Minister. A private advisory council for the King was formed, headed by Prince Savang Vatthana.

The new arrangement, it was thought, put to rest the long-running rivalry between the *vang na*, the 'front palace', and the *vang luang*, the 'main palace', which had been there since Sisavangvong was chosen over Phetsarath's father for the throne in 1904. Chao Boun Khong had been the *ouparat* (viceroy) at the time, and under the system which had been adopted from Ayudhya, stood a good chance of becoming king on the death of the incumbent. Boun Khong, however, was passed over by the French, no doubt because he had been a loyal vassal of Siam and had ridden against the Haw with their armies, and the young Sisavangvong had been trained in France. When Boun Khong died in 1921 no new *ouparat* was named and it looked as though the position would slip into oblivion, just as it had under King Chula-longkorn in the late nineteenth century. In 1941, however, Phetsarath regained his father's old position as 'second king', as it has often been translated. Through the power he exercised in the French adminis-tration Phetsarath was already known as the 'king of Vientiane'. Over the previous 20 years Phetsarath had probably become the most pow-erful Lao in the country. In 1923 he had become head of the Lao Civil Service and in this capacity had organised the Indigenous Consultative Assembly. In 1927, while the King of Luang Phrabang was ill, he took the opportunity to reorganise some of the affairs of the Kingdom. In 1932 he was appointed to the Indochina-wide Council of Economic and Financial Interests, and around the same time became head of the Buddhist Council of Laos. In these various capacities he moved all around Laos, making contacts and dispensing patronage, and building up a substantial entourage throughout Laos, while the King moved in a more restricted circuit. In retrospect it is clear that Prince Phetsarath understood the re-organisation of the kingdom in 1941 to be some-thing similar to the formation of a constitutional monarchy, as had happened in Thailand, with him as head of the government. Lack of clarity in this matter, however, would later lead to serious misunder-standings between him and the Luang Phrabang court.

The ascension of Phetsarath was important for another reason; because his investiture as Prime Minister in Luang Phrabang was the first real occasion of high regal pageantry since the coming of the French. *Chao khwaeng* (provincial governors) from all over Laos, not just Luang Phrabang, were invited to the rituals spread over several days, thus making a claim to the whole of Laos, and to the Luang Phrabang monarchy's central position. Lao officials from elsewhere were clearly overwhelmed by the pomp of the occasion. Phoui Sananikhone, then a young official from Vientiane, writes about how wonderful the parade of elephants and officials was, with the latter resplendent in their traditional costumes covered with medals, followed by a traditional Lao orchestra.

## French sponsored nationalism

In early 1941 a plan of action was drawn up by the French to counter the Thai challenge. Admiral Decoux wrote to the Résident Supérieur, M. Roques: 'The Lao who have rarely bothered to see beyond the trees which surround their villages, must realize from here on that they belong to the great Lao people . . .' and went on to speak of the culture's 'resurrection'.[19] This quasi-biblical imagery was also applied to the upgrading of the École d'Administration, which should be a 'temple for the National Idea of Laos'. The belated recognition of the importance of education for nation-building was shown by the fact that between 1940 and 1945, more schools were built in Laos than had been for the past 40 years. As yet another French report on the situation put it: 'If the protectorate government does not succeed in creating an autonomous Laotian individuality—at least among those who have received education—then they will feel themselves increasingly attracted towards the neighbouring country and this situation will create new difficulties.'

In charge of much of this work was a M. Rochet, Head of the Educational Service in Laos, who was authorised to establish a propaganda arm whose aim was 'to awaken in the Laotians a national spirit and to progressively achieve the moral unity of the country'. The principal instrument of this policy was a Lao language newspaper, *Lao*

*Nyai*, 'Great Laos', which began publication in January 1941. It was an irregular bi-weekly, several thousand copies of which were printed and distributed free. S.P. Nginn, Katay Don Sasorith and others, participated enthusiastically in this enterprise. Rochet, in his memoirs *Pays Lao*, sketches the atmosphere at a typical meeting at one of the *cercles Lao* associated with the paper, and which were formed all over the country, mainly among civil servants:

> It was up to the president of the evening to invite the gathered comrades to begin work as soon as the first dish had been eaten. That was done by Thao Nhot. He stood up and made himself heard over the racket:
> 'It's the time for reports . . . We will begin with the Literature Committee. Boun Tieng has the floor.'
> The tumult died down. Each person took out of their pocket some papers and prepared their presentation. Boun Tieng rose:
> 'During the previous month the Literature Committee has met three times. The first meeting was taken up by the poetry competition: 31 entries have come from all provinces. The jury has made its decision on the winner.'
> Who is it? Came the demand from all sides. Boun Tieng hesitated. Did he have the right to divulge it? . . . They persuaded him and he revealed the name of the winner: Thao Nong, a young functionary from the south of Laos. Everyone clapped. Then they asked for the title of the poem. Boun Tieng pronounced:
> 'It is "The Lao Nation".'
> Tumultuous applause. They called for it to be read. But Boun Nhot rose:
> 'No, not now. First we have the reports.'[20]

ຫັດກາຍບໍລິຫາຮ

A *cartoon from* Lao Nyai *in 1943. The top caption reads 'Physical Fitness'.*
*To the left the sign reads 'dissipation', to the right 'modernisation'.*
*The bottom: 'For the modernisation of the nation'.*

While the content of the paper was never allowed to stray beyond
French policy, nor to become explicitly nationalist, its most important
function was to instil in its readers a sense of Lao space and to create
a sense of identity across this space. It ran poetry competitions that
celebrated Lao culture and history, and it ran columns that propagated

the 'glorious lineage' of the modern Lao from the time of Lan Xang. The inauguration of the renovated Vat Phra Keo in 1942 was publicised as a symbol of general renovation. It, along with the That Luang, the central stupa in Vientiane, would feature as a symbol alongside the paper's masthead. It advertised a newly written and recorded 'Hymne Lao': 'For the first time a revived Laos sings on a gramophone, and to think that tomorrow—from the banks of the Khong to the lost mountains of Phongsali—the same notes will ring out in our hearts and we will hear the very voice of our nation.'

One of the main tasks of an emerging Lao nationalism was to demarcate the Lao from the Thai. For more than 30 years the Thai had been developing their own brand of nationalism, culminating most recently in the Pan-Tai claims emanating from Bangkok. But like all claims based on a mandala past, the game could be played both ways, and inevitably the Lao began to make their own counter-assertions, including claims for the 'lost territories' on the Khorat Plateau. Little of this made its way into the pages of *Lao Nyai*, except obliquely in the form of debates about the nature of the Lao language. At this time Katay Don Sasorith began to emerge as one of the most articulate polemicists for Lao nationalism. In his articles, and especially in the pamphlet *Alphabet et ecriture Lao*, published in 1943, he turned the tables on the Thai to claim not only that King Ramkhamhaeng of Sukhothai was a Lao king, but that the Thai language, often considered at the time to be 'superior' to Lao, in fact was derived from Lao! Katay proclaims: 'Have we ever come across the vestiges of a specific Thai past? No. It is said that even the Thai themselves, when speaking about old traditions and their old secular literature, always refer to old Lao traditions—to the classical Lao literature.' These claims are historically no more accurate than the opposite hyperbolic claims then being made in Bangkok, but they nevertheless expressed a confident and ebullient Lao nationalism.

Given the recent expansion of the kingdom of Luang Phrabang, and French off-the-record assurances that the kingdom could be expanded in the future, it is not surprising that in its early years *Lao Nyai* featured the movements of King Sisavangvong. No doubt in an attempt to placate unease in the south, the King made his first ever trip to Thakhek, Savannakhet and Paksé in 1941, en route to Phnom Penh, and this was covered in the paper. But regal movements did not remain a feature of the paper. One must recall that ever since the overthrow of the absolute monarchy in Siam in 1932 anti-royalist statements would occasionally emanate from Bangkok, especially after the rise of the military regime of Phibun Songkhram in 1938. More-over, the emergent Lao intelligentsia was subject to propaganda from the pro-fascist Vichy regime in France, and a central symbol of the new movement in Laos, a shield inscribed with an L, bore a striking resem-blance to right wing iconography current in Europe. We can therefore see a secular nationalism becoming more pronounced among these Lao, along with muted expressions of egalitarian and democratic sen-timents. Thus an article in *Pathet Lao* in February 1944, 'Reflections sur l' "élite" laotienne', reminds them about how their education fees are paid for by the hard work of the peasantry, and of their responsibilities to the country. 'The new Laos has no need for these representatives of the elite who, both egotistical and ungrateful, scorn-fully isolate themselves and forget the debt that they owe.' These were premonitions that the old world would soon change, forever.

## The Lao Issara movement

On 9 March 1945 Japanese forces overthrew the Vichy French col-onial regime throughout Indochina, and then had the various states declare their independence. Thus, in Luang Phrabang on 8 April, King Sisavangvong proclaimed that 'from this day our Kingdom has been delivered from French domination and become once again a fully independent state'. During negotiations over statehood, differences had emerged between Phetsarath and the palace over their respective roles. According to Phetsarath, Crown Prince Savang Vatthana wished to make the proclamation, but Phetsarath objected that this 'was the opposite of the procedure used in Thailand, where in government matters the Japanese spoke with the Prime Minister and did not intrude on the King. Because of his rank, the Crown Prince is not at government level . . . He should put himself above politics . . .' Dissension over the rights of the monarch and the rights of the prime minister would only deepen in the coming months.

On 27 August 1945 the Japanese forces surrendered to the Allies, and with this Phetsarath moved to bring the southern provinces under the umbrella of a single government and kingdom. This action placed him on a collision course with the court in Luang Phrabang, which had already agreed with the French on the revocation of the earlier proclamation of independence and to the re-establishment of the protectorate. On 15 September Phetsarath went ahead and declared the unification of the Lao Kingdom. For this the King dismissed him from his posts as Prime Minister and Viceroy on 10 October. On 12 October the Lao Issara (Free Lao) government was formed to uphold the April declaration of independence. Katay, a minister in the Issara government, wrote in his history of the movement, published in 1948:

> The formula: 'There is a continuity pure and simple of the protectorat Français in Laos', dictated by colonel Imfeld to prince Savang, implies the maintenance pure and simple of the status quo. This was perhaps for prince Savang—who had never worked in his life and who had never been concerned with the needs and aspirations of the Lao people—a convenient and easy solution, but for us it was a total misunderstanding of the evolution of our sentiments and views since the Siamese aggression of 1940 and the Japanese action of 1945. We could not allow it.[21]

And indeed it was a 'profound misunderstanding', for as we have seen, in Vientiane in particular a Lao nationalist intelligentsia had begun to form (among civil servants, students, military men and others), and Phetsarath was more attuned to their desires than was the palace in remote Luang Phrabang. Even there, however, there was a substantial group of supporters of the Lao Issara, although dynastic politics had inevitably become mixed up with national politics. On 20 October the Lao Issara government asked the King to step down and await a decision of the provisional assembly on the future shape of the monarchy. In Luang Phrabang on 10 November a group of around 30 armed men, led by Prince Sisoumang Saleumsak and Prince Bougnavat, marched on the palace and placed the royal family under house arrest.

The calculations and motivations of the participants in these events were complex for a variety of reasons, not least because of the number of players that had become involved during this short period. After the surrender of the Japanese, the Chinese 93rd Division of 16 000 poor peasant soldiers was dispatched from Yunnan by the Allies to disarm the Japanese in the north, while below the 16th parallel the British were in charge. The British facilitated the return of the French, but the Chinese obstructed it. Most disruptive, however, were the activities of the communist-controlled Viet Minh among the Vietnamese population of the country. In short order, one found pro-French, pro-Thai and pro-Vietnamese supporters in Laos. The political manoeuvring was intense and confused, and no one could really claim to have a clear view of the balance of forces inside the country over that period.

The Luang Phrabang monarchy, which had been treated benignly by the French, felt that, given French promises of a united Lao Kingdom (reconfirmed by de Gaulle), it was best to manoeuvre from under their protective wing, especially in the face of perceived threats from China and Vietnam. The inability of Laos to protect itself from invading armies was abundantly obvious, and not only did Luang Phrabang find the 93rd Division reminiscent of the Haw pillagers of the last century, but the growing power of Vietnam also alarmed them. Fear of Vietnamese intentions was also a major motivation for Lao Issara supporters, many of whom believed that the Vietnamese wished to swallow up Laos (although paradoxically they often found themselves relying on the better organised Viet Minh forces to keep the encroaching French at bay). With his eye on the Vietnamese in his midst Phetsarath, in his October 1945 appeal to the Allies, would say that the Lao 'had become, on their own soil, a poor and backward minority'. Previously, he and the Lao Issara had been depending on America opposing the return of the French to Indochina, which was the policy of President Roosevelt. Roosevelt's death in April 1945, however, had dashed these hopes.

In the cities of Laos distrust became endemic between Lao and Vietnamese. Houmphanh Saignasith, a young Issara supporter, writes in his memoirs of those days:

> I still remember well the climate of tension between the Lao and Annamites of Vientiane one day in June 1945, when the 'Annamites' of the village Ban Ilay (26 km north of Vientiane) marched on Vientiane to show their opposition to the return of French power in Laos . . . All the pagoda drums of Vientiane sounded and one saw the Lao come out of their houses armed with knives, sabres, sharpened bamboo poles, hunting rifles, in short with anything that could be used as a weapon, and that had the effect of discouraging any adventurous action by the Annamites.[22]

As we have already observed, all the major towns of Laos except for Luang Phrabang were dominated by the Vietnamese, and during this time of nationalist upheaval throughout Indochina they were the main force to be reckoned with by everyone.

## The Viet Minh gain their first recruits

The French were prone to brand all nationalist activists as 'communists', but they had a point because communist cadres were very active among the Vietnamese population of Laos. Issara activists, however, seemed unaware of this, and Katay would dismiss such claims out of hand. Nevertheless, their propaganda did influence that of the Lao Issara. There were also individuals like Prince Souphanouvong, the younger half-brother of Phetsarath, who had been working in Vietnam, had married a Vietnamese wife, and had come under the influence of the Viet Minh. He was strong anti-colonial nationalist who believed that only an alliance with the Viet Minh could remove the French. On his arrival in Laos with his Viet Minh bodyguard, some three weeks after the formation of the Lao Issara government in which he had been named a minister, he obviously expected to be treated as an important figure by the leaders of the Lao Issara despite many years' absence. Many of them, however, saw him as an arrogant upstart aristocrat. Katay would write in 1949 of Souphanouvong: 'He, the great man, the little god, . . . He forgets only one thing, unfortunately: for the great masses of the Lao people, he is an "illustrious unknown" . . .' The antagonism was such that Souphanouvong stayed in Vientiane only a short time, relocating himself further south to Thakhek whose population was 75 per cent Vietnamese. In Vientiane he had used his connection to Phetsarath to gain the portfolio of Minister of Foreign Affairs, but not control of the Issara army, as no doubt his mentors hoped. In Thakhek he formed a Committee for an Independent Laos which later communist historians would claim was the foundation committee of the Lao Issara.

It is probably true to say that there were no Lao communists at the time. Kaysone Phomvihan, for example, the future leader of the Lao Peoples' Revolutionary Party, was born in Savannakhet to a Lao mother and a Vietnamese father, and grew to maturity in Vietnam. Somewhere around the age of ten he left Laos to study in Vietnam. In

1943 he entered law school in Hanoi and studied there until the school was closed due to the political turmoil of 1945. From the late 1930s Kaysone was influenced by the political ferment in Vietnam concerning independence, and then by the Viet Minh, with whom he became actively involved in 1944. He returned to Savannakhet in 1945 and organised among the Vietnamese and Lao there. On his return to Vietnam in 1946 he met Ho Chi Minh, and from then on worked in the north of Vietnam and in northeastern Laos with the Viet Minh, becoming a member of the Indochinese Communist Party in July 1949. It is important to understand that at this time people like Kaysone had two identities open to them—both Vietnamese and Lao. As Vietnamese they had the option of a Vietnamese identity that was Indochina-wide. Lao (and Khmer), by contrast, had more spatially restricted identities, although some, like the Issara leader Oun Sananikhone, were at one time influenced by Pan-Tai ideas. It is reasonable to argue that Kaysone's Vietnamese identity was uppermost at this time. He probably used his Vietnamese name as a matter of course, and was indistinguishable from other Vietnamese. A clearer Lao identity only emerged as political imperatives dictated it.

Although communists played no direct role in the Lao Issara movement, the movement's failure and the ensuing recriminations would ensure a core of recruits for the future Lao communist party. And failure of the Lao Issara was ensured once the Allies agreed to the return of the French, which among other things meant no foreign aid to support the new government. Within a very short period of time the Issara government ran out of money to pay for its own running, let alone anything else, like an army, for example. It had asserted control over the opium trade, but in reality could not control it. In an attempt to rein in fiscal expenditure and inflation, the Minister of Finance in the Issara government, Katay Don Sasorith, issued new money in early 1946, which quickly became known as 'Katay's dried banana leaves' for the poor quality of the paper on which it was printed, and its uselessness. There were problems of lack of competence and knowledge, but the fundamental weakness of the Lao Issara was that it remained a small urban-based movement. As Houmphanh Saignasith would later admit: 'As for the population, it was mostly silent, used to the established order and did not appear hardly concerned by this aspiration for the country's independence, and personally I think that it was mostly loyal to the *ancienne* administration, that is to say, the French!' French guerillas operated from the countryside, and from the south a main French force, supported by Prince Boun Oum Na Champasak and other pro-French Lao, slowly rolled up the cities along the Mekong. A bloody battle took place at Thakhek, on 21 March 1946, where the Viet Minh, Souphanouvong and a small Lao contingent stood their ground. Four fighter planes called in by the French caused perhaps hundreds of casualties among the civilians, mostly Vietnamese, and Souphanouvong himself was wounded while withdrawing from the engagement.

In a last desperate attempt to legitimise their government the Lao Issara asked King Sisavangvong to re-ascend the throne as constitutional monarch, to which he agreed. It had only been the continued presence of the Chinese 93rd Division that had stopped a final French assault on Vientiane, but in April the Chinese announced the Division's withdrawal. At the end of April the French took Vientiane, by May they had entered Luang Phrabang, and the Lao Issara leadership fled into exile in Thailand.

# The end of colonialism

The French decision to re-assert colonial control in Indochina and elsewhere was not inevitable. Indeed, in the face of the rise of anti-colonial sentiment inside France and the broadly anti-colonial stance of America, now the most powerful nation in the world, France almost did grant her colonies independence. Once France took the decision to return, it only begrudgingly conceded greater internal autonomy in

*Lao urban activists demonstrate their independence from France, 1950.*
*(Courtesy French military archives)*

Laos, and there were many Frenchmen in the colonies who were reluctant to give up their colonial privileges.

But Laos had changed more than they realised, and even those Lao who were prepared to work with the French saw their presence as a temporary, albeit necessary, compromise before the granting of full independence. On 27 August 1946 a *modus vivendi* was signed that endorsed the unity of Laos as a constitutional monarchy within the French Union. To ensure the ascendance of the Luang Phrabang monarchy a protocol, kept secret at the time, had Prince Boun Oum renounce claims to a separate principality in the south in return for a position as Inspector-General of the kingdom for life. In November the 'lost territories' of Xaignabouri and parts of Champasak were returned by the Thai. In December 1946, elections were held for a 44-seat Constituent Assembly, which met for the first time in March 1947 and endorsed a Constitution. New elections were held in August, and the National Assembly of the first Royal Lao Government endorsed Prince Souvannarath as Prime Minister. A new political party quickly took shape—the Lao National Union, under the leadership of Bong Souvannavong and Kou Voravong, who raised criticisms of the continuing role of the French in the country's administration. Similar criticisms were broadcast by the Issara members in exile.

*Issara members (l–r), Katay Don Sasorith, Prince Souvanna Phouma's wife Aline, Phanya Khammao and Souvanna Phouma, celebrating New Year in 1949 just before their return from exile in Bangkok. (Courtesy Khammao family)*

*Prime Minister Phoui Sananikone reads a speech outside the Opera House in Vientiane on the occasion of the transfer of powers from France to Laos, April 1950. Immediately to his right (standing) is recently returned Issara leader, Phanya Khammao; fourth from the left (standing) is Prince Souvanna Phouma. (Courtesy French military archives)*

The Lao Issara would eventually go the way of most exiled political groups, fragmenting into factions blaming each other for their lack of success. Initially they were welcomed by the post-war Thai government of Pridi Banomyong and assisted by Thai friends and officials. Their activities were largely propagandistic, a task that fell to the prolific and polemical Katay. Small guerilla actions were launched against the French, from Thailand and areas controlled by the Viet Minh. The right-wing coup in Thailand by Phibun Songkhram in November 1947, and his subsequent rapprochement with the French, meant that Lao Issara military activities from Thai soil had to cease. This allowed

Prince Souphanouvong to play the Viet Minh card, arguing that all operations should be relocated to Viet Minh-controlled territory. But most of the Lao Issara leadership were, if not anti-Vietnamese, at least suspicious of Vietnamese intentions, and anti-communist to boot. Souphanouvong denounced his Bangkok-based colleagues as spineless, inviting counter-charges of arrogance from Katay, and in early 1949 resigned from the Lao Issara to throw in his lot with the Viet Minh. Meanwhile a window of opportunity had opened for the Lao Issara leadership's return to Vientiane.

In July 1949, under pressure from within and without, a new General Convention was signed between France and the Royal Lao Government (RLG), which granted Laos much greater autonomy than previously, and was enshrined in a new Constitution in September. This satisfied the demands of most of the Lao Issara leadership, who returned to Vientiane under an amnesty. Laos could now join the United Nations, although foreign policy and defence remained largely in French hands. At that time this was not as unusual as it may seem. Australia, for example, had become independent in 1901, but Britain remained in charge of its foreign policy until 1945. But, the old verities of a colonial world were disintegrating; this kind of divided sovereignty had become anachronistic, and so in October 1953 full sovereignty was attained by the RLG. The military defeat of the French at the hands of the Viet Minh in 1954 saw the end of French colonialism throughout Indochina.

# 3
# THE ROYAL LAO GOVERNMENT

Under an unusually cosmopolitan elite, Lao in the 1950s looked forward to building a modern nation. Soon, however, they were faced with the fact of poverty and the reality of geography which placed Laos in the middle of the Cold War. American aid poured into Vientiane for development, but caused corruption and an unwarranted growth in the power of the military. Many Lao opted for a policy of neutralism, while a small Lao communist movement opposed any alignment with the USA. They were backed by the North Vietnamese who, determined to use trails through Laos to infiltrate into South Vietnam, ignored Lao desires for neutrality. A series of military coups and counter-coups in Vientiane in the early 1960s gave the Lao communists a chance to grow and they made significant inroads on RLG control of the country. Alarmed, America began its air war, and Laos was swept into the Vietnam War.

# The 1950s: years of optimism

One of the most striking changes in the immediate aftermath of the collapse of the Lao Issara government was the Lao-isation of the main cities in the country, as perhaps more than 80 per cent of the Vietnamese population fled back to Vietnam or into Thailand. This meant that Lao would now play a greater role in the running of their country, taking over the positions previously occupied by Vietnamese in the colonial administration. As welcome as this was in theory it was, however, difficult to put into practice because of the failure of the French colonial education system to train sufficient numbers of bureaucrats, despite the educational reforms of the early 1940s. This fact, plus the limited autonomy granted by the French in 1946, meant that French bureaucrats continued to play an important role in state administration up until 1949, when Lao asserted control over all of their ministries. The early 1950s were a time of great optimism in Laos. Most of the Issara luminaries had returned and been reintegrated into society; the government and the Lao leaders, still with considerable French collaboration, set about constructing the new state. 'We were so optimistic. Everything was in front of us. The country was peaceful and we felt we could create the world anew,' Panh Ngaosyvathn, now in his eighties but in charge of handicrafts and industry back then, explained to me in 1998. In 1951 a national police force was created, a national treasury, a post office issuing its own stamps, and various cultural institutions dealing with Buddhism, national monuments, and language and literature. New public buildings were begun, the first stone of the new National Assembly building being laid at the end of 1952. Of course, setting up new state organisations was one thing—and many Lao took great pride and joy in doing so—but paying for them and running them effectively was another thing entirely.

Independence had not changed the basic economic realities of Laos, but the state could no longer expect budget deficits to be covered by a French-controlled central Indochinese budget. How was the shortfall to be managed, especially when the creation of the new state demanded even greater expenditure? One ready source of income was opium, whose production had been encouraged by the French, especially during World War II. Although the Lao themselves did not use opium they had no compunction about selling it to people who did—they had not been subjected to the moral debates in Europe and America about the 'scourge of opium', and therefore felt no guilt in this matter. Thus Thao Leum, the new Minister of Finance in the Royal Lao Government (RLG), boldly told gathered provincial governors in 1948 to lift opium production to 1944 levels: 'The interest of collecting opium is thus of national priority. Every functionary and citizen who lends his collaboration can be proud to have performed useful work.' The withdrawal of the French, however, meant not only a winding down of French aid but also the closure of the opium corporation. Opium could no longer be an official source of revenue because the Americans, who would from the mid-1950s provide crucial support to the Lao budget, found it morally unacceptable. Even so, the growing of opium was not made illegal until 1971 (under American pressure) and trade in opium has remained a tempting source of illicit finance in Laos up until today.

## Underdevelopment

Despite the post-war flurry of activity in Vientiane and other towns along the Mekong, most of the approximately 1.5 million people in Laos in the early 1950s lived as peasants. Unlike the Thai peasantry of the Chao Phraya valley, the lowland Lao had not become drawn into significant commercial production of rice, or indeed any other crop. Commercial rice growing had made acquisition of rice-growing land attractive to commercial farmers and landlords in Thailand, but nothing like this happened in Laos. Lao peasants lived in a basically subsistence economy, in which families produced most of what they needed and bartered and traded for the few products they did not have, often with forest products. Trading was mostly confined to occasional markets that rotated through villages surrounding the market towns usually associated with *tasseng* and *muang* administrative centres. Some industrial products found their way into these networks, primarily through itinerant Chinese traders. Through these small markets the different ethnic groups of Laos came into contact with one another, with highlanders carrying their produce to markets on their backs and gathering there the few items they needed back in their villages. Paradoxically, while the importance of opium in the colonial economy meant that it was some of the most remote groups, such as the Hmong, which were most drawn into commercial agriculture, the wealth that flowed back into their communities, mostly in the form of silver, did not substantially transform the Hmong way of life. They employed some adjacent minority individuals, often opium addicts, as labourers in their fields, but at no point did they turn to large-scale commercial farming.

Leaving aside natural conditions, the major obstacle to greater commercial development was the serious lack of communications infrastructure in the country. In the mid-1950s Laos had around 5600 kilometres of roads, of which around 800 were surfaced and therefore useable in the rainy season. In 1945 there were only nineteen registered vehicles in the country, a figure which had risen to around 100 by the early 1950s. The Mekong River and its tributaries constituted the main travel arteries, but only in some instances were boats driven by motor power. Air transport was minimal, and telecommunication was confined to the main centres. Telephone calls to provincial centres would not become possible until 1967. Communication throughout the country, therefore, was slow and intermittent. Without improvement there could be no serious commercial development of agriculture or exploitation of natural resources, and thus no revenue to initiate serious economic development. Thus the RLG made few economic demands on the rural population and essentially left the peasants untaxed for the whole of its existence.

Given the absence of any important sources of wealth, it is fair to say that at the beginning of the 1950s there were no really rich people in Laos, certainly in comparison with the countries surrounding it, and therefore no elite with capital to invest for economic development. The richest group was the Chinese merchants, but even they had no large funds or obvious outlets for investment. As in Thailand and Cambodia, commercial activity had been largely left to the Chinese while Lao sought a career in the state. The Lao political elite was composed of aristocrats and people whose fathers had held significant administrative positions in the state as either *chao muang* or *chao khwaeng* and had gained some education as a result. Some came from Sino-Lao or Viet-Lao backgrounds, and had chosen to work in the bureaucracy. In these early years traditional hierarchical status differences remained strong within this largely urban-based elite, but there were not yet striking differences of wealth. Those at the very top might have acquired cars, but it was a time when vice-ministers could be seen cycling to work, while many others simply walked. The women on the streets at the time would be going to market because bureaucratic jobs were still mainly a male preserve.

Graham Greene, the author of the acclaimed novel on Vietnam, *The Quiet American*, made a short visit to Vientiane in January 1954. It was, he felt,

> a century away from Saigon . . . an uninteresting town consisting of only two real streets, one European restaurant, a club, the usual grubby market . . . Where Vientiane has two streets Luang Phrabang has one, some shops, a tiny modest royal palace (the King is as poor as the state) and opposite the palace a steep hill crowned by a pagoda . . . One can see the whole town in a half an hour's walk . . .[23]

Little had changed a few years later when Oden Meeker of the international aid organisation CARE arrived in Laos for a one-year assignment:

Vientiane is a wandering village and a few lines of weathered, one-story wooden shops selling pressure lamps, cotton goods, tinned French delicacies, and a scattering of notions. Here and there on one of the three parallel main streets which make up the center of town there are a few two-story buildings. Most of the houses are built of wood and thatch and plaited bamboo, on stilts high off the ground, set back in clumps of thin bamboo and pale-green, oar-bladed banana trees. Everywhere there are pagodas . . . There are a number of pedicabs but few automobiles. This is the capital of Laos . . .[24]

# The American mission civilatrice

The Americans believed they were different from the 'bad old' colonial powers of Europe. Indeed, the Lao Issara initially believed they were too, and looked to the USA for support. The rapid polarisation of Europe into communist and non-communist camps following the ending of World War II and the beginning of the Cold War compelled America to support the French return to Indochina in the name of anti-communism. It was their first major mistake in the region. The USA's emergence from World War II as the most powerful country in the world brought with it imperial responsibilities that many Americans were unprepared for. The cultural shock of this shift from isolationism possibly explains the intensity and indeed hysteria of anti-communist rhetoric in America in the 1950s compared with its other Cold War allies. In schools and on film, communists were presented as radically and frighteningly totally Other, like monsters from outer space, the opposite of 'the American way of life'. Yet the 1950s were also optimistic years; Americans were fiercely proud of their liberal democratic system and the affluence that their brand of capitalism had created. Not unlike the colonial powers they had replaced, they believed that their system was the best of all possible worlds, and many felt they had a mission to spread the 'gospel' of 'the American way of life'. Slowly, however, many in the USA became deeply disturbed by the fact that the use of military power to spread or 'defend' this way of life looked awfully similar to the bad old days of colonialism, at no time more so than during the Vietnam War.

America's support for the RLG in late 1954 was in conscious opposition to French colonial influence. The US mission in Laos in 1954 encompassed less than 20 people; by 1957 there were 100. Laos was not a high priority in American foreign policy, and the few Americans who arrived in Vientiane in those early years knew little about the country—it was simply a far-off place to which they had been sent, a 'hardship posting', which it remains even today for many foreign legations, with 'hardship' bonuses and perks. Anthropologist Joel Halpern, who spent 1957 in Luang Phrabang as part of the US aid mission, wrote of how Americans in Vientiane simply created a 'Little America' there. Of course, all well-off expatriate communities tend to live in a social bubble, but the rapid growth of the American community saw them create their own compounds with American ranch-style homes, a commissary supplying American foods, and even an American restaurant. At this time Vientiane had only two French restaurants and two hotels and there was little night life. Few Americans spoke French, still widely used in the Lao bureaucracy, and almost none knew Lao, thus socialising was confined to the small English-speaking community. The insularity of the American community is reflected in the intense concern with protocol within the community set out at length in the 'Welcome to Vientiane' guide produced by the American Women's Club in 1957. That the 1950s was a world away from the USA of today is underlined by the fact that American women were advised in the guide that: 'Although hats are seldom worn in Vientiane, it is customary to wear a hat and gloves when paying your formal calls, if convenient.' Of course there were some who threw themselves into their work, living outside the confines of 'Little America' or in the provinces, and they became more numerous as time went on, especially in the 1960s as International Volunteer Service (IVS) volunteers fanned out through the country. In these early years few Americans in Laos appreciated the complexities of the land they were to 'save' from communism.

For their part, many Lao actively courted American involvement. The irrepressible Katay, who became Prime Minister in November 1954, penned a tract entitled *Laos—Ideal Cornerstone in the Anti-Communist Struggle in Southeast Asia*, which was clearly aimed directly at American hearts and minds. Having gained independence from the French, the depressing reality had begun to dawn on many that Laos was unable to sustain that independence economically. Furthermore, with the communist revolutions in China and North Vietnam, they were made brutally aware of their political vulnerability. Some like Katay made clear and resolute decisions to seek help from the 'free world', others felt that there must be another way, although they found it hard to articulate what it might be. In the late 1950s the idiosyncratic Bong Souvannavong produced for his Lao National Union party a long and obscure codification of this sentiment in a booklet entitled *Doctrine Lao ou Socialisme Dhammique* (Lao Buddhist Socialism). It attempted to draw on indigenous religious concepts to make sense of the Lao situation, but presented no practical solutions to the country's fundamental dilemmas. Just as America's break with isolationism had created cultural shockwaves of anticommunist hysteria, so the demands in Laos for rapid social and economic change, along with the danger of being sucked into the vortex of the Cold War, sent shivers of cultural anxiety down the spines of its leaders and cultural institutions such as the Buddhist *sangha*. It triggered off a nostalgic preoccupation with 'traditional values' which has still not subsided today.

*Mr Charles Woodruff, Plenipotentiary of the United States, hands over to Prime Minister Katay a cheque for $1 million on 3 January 1955. (Courtesy French military archives)*

## Irresponsible US aid

Consistent with Cold War aims of stemming the 'communist tide', the USA was initially concerned with paying the army numbering 12 800–15 000 men that the French had created as a police force, and they did this from November 1954 onwards. As in the bureaucracy, the departure of French officers left a gap in the command structure that was difficult to fill because the educated class from which officers could be drawn was so small. The USA was drawn inevitably into a much larger aid programme. In the mid-1950s they explained their actions this way:

> The Lao government does not earn enough money to pay the salaries of the soldiers, policemen, teachers, and civil servants it needs. The United States has decided to help, not by paying these people dollars, but by providing dollar exchange to the Lao Government for which the Lao Government provides *kip* at the rate of 35 to one.[25]

What this scheme produced, however, was a wildly overvalued kip that was quickly scooped up by Chinese trading networks throughout the region. The economic consequences were outlined by a scathing *Wall Street Journal* survey in 1958:

> A Laotian trader can buy 100,000 *kip* in the free money market for $1,000. He then applies for an import license for say $1,000 worth of building cement, but puts up only 35,000 [*kip*] to get the $1,000 from the government at the official rate. This leaves him 65,000 *kip* before he has even moved the goods . . . items arrive in Vientiane only to be shipped out again for greater profits. Thus industryless Laos has become an exporter of automobiles and outboard motors.[26]

Many of the goods were simply diverted in Thailand by the trading networks, whose controllers were laughing all the way to the bank. So too were those in charge of import licensing in Laos, as were the Lao political patrons of Chinese merchants who were invited onto the boards of their companies. In a few short years millions of dollars had rained down like manna from heaven on the cities of Laos, making some Lao wealthy, while many others in political positions could at least afford a car or a new house. The bulk of the profits, however, melted into the Chinese business networks. This fools' paradise came to an abrupt halt in 1958 when the Americans insisted on a devaluation of the kip against strong opposition from many in the Lao elite who had become intoxicated by this fabulous infusion of wealth. The corruption and wealth disparities created by the careless dispensation of American aid caused serious political rifts in Laos. What was for the USA a relatively small aid programme amounted to the difference between economic life or death for the RLG, and its dependence on US aid created resentment towards the Americans.

*By the late 1950s Laos had become totally reliant on US foreign aid in all forms. Here USAID is distributed on the ground. (Courtesy Joel Halpern archive).*

The provision of US aid, which had been politically motivated from the outset, became a central issue in Lao politics, contested most adamantly by the communists. In the late 1940s the Indochinese Communist Party or ICP (effectively the Vietnamese Communist Party) had begun recruiting Lao and Lao-Vietnamese adherents, most notably Kaysone Phomvihan in 1948. It was also around this time that Prince Souphanouvong broke with the Lao Issara and joined forces with the Viet Minh. In August 1950 these leftist nationalists and newly recruited communists, numbering around 100 in all, were formed into a new organisation, the Neo Lao Issara (the Lao Freedom Front), which in turn became the kernel of the Lao Communist Party, established in 1955. Souphanouvong himself became a member of the ICP in 1954, a fact he kept well concealed from both the Lao people and his half-brother Prince Souvanna Phouma who, it seems, up until the final communist takeover in 1975 could not believe that a Lao of 'royal blood' could ever become a communist. This belief was more general, and Souphanouvong and his movement would capitalise on it to the end, parading him simply as a Lao nationalist. At the time of the Geneva Conference on Indochina in May 1954, called by the Great Powers to settle the war between the French and the Vietnamese, the Lao communist movement was tiny. But it was backed by the militarily powerful Viet Minh, which had occupied large areas of northern Laos and had helped in the recruiting of more Lao cadres. It was the North Vietnamese who secured recognition for the Lao communists at this conference, as a guerilla movement which had rights to assembly areas in the provinces of Houaphan and Phongsali, both of which shared a border with north Vietnam. Subsequent negotiations with the RLG would determine the communists' integration into the mainstream of Lao political life. Just how they would be integrated was the key issue of Lao politics for the next three years.

# Phu nyai politics

Political parties were new to Laos. As in other developing countries, they seemed to ramify and factionalise endlessly along personal lines, as indeed they had in the early years in western democracies. The Americans at the time, and subsequent historians of Laos, have often tried to make sense of this chaos by attributing key roles to 'great families' and 'clans'. The inadequacy of these concepts for understanding the Lao reality is underlined by the fact that one is forever confronted by examples of family members on opposite sides of the political fence. The most visible case is that of Souvanna Phouma and Souphanouvong. Family ties and obligations did continue to bind these two, and sometimes a family idiom was used by outsiders to understand their actions (and no doubt by the individuals themselves), but these ties were challenged by other imperatives. A key role has also been attributed to regionalism, in particular competition between the north and south of the country, but this too was only a tendency, not a hard and fast rule.

An equally enduring and salient concept for Lao political culture is that of the *phu nyai*, the 'big man', and his volatile entourage. In the Lao cultural world there is an ambiguous relationship between power and righteousness, one which often veers strongly in the direction of 'might is right'. People with power and wealth have maybe acquired them because of their Buddhist merit, or *boun*. The reality of *boun*, however, can only be revealed through the lapse of time as the *phu nyai* redistribute wealth and dispense patronage to their followers on a continuous basis. The *phu nyai* are expected by these followers to adhere to the etiquette of their elevated station, which means driving good cars, eating good food, leaving large tips, and the like, as a way of continually reaffirming their status. In this world followers are also always looking for signs of sudden decline, and are prepared to quickly desert a former patron. In this sense the *phunyai* system is not 'feudal' because followers are not bound to an overlord, it is rather a form of patron–client relations typical of modernising political systems. As in all developing countries, politics in Laos was largely confined to a small urban elite, where real political differences were minimal, and entourages formed and reformed around individuals in endless manoeuvres for the spoils of power.

In these circumstances the ability to gain high position and channel US aid towards one's entourage was a central political aim of the 1950s, and no doubt accounts for the facility with which some politicians began to reproduce American-inspired anti-communist rhetoric. Certainly, among some politicians and generals these sentiments were heartfelt, but others opportunistically expressed the same views in order to manipulate the USA. Indeed, far from American influence being a one-way street, Lao became masters at channelling and twisting US rhetorical and policy imperatives to their own aims. It is this that confounds simplistic models of 'neo-colonialism' for Laos.

## Neutralism

Neutralism as a political option first emerged at the Geneva Conference, and the politician who came to embody this policy for the next 20 years was Prince Souvanna Phouma. Aristocratic, mild-mannered and cosmopolitan, he was never seen to be venal although he and his followers clearly benefited from the perks of office. But in Lao eyes this was appropriate, as Souvanna was seen to be a 'man of merit'. Other neutralists, such as those grouped around Bong Souvannavong, were in American eyes 'leftists' because they did not support alignment with the USA. The communists opportunistically supported neutralism, because in the context of Lao politics they could not openly call for alignment with communist North Vietnam or China. It was their verbal support of the concept that made it so much easier to brand other neutralists as 'leftists'. Politicians like Bong in fact reflected the deep cultural reservations of some Lao about the impact on traditional values of the modern world, which American culture represented. Lao, they implied, would be better off if they simply kept to themselves.

Souvanna's view was more sophisticated, for he realised that none of Laos's neighbours, nor the Great Powers, were likely to allow this little country, which now shared borders with 'Red China' and the Democratic Republic of Vietnam, to go it alone. He also believed that a tiny country like Laos could not afford to openly take sides. The key to interference by outside powers was their ability to find clients inside Laos, thus the key to neutrality was to draw these clients away from their patrons, in particular Souphanouvong and his followers away from the North Vietnamese. Souvanna Phouma was anti-communist, although in the mid-1950s his opposition was not sufficiently strident for US taste. He believed, probably rightly at that time, that communism had still not sunk solid roots in Laos and, influenced by a somewhat romanticised view of Lao culture, that no real Lao could be a communist, because of the importance of Buddhism, among other things. After Geneva, Souvanna as Prime Minister devoted his energies to drawing the Neo Lao Issara supporters back into the mainstream of Lao politics and society. When Souvanna was briefly ousted from the prime ministership by Katay in late 1954, negotiations with Souphanouvong stalled, partly because of the strong personal antipathy between Souphanouvong and Katay (a hangover from their Lao Issara days) but also because the leftists refused to return Houaphan and Phongsali to RLG administration. Souvanna Phouma returned to power in early 1956, and by August had reached agreement with Souphanouvong for the return of the two provinces, the integration of guerilla soldiers into the RLA, and for supplementary elections to be held, preceded by a Government of National Union. A year earlier the Neo Lao Issara had been transformed into the Neo Lao Hak Xat (NLHX), the Lao Patriotic Front, in order to contest future elections.

Regional conditions for pursuing a neutralist course were relatively favourable in 1956. The Bandung Conference of Asian and

African nations in April 1955 had raised the profile of 'non-alignment'; in Thailand, the regime of Phibun Songkhram flirted with rapprochement with China and newspapers debated neutralism. This caused consternation among Thailand's American backers—besides being strongly opposed to any overtures to China, they felt that the Thai stance was undermining their opposition to Souvanna Phouma's policies in Laos. (When in August 1956 Prince Souvanna Phouma set off on goodwill missions to Hanoi and Beijing, he did so hard on the heels of several Thai emissaries to Beijing.) The more moderate and democratic mood that emerged in Thailand in the period 1955–58 facilitated Souvanna's attempts at reconciliation in Laos.

*Prince Souvanna Phouma meets Mao Zedong in Beijing in 1956.*
*(Courtesy Prince Mangkra Souvanna Phouma)*

Indeed, reconciliation was in the air. In March 1957 Prince Phetsarath returned from ten years of exile in Thailand. In a sign of settlement, the now aged King Sisavangvong restored to him the rank of *ouparat*. While Phetsarath endorsed Souvanna's policies, this man who once towered over Lao politics now had little influence. This did not stop him from casting a caustic eye over the Lao political scene:

> Our greatest danger of Communist subversion arises from the bad use of foreign aid we receive ... It enriches a minority outrageously while the mass of the population remains as poor as ever ... Laos maintains an army of 30,000 men, including the police force. This army costs us dearly. It takes men from agriculture and industry. And it could not possibly defend the country from foreign invasion.[27]

Phetsarath retired to Luang Phrabang, and although he died only two years later, his return suggested that the Lao could finally put past divisions behind them.

## Cold War politics in Laos

The Americans were opposed to Souvanna's inclusive position on the communists because they felt it would lead to 'conquest by negotiation', as had occurred in Czechoslovakia in 1949, a failure which loomed large in their imagination. The difference was that the Czech communists had a large following, the Lao communists did not. Even so, US aid was not withdrawn when the NLHX handed over the two northern provinces to the RLG on 18 November 1956, and Souphanouvong and his associate Phoumi Vongvichit joined the government as Minister of Planning and Minister of Religion and Fine Arts respectively. In an attempt to support non-communist candidates in the build-up to the supplementary elections, scheduled for 8 May 1958, the US Ambassador, Graham Parsons, in American electioneering style launched Operation Booster Shot to get some aid out to 'the people'. Oden Meeker of CARE observed how the candidates 'caught on quickly, dandling babies and handing out aspirin, showing movies, throwing parties with free drinks and dancing, and putting their pictures up everywhere, including the backs of pedicabs. Representative government had arrived'.

The NLHX did well in the supplementary elections, scoring nine out of a total 20 seats; their ally Satiphab (the Peace Party) scored four; their anti-communist opponents scored only seven. Yet the NLHX had gained only 32 per cent of the vote. The secret of their success was simple—their opponents had continued to play personal politics and fielded 84 candidates for the 20 seats, thereby seriously fragmenting their electoral support. It was a sobering lesson in party politics and the non-communist groups quickly consolidated themselves into the Rally of the Lao People, to hold 36 of the overall 59 seats in the new Assembly, easily outvoting the NLHX and Santiphab. The now legendary Prince Souphanouvong had gained the highest individual vote, while Kaysone Phomvihan, future communist strongman of Laos, had lost, in the only free and relatively fair election he ever participated in.

Throughout the Third World Leninist parties were formidable opponents, whether in elections or armed struggle, because of the discipline they exercised over their members. The disciplined unity of these parties for many seemed to embody the nationalist ideal of unity. Their modern, apparently rational bureaucratic structure and egalitarian recruitment also seemed to be a break from the 'feudal' nature of parties that were organised around the *phu nyai* and patronage so typical of Laos and other developing countries. A further reason for the effectiveness of the NLHX against the other parties in Laos was that in structure it provided a parallel 'government', unlike the RLG parties which, for all their nepotism, kept party structures and government structures largely separate, as at least a gesture towards liberal democratic practices. Communist support was also spread by terror, that is, by the execution of 'reactionary' leaders at the village and district levels. Not only was this an effective form of intimidation, but it was familiar—the use of force by outsiders to assert political and social power was all the peasants had known. They had no experience of liberal democracy. The NLHX was also able to effectively redirect resentment against outsiders by mobilising sentiment against 'foreigners', who were allegedly corrupting and wrecking the country. The maladroit American aid effort made this task all the easier.

Even with all these factors working for the communists, their influence in Laos remained small in 1958—not that one would have thought so from the reactions of both the Americans and the right wing Lao parties. The result of the May 1958 election sent shock waves through the US establishment, triggering among other things the reappraisal of aid that torpedoed the exchange rate scam. Under the pretext of this reappraisal, which had also uncovered corruption among American contractors, the USA suspended its now vital aid, with the aim of forcing Souvanna Phouma and his coalition government from office. They succeeded when in August 1958 Phoui Sananikhone became Prime Minister and excluded the NLHX from ministerial posts. Phoui, described by the perceptive British military attaché at the time, Hugh Toye, as 'one of the two or three Laotian politicians capable of holding his own in the world of statesmen', launched a campaign against corruption and against sympathisers of the NLHX in the administration. A lurch to the right began.

Phoui was by now a veteran on the Lao scene, a member of the generation which had grown up under the French. By the late 1950s a new generation of leaders was emerging, people formed by decolonisation who were enthralled by the promise of modernity held out by the 'American way of life'. In 1958 they came together in the Committee for the Defence of the National Interest (CDNI), a strongly pro-American political organisation committed to a western vision of modernisation. They campaigned against corruption and called for 'reform of our public service, with promotions based on merit and not on ancestry or nepotism'. The CDNI's power base was primarily in the Defence and Foreign Ministries. The key military figure in the CDNI, which secured four positions in Phoui's cabinet, was Colonel Phoumi Nosovan, recently returned from officer training in France.

## The army enters politics

As in many other Third World countries, the army appeared to be one of the few national organisations that could get things done in Laos. For uneducated lower class recruits, armies were schools for modern skills and for nationalism. In the context of the Cold War the army was thus a natural target for American aid, but the disproportionate amount of money that flowed towards it had the *phu nyai* effect of creating politically ambitious officers. By 1958 army salaries, which were paid for by US aid, had become the main source of liquid cash in the Lao economy and were driving commercial development. Despite this, the Lao army remained a young, poorly trained force, with officer training shared between the Americans and the French—which became a source of division. Furthermore, officer training concentrated on conventional warfare rather than the guerilla warfare more appropriate for Lao conditions. Thus Royal Lao Army (RLA) troops were scattered in small platoons and companies across the length and breadth of Laos, in fixed positions, only in contact with their rear areas by messenger or infrequent liaison plane. They were easy prey for guerillas able to concentrate their forces for an attack, who in the border regions could always panic small garrisons by spreading rumours of North Vietnamese soldiers on the march. Unable to easily call in reinforcements, the RLA made frequent recourse to standing orders to abandon posts when confronted by superior forces.

The evolution of events in Laos was being watched keenly by Hanoi, which was able to maintain much stricter control over the NLHX than the Americans were ever able to assert over their clients. During 1958 the Vietnamese Communist Party moved towards a policy of armed reunification with the South. To maintain contact with their sympathisers in the South, to infiltrate northern cadres and receive southerners for training, they depended on a series of trails that ran through eastern Laos that came to be known collectively as the Ho Chi Minh Trail. A key entry point was near the town of Xepone in Savannakhet Province, and in December the Democratic Republic of Vietnam (DRV) dispatched two battalions of regular soldiers to secure the area from RLA patrols. This caused uproar in Vientiane. In the face of this threat from the North Vietnamese army, in January the National Assembly gave Phoui special powers for a year to deal with problems of subversion, and Phoumi Nosovan was brought into the Cabinet. In the following months tensions escalated between Vientiane and Hanoi and Beijing. In May Phoui's government insisted on the integration of 1500 NLHX troops into the RLA, as had been agreed before the election, and the demobilisation of the rest. One battalion near Luang Phrabang complied with the reintegration order, another on the Plain of Jars fled back into North Vietnamese protected territory. It was an act of 'rebellion', said Phoui, and the NLHX members in Vientiane were arrested. Had it been elsewhere they probably would have been shot, and perhaps it was only Souphanouvong's magic circle of royalty that saved them from this fate.

The NLHX guerillas, with support from North Vietnam, set about reasserting control over Houaphan Province by attacking the dispersed RLA garrisons there. The Vientiane government's move to the right had given impetus to the North Vietnamese desire to secure the border provinces inside Laos. The poor state of communications across the country made it hard to know the real situation in the provinces, and wild rumours of Vietnamese invasion circulated in Vientiane. This stiffened the resolve of the rightists there to request greater US military aid and to crack down on the communists.

Punctuating this crisis atmosphere in 1959 were the deaths of three major figures. First to go was Prince Phetsarath on 15 October, followed by King Sisavangvong on 29 October, after more than 50 years on the throne. On 29 December Katay died suddenly, at the age of 55. The new King Savang Vatthana, a conservative but very careful man, would play a crucial behind-the-scenes role in the coming turbulent years. Often considered pro-French like his father, in fact he was sometimes intensely critical of France's post-World War II role in Indochina. He would angrily tell the American Ambassador in the 1960s that 'it was France which started the [Vietnam] war by its stupidity in attempting to re-establish its colonial control in 1945. It was France that created the Viet Minh'.

In an attempt to allay the crisis atmosphere, on 15 December Phoui renounced his special anti-subversion powers, while the Assembly voted to prolong its mandate until elections scheduled for April 1960. Phoui also foreshadowed the removal from his Cabinet of CDNI members, who had become strident and assertive over the past year. In reaction the CDNI made their move on 31 December, with Phoumi leading a putsch to force Phoui's resignation. Many felt that only Katay with his strong army connections could have averted this, and Phoui would say at his funeral in Paksé in mid-January, attended by thousands of mourners: 'His loss at this crucial moment for the future of our country has been sorely felt. There is no doubt that if he were alive, things would not have the same aspect as they do today.' The CDNI had been emboldened by Sarit Thanarat's imposition of martial law in Thailand in October 1958, declaring that Thai problems needed Thai not western solutions. Sarit's 'Thai solutions' required American backing for the army, and thus he crushed all neutralist and leftist debate to swing strongly behind US foreign policy aims in the region. Crucially, Sarit and Phoumi were related by marriage, a tie which further emboldened the would-be Lao military strongman. But Laos was not Thailand, and the balance of political forces was different. The Lao king at that time exercised relatively greater power than the Thai king, whose effectiveness since he had ascended the throne had been hamstrung by the government of Phibun Songkhram; moreover, the Lao king was a fervent defender of constitutional rule. In Thailand a strong and hierarchical bureaucratic polity had been put in place over the past half century, and since the overthrow of the absolute monarchy in 1932 the Thai army had secured for itself a central and powerful place in Thai politics. In Laos, by contrast, the bureaucracy remained weak and ramshackle, while the army was still in its formative years, weaknesses enhancing the role of *phu nyai* politics.

The putschists declared their allegiance to the constitution before the King, who named the venerable head of the King's Council, Kou Abhay, to head an interim government to arrange for elections. Ominously, Phoumi was named Minister of National Defence. Formerly a young Issara member, he became the communists' *bête noir*, and was endlessly denounced as an 'American puppet'. But Phoumi epitomised a particular cultural ideal of the tough *phu nyai*. Toye described him as having 'an open smile and a persuasive manner . . . His voice was deceptively soft, his speech disarming. But in fact he was as ruthless as his appearance suggested. When among his own people, there was an air of muted violence about the man, a scarcely hidden enjoyment of power over people, a hint of conscious physical restraint.'[28] As Minister of National Defence he was now one of the most powerful men in the country. And he and his CDNI colleagues used this power to rig the forthcoming elections through gerrymandering, toughening the criteria for candidacy, vote buying and intimidation. Not surprisingly, they swept the polls held in May.

Prince Somsanith, a cousin of Souvanna Phouma who was now head of the Assembly, became Prime Minister. Somsanith was a former young Issara man too, respected former Governor of Luang Nam Tha Province. While the real power in his government lay with Phoumi, the fact that Phoumi did not hold the top post was one indication that, unlike Sarit in Thailand, he could not impose his will on the Lao political scene. His attempt to do so, however, detonated a political crisis from which the RLG never recovered.

## The Kong Le Coup

Before dawn on the morning of 9 August 1960, the crack troops of the 2nd Paratroop Battalion fanned out through Vientiane and quietly but firmly took control of government offices, communications and the power station. This was the Kong Le Coup whose consequences were such that its leader, Captain Kong Le, became a modern legend. In the days following the coup he would tell his audiences: 'We have only seen Lao killing Lao without cause. In my experience, many past Lao governments have told us they wished to follow a neutral course, but they never did so. My group and I decided to sacrifice everything, even our lives, in order to bring peace and neutrality to the nation.' The coup was totally unexpected. The day before, the entire Cabinet, including Phoumi, had decamped for Luang Phrabang to discuss with the King final plans for the funeral of the late Sisavangvong, whose embalmed body had rested in an ornate sandal-wood bier since October 1959, awaiting a propitious time for cremation. The Americans, who thought they had a privileged relationship with the army, were also taken by surprise. Like many neutralists, Kong Le distrusted US influence on the Lao army and politics, and he drew on a deep cultural wellspring fearful of Laos's rapid ascent into the vortex of the Cold War. As a soldier he was disgusted to see politicians and generals in Vientiane growing fat on US aid while his soldiers faced hardship and death. This diminutive figure, who emerged out of nowhere like a *phu mi boun* to 'save the country from foreigners', became immensely popular. Arthur Dommen, a witness to these events, wrote: 'Kong Le, plucked from the familiar milieu of his trusted soldiers and thrust into the public limelight, acted with a strange mixture of humility and flamboyance. He delighted in pleasing the people; while in Vientiane he passed out hundreds of photographs of himself in his captain's uniform.' Iron-ically, the coup that Phoumi would have loved to pull off, but never could because of American restraint, was finally carried out by the neutralist Kong Le, and it moved the military to centre stage in Lao politics.

Kong Le's politics were simple, even naive, and he and his comrades had little idea of what to do next. Colonel Oudone Sananikhone, arrested temporarily by the coup makers, commented: 'When I asked about their plans for the economic and commercial life of the country, it became clear that they had no idea at all of economic planning, other than to raid the banks.' Kong Le called for Souvanna Phouma to be reinstated as Prime Minister, and indeed the Prince attempted to lead the coup back onto the path of legality, on 13 August having the National Assembly pass a censure motion against the Somsanith government. Somsanith then stood down in favour of Souvanna, who formed a government that excluded the CDNI. The crisis seemed to have been averted, and even Phoumi appeared to have acquiesced. However, the dynamics of *phu nyai* politics would not allow Phoumi to return to Vientiane and have his actions circumscribed by a soldier who was his subordinate. He still controlled most of the supplies of the Lao army, had the allegiance of the commanders of four of the five military regions (excluding Vientiane), and could promise to pay the salaries of those who supported him because the CIA at least had promised continued funding. Moreover, Sarit in Thailand was urging a hard line against what seemed to him a pro-communist coup. Phoumi therefore flew from Luang Phrabang to Bangkok for consultations with Sarit, and then to his home town of Savannakhet to organise opposition to the coup.

American reactions to the coup were split. Divisions had already emerged under Horace Smith, appointed Ambassador in March 1958, who had feuded with the CIA chief of station over policy options in Laos, with the CIA favouring their military contacts. Smith was replaced one month before the coup by Winthrop Brown, whose attitude to Kong Le was sympathetic, once again in contrast to Phoumi's CIA and Pentagon backers. The black-and-white verities of the Cold War were under challenge. The 1958 release of *The*

*Ugly American*, the bestselling semi-fictionalised critique of American aid modelled on Laos and Thailand, signalled the beginning of a more subtle approach to the region. But for the moment US policy on Laos was divided.

Souvanna Phouma, with the backing of the new American ambassador, swiftly moved to open negotiations with both the left and the right. In particular he realised that Phoumi had to be accommodated, or the country would be at risk of civil war. Thus Phoumi was brought into a new Cabinet as Deputy Prime Minister and Minister of the Interior on 17 August. This Cabinet, however, was stillborn. Rightists were already wary of returning to a capital controlled by Kong Le's troops, and Kong Le himself did not help matters when he denounced the new Cabinet in an emotional broadcast over Vientiane radio, an action for which he was reprimanded by the ever-tactful Souvanna Phouma. *Kiat*, pride and respect, had to be nurtured at all times in this volatile environment, yet Kong Le had offended Phoumi once again. Back in Savannakhet, surrounded by his entourage, Phoumi was obviously convinced that his failure to gain the Ministry of Defence was reason enough to not participate in the new government, particularly when he retained the support of most of the army, Sarit and the CIA. Prince Boun Oum, who commanded loyalty throughout most of the south, joined with him in a Counter Coup d'Etat Committee to oppose Kong Le and the new government by force of arms. Unmarked planes began to deliver war material to Savannakhet and Marshall Sarit in Thailand imposed an unofficial blockade on Vientiane.

In October, America suspended its cash grant aid to Souvanna's government and dispatched former Ambassador and now Assistant Secretary of State J. Graham Parsons, a Cold War stalwart, to talk with Souvanna. Parsons insisted that negotiations with the NLHX, or Pathet Lao (PL) as they had come to be known, be broken off, but the Prince could not agree to this. Ambassador Brown tried to broker a compromise by pointing out the threat posed by the PL while the two anti-communist forces squabbled. He got aid flowing again by having Souvanna agree to the continuation of deliveries of arms to Savannakhet, on condition that they were only to be used against the PL. But all attempts to broker deals between the belligerents failed. The Thai blockade had compelled Souvanna Phouma's government to turn to the Soviet Union for airlifts of fuel to support the running of Vientiane, a move which further inflamed rightist suspicions, and foreshadowed the crucial role the Soviets would play over the coming year. Even though the USA cut off its supplies to Phoumi on 30 November, it had lost any control over events.

In the first week of December Phoumi's troops marched on Vientiane and in two weeks of fierce fighting some 600 people were killed and large sections of the city wrecked. On 9 December, Souvanna Phouma flew into exile in Cambodia. On 10 December one of his leftist Cabinet Ministers, Quinim Pholsena, flew to Hanoi and signed an agreement for the airlift of arms and supplies to the forces opposing Phoumi (which included North Vietnamese manned artillery). Even so, the neutralists were outgunned. Kong Le and his troops retreated up the highway towards Luang Phrabang, finally establishing their headquarters on the Plain of Jars, where they were joined by PL troops. On 11 December the National Assembly convened in Savannakhet to censure Souvanna's Cabinet, and a few days later a Boun Oum-led government was entrusted by the palace with the 'temporary conduct' of the Kingdom's affairs. From Phnom Penh, Prince Souvanna Phouma bitterly denounced Parsons: 'He understood nothing about Asia and nothing about Laos. The Assistant Secretary of State is the most nefarious and reprehensible of men. He is the ignominious architect of disastrous American policy toward Laos. He and others like him are responsible for the recent shedding of Lao blood.' In fact, rightist policy had been totally counterproductive in its own terms because it led to a rapid expansion of communist influence in Laos.

*The coup by Colonel Kong Le (right) in August 1960 had
profound repercussions for Lao politics. His neutralist soldiers
were forced to retreat to the Plain of Jars, where he was joined
by neutralist Prime Minister Prince Souvanna Phouma (left)
in 1961. (Courtesy Prince Mangkra Souvanna Phouma)*

## Communist influence grows

Up until the time of the coup PL forces in Laos remained small, maybe
several thousand strong. Their objectives throughout remained
subordinate to those of the Vietnamese Communist Party, whose main
aim was to ensure that no foreign bases could be installed in Laos (also
a condition of the Geneva Accords). The prospect, for example, of a
US airbase on the Plain of Jars within easy striking distance of
Hanoi was a strategic nightmare for the DRV. If a neutralist coalition
government in Laos could keep foreign bases out the DRV would
support it. If rightists won the day in Laos and tried to deny access to

the Ho Chi Minh Trail, the DRV was ready to commit regular forces under a PL umbrella to secure that access. In 1958, however, both Souvanna Phouma's government, and then Phoui's, insisted that the conditions of the 1954 Geneva agreement had been fulfilled in Laos. This was unacceptable to the North Vietnamese who, through Prime Minister Pham Van Dong, declared in early 1958 that solutions to the problems of the three states of 'Indochina', as outlined at Geneva, 'were one and indivisible'. In other words, try as the Lao might, the North Vietnamese would not allow them to separate their internal problems from those of the DRV. It was this ruthless determination which would drag Laos into the maelstrom of the Vietnam War. During 1959, against the background of a shift to the right in Vientiane, the PL and the DRV intensified their armed engagements in the northern provinces. The split in the anti-communist forces caused by Kong Le's coup was a godsend for them because it made possible a military alignment with the neutralist forces against the right. When Kong Le established his headquarters on the Plain of Jars the Soviets, claiming to carry out their commitments to Souvanna Phouma's government, were able to fly in not only military supplies that supported Kong Le's army but also PL units which were able to transform themselves into a regular army. This alliance spread the field of operation of the PL and extended their control of village administrations. Furthermore, many of the young students and others who rallied to Kong Le in Vientiane had been airlifted up to the Plain, where large numbers were recruited by the PL. Beijing's declaration of support for 'liberation movements', spurred on by its competition with the USSR for hegemony in the world communist movement, during 1960 saw the Chinese provide the PL forces with enough weapons and supplies to equip 20 000 men.

The split in the anti-communist forces caused disarray and demoralisation in the RLA which, under Phoumi, fought uninspiringly. They were no match for North Vietnamese regulars, who were often used to spearhead assaults while PL troops were used to mop up or pursue the panicked RLA soldiers. The lacklustre performance of Phoumi's forces dashed rightist hopes of a military solution to the Lao crisis. King Savang Vatthana came under increasing behind-the-scenes pressure to enter the political fray to form a broadly based government. He refused because to do so would compromise the constitutional monarchy, perhaps fatally, and he felt he could be more effective where he was. On 19 February he addressed the nation: 'Lao people, the misfortunes which have befallen us have been the result of disunity among the Lao on the one hand and of foreign interference on the other. Foreign countries do not care either about our interests or peace; they are concerned only with their own interests.' This speech encouraged Prince Souvanna Phouma to fly to the Plain of Jars from Phnom Penh and begin yet another search for a political solution. Indeed, he managed to arrange a meeting with Phoumi in Phnom Penh in early March, but the communist side, wishing to capitalise on its battlefield successes, was reluctant to join talks. The momentum towards new peace talks was given a boost on 23 March when the new US President Kennedy threw his weight behind a neutralised Laos, and US support fell in behind Souvanna Phouma. A month earlier Souvanna had observed morosely:

> The Americans say that I am a Communist. All this is heartbreaking. How can they think I am a Communist? I am looking for a way to keep Laos non-Communist. To be pro-West, on the other hand, does not necessarily mean to be pro-American. To be anti-American does not mean to be pro-Communist. When we say we are anti-American, we are against the American policies of the moment. We are anti-American because these Americans don't understand Laos, they have regard only for their own interests.[29]

Under Kennedy the USA finally woke from its Cold War nightmare, and began to see the world more clearly, including Souvanna's vital role in Laos.

The Soviets responded favourably to the US shift, and in April they and their co-chair of the 1954 Geneva Conference, the UK, issued invitations to twelve countries to attend an 'International Conference on the Laotian Question'. But on the ground, fighting continued as the communist forces attempted to maximise their gains, and Phoumi doggedly refused to accept moves towards a second coalition government despite US pressure. Finally, in January 1962 the three Princes, Boun Oum, Souvanna Phouma and Souphanouvong, met in Geneva and agreed on equal representation of the right and the left in the coalition. In an attempt to force Phoumi's government to agree to this proposal, the USA suspended economic and military aid. Phoumi had already turned to that old staple of Lao finance, the opium

*The three princes, Boun Oum, Souvanna Phouma and Souphanouvong, 1963, following their final peace agreement. (Courtesy Prince Mangkra Souvanna Phouma)*

123

trade, to forestall US pressure, but it was not nearly enough to pay for his soldiers and government. This deficit, combined with a military debacle for the RLA in Luang Nam Tha, left Phoumi with little to bargain with and he agreed to talks with Souvanna. In the meantime he and Boun Oum, accompanied by Sarit, had held talks with the Thai King who, familiar with American accounts of what had taken place in Czechoslovakia in 1949, was deeply worried by developments in Laos. The two Lao expressed their bitterness about what they saw as 'American betrayal' to the King, and a few days later he would lecture the US Ambassador to Thailand on the need for Americans to understand the 'different temperament and mentality' of the Lao. The Ambassador reported:

> The King told me he could well understand Lao emotional reactions to Americans because Thais went through similar experience several years ago when there were many deep and bitter clashes between American and Thais. Today Thai–US relations are good . . . Americans now show tact and consideration for very sensitive people in this small Asian country. Lao people are no different than Thais in this regard. The King said he hoped Lao and Americans would achieve a similar relationship.[30]

## The eclipse of neutralism

In June agreement was reached on a Provisional Government of National Union, made up of eleven neutralists, four rightists and four Pathet Lao. Souvanna was Prime Minister and Minister of Defence, and was flanked by Souphanouvong as Deputy Prime Minister and Minister of the Economy, with Phoumi as the other Deputy Prime Minister and Minister of Finance. Prince Boun Oum retired from politics. Many of the conditions from the original Geneva Conference were stipulated, including no foreign bases and a timetable for the withdrawal of foreign troops. The government would exist only until a permanent government could be properly established through elections. The two sides would continue to administer their respective zones, although this meant, among other things, that the withdrawal of 10 000 Vietnamese troops from PL zones could never be verified. American and Thai military personnel left under international scrutiny, although the CIA continued to supply clandestine support to a burgeoning irregular army around the Plain of Jars, under the command of the Hmong, Colonel Vang Pao. While Souvanna Phouma hoped to be able to build up a strong centrist party, constructed partly out of defectors from the right and the left, this plan foundered when his military power base, Kong Le's neutralist army, split over the acceptance of US military aid. The Soviet airlift to the Plain of Jars had ended, Kong Le's forces needed re-supplying, and Souvanna agreed to have Air America, a CIA-funded airline, ferry in US supplies. The Pathet Lao objected, and when in November a plane was shot down by a neutralist faction under Colonel Deuane Sunnarat, who had grown close to the PL, Kong Le's closest comrade Colonel Ketsana tried to arrest those responsible. He was prevented from doing so by the PL, and two months later was assassinated. In retaliation the leftist-neutralist Minister of Foreign Affairs, Quinim Pholsena, was assassinated in Vientiane on 1 April 1963, by one of his own guards. Other scores were settled, and in fear of their lives Souphanouvong and Phoumi Vongvichit left the capital. On the Plain of Jars, the PL and Deuane's troops launched a major assault on Kong Le's soldiers who were driven to the western margin of the plain and to the margin of Lao politics. The neutralist armed forces role had effectively ended, and with it the prospects of a neutralist government as envisaged by Prince Souvanna Phouma.

In response the USA stepped up its support of the Hmong forces under Vang Pao and of the RLA, still the main power base of the right. A new element had emerged in the form of General Siho Lanphoutakun, the Director of the Lao National Police, whom Boun Oum

125

*As part of a thirteen-nation tour to seek support for the Geneva agreement, King Sisavang Vatthana met with President Kennedy in Washington, DC, in February 1963.*

would refer to disparagingly as trying to emulate the career of the infamous police chief Phao in Thailand in the 1950s. Siho was described in one US Embassy dispatch as 'a political figure with no ideology no political scruples, and no convictions'. Like Phao and other unrestrained police chiefs the world over, Siho engaged in gambling, prostitution and extortion. Phoumi, his ally at least for the moment, also opened a casino, in Vientiane, but this appears to have been part of his ongoing search for fiscal independence from outsiders, rather than the pure venality of Siho. Denouncing rivals in business and in politics as pro-communist, Siho brought Laos as close as it would come to a police state under the RLG. On 18 April 1964, Siho and General Kouprasit Abhay attempted a *coup d'état*. All government ministers were dismissed, including Phoumi. The plotters had no international support, however, and the coup collapsed.

The following year would see the final working-out of *phu nyai* politics as moves and counter-moves first forced Phoumi and Siho to flee to Thailand in 1965, and then Kong Le to Paris. General Ouan Rathikhoun, who was close to the King, took over as Commander-in-Chief of the army, but the compromise was that regional commanders ran their regions with as little interference from the centre as possible. 'The military region commanders,' wrote Colonel Oudone Sananikhone, 'and the forces they controlled, quickly became the centers and sources of all power in the provinces. The civil administration looked to the military for support and the means to carry out all civil projects.' This finally dampened down *phu nyai* rivalry, but at the expense of coordination against their mutual enemies, the Pathet Lao and the North Vietnamese. This would only change in 1971 when Sisouk Na Champasak became Minister of Defence and set about re-centralising military power.

The fragmentation of power in this period was partially a result of the new Lao state having not consolidated its bureaucratic apparatus, which might otherwise have acted as a counterweight to the army's organisation. It was a structural weakness that enhanced *phu nyai* politics and caused the various politicians and generals to act in the way they did. It has become almost a cliché of commentary on Laos to say that these men could not suppress their personal interests and rivalry for the national good—but in fact they all held deep and strong nationalist beliefs, and fought for them. Short of outright military or communist dictatorship, the inherent divisiveness of the structure could not be overcome in the short term. Had the small, weak Lao state not come under tremendous outside pressure, it would have finally overcome some of these problems—but in the coming decade the RLG would be subject to pressures that even stronger states could not have withstood.

The end of Police Chief Siho presented foreign observers with yet one more cultural conundrum. Advised by a Thai Buddhist monk that he would be safer back in Laos, Siho, festooned with protective amulets, turned himself in to the authorities in Paksé on 17 April 1966. He was jailed at Phu Khao Kwai, just north of Vientiane, and shot 'while attempting to escape' on 4 September. No one mourned his passing. In Lao eyes, his *boun* had run its course.

# Life under the Pathet Lao

Unlike the RLG-controlled areas, which were open to scrutiny by outside observers and journalists, the Pathet Lao zones were off limits, except for carefully controlled guided tours for the occasional diplomat, journalist or fellow-traveller (a prelude to the totalitarian controls imposed after the revolution). The glare of publicity thus fell on the politicians and generals of the RLG, exaggerating their failings and minimising those of the other side. Nevertheless, it is possible to paint in broad brush-strokes the situation in PL areas.

By the collapse of the second coalition government in 1964, the PL zone covered roughly half the country, mostly mountain areas and therefore sparsely populated. Somewhere between a quarter and a third of the population lay within this zone, most of them belonging to various ethnic minorities. The PL and their North Vietnamese backers controlled this zone largely in the sense of being able to deny RLG access. They could not directly control all the villages in the zone, however, as the dispersal of the population far exceeded their administrative capacity.

PL control was strictest in Houaphan and Phongsali, two provinces that had been under their control for a long time, and to the east of the Boloven Plateau in the south. At the frontier between the two zones control was much less tight, and indeed many villages were in a kind of no-man's-land. The PL takeover of *muang*, *tasseng* or *ban* administration was either by straight-out assassination of the incumbents, or by their removal through stage-managed 'struggle sessions' and 'people's courts', after which they might be shot or imprisoned. 'Appropriate' people would be selected as the new heads and elected by acclamation—in other words, in a public context in which any dissenting voters could be easily identified. Dissenters had to explain themselves and were shown the 'error' of their ways in propaganda sessions. Party control of political positions in the PL areas meant that the free elections proposed for the second coalition could never have taken place.

The undemocratic practices of the communists were nothing unusual for the peasants—they had never experienced any other form of government. The RLG-sponsored national elections, however, saw the beginnings of the propagation of a new idea of political rule in which all the citizens of a nation had equal political rights over its destiny. In this regard, the several election campaigns run by the RLG, whatever their failings, were an exercise in mass education on the subjects of nationalism and citizenship. Unfortunately, these elections reached at most only half the population, and the new concepts of democracy and freedom were alien and only half-understood. The Pathet Lao spoke the language of nationalism and equality too, and thus the legitimacy of these ideas, whatever their source, gradually spread. The ideals of liberal democratic politics were best understood in the cities, and least understood in the countryside, where the response to excessive authoritarianism was the old one of moving away rather than standing up and demanding one's rights.

The communists set up 'mass' organisations in the villages of women and youth, and committees for seemingly everything. (Many people after the revolution in 1975 would complain of endless political meetings, as did refugees from the communist zone before 1975.) Youth organisations were especially important, as young people were seen as the seeds of the 'new society'; many were sent to Vietnam for further education, as mechanics, as nurses or doctors, and for political indoctrination. The PL efforts at education were appreciated, as was the suppression of even petty corruption. As everything was subordinated to the 'higher aims' of the struggle, however, any 'surplus wealth' had to be redirected to supporting the PL army. Thus the PL frowned upon 'wasteful' expenditures on such things as ritual and the support of the Buddhist monkhood. Cooperatives were established to control marketing of agricultural produce and to displace small traders. A rice tax of 15 per cent was imposed, unpopular in these upland regions where yields were low, and pressure was also exerted for donations of rice 'from the heart'. Naturally, there was evasion. People began to dress as poorly as possible, no longer wearing jewellery, to avoid charges that they were rich (this appearance was seen generally after 1975). In older PL areas individuals carried 'work result books' in which were recorded taxes paid, voluntary contributions made, celebrations and rallies attended, labour contributed to the revolution—in short, a catalogue of their assets as a PL citizen. Personal dossiers were also compiled, especially for 'unreliable' individuals. What was most resented was communist corvée, in particular the portage system for the army. Almost no one was exempt from numerous 'short trips' of up to a week's duration, and everyone with enough strength was required to make at least one 'long trip' per year of around 30 days. On top of this, labour was demanded for road building and maintenance, though some key routes were left to North Vietnamese engineering units. Military conscription applied to those aged fifteen and older; there were reports of boys as young as thirteen being recruited. (It must be remembered that in thinly populated Laos manpower was short on both sides.)

As in nineteenth-century Europe the army functioned as a school for nationalism as well as modern skills. It carried people beyond their village and ethnic group and introduced them to strangers whose affinity was 'nation', who were all called 'Lao'. Furthermore, war helped to constitute a 'we' against a foreign 'them', in this case the Americans and their 'lackeys' in Vientiane. The propaganda of the PL was simple and anti-foreign. As one refugee in the late 1960s reported:

> I was repeatedly told that I was the owner of Laos. Laos is a beautiful country, with an abundance of rivers and streams and natural resources. The Lao people could not do anything to use these resources because of the aggression and oppression of foreign countries. The French, for instance, ruled Laos for more than sixty years ... They told us how the principal enemy of the Lao people is the American imperialists.[31]

Or as another refugee put it, they were taught 'we are Lao and whatever is foreign is not good for us'.

The qualities of the PL army were often overestimated by outside observers who made little or no distinction between PL and their Vietnamese allies. But a British diplomat, Mervyn Brown, who was held captive for a month by the PL in June 1962, concluded: 'By world standards the Pathet Lao are incompetent and lazy soldiers. By comparison with their actual opponents they are a tough and effective guerilla force.' Defectors or captives from among the thousands of North Vietnamese advisers on the PL side were among the PL's sternest critics. One told interviewers:

> The Vietnamese are disciplined and well-organized. The Lao are not. Sometimes the Lao troops will say frankly that they want to defect or that they don't want to work. Their chiefs will often just listen and smile. If that

> happened in a Vietnamese unit—watch out . . . But in the
> Pathet Lao, a cadre who would discipline such a man
> would have to fear being shot, either by the man or
> another soldier in the unit.[32]

He also spoke about how Vietnamese officers were disdainful of Lao officers: 'They mocked the Lao officers, who often carried their pistols in a holster far down on their hips, with a swaggering walk.' The Lao, on the other hand, were somewhat overawed by Vietnamese discipline and puritanism, said the Vietnamese adviser.

> As for the Pathet Lao soldiers, their morale was low; they
> were poor fighters and poor shots. Sometimes they still fired
> when there was no enemy present at all. Their cadres were
> unable to control the soldiers during combat. They could
> not keep operations secret . . . The Vietnamese did not
> trust the Lao, and the Lao relied on the Vietnamese, so that
> coordination in battle was not tight enough to defeat the
> enemy. The Pathet Lao forces were weak. If they were sent
> somewhere, a Vietnamese unit had to be sent with them.[33]

These complaints are strikingly similar to complaints made by American advisers about RLA soldiers.

A kind of *phu nyai* politics also played a role in the PL zones. Among the minorities, big men thought to possess special 'soul stuff' emerged to assert their authority over their followers. A classic case was the Loven leader, Sithone Khommadam, whose father had led a longstanding rebellion against the French. Sithone was jailed by the French following his father's assassination and was later recruited to the anti-colonial cause by Souphanouvong. Elected as one of the NLHX deputies from the south, he was jailed again in 1958 but escaped with them and made his way back to the southern mountains. Sithone combined the qualities of a traditional chief, by calling on kinship and ethnic alliances, with the modern party organisation of the PL. He was charismatic; Mervyn Brown, who was held by his men, described him as having 'a natural air of authority, a stern but not unhandsome face, direct eyes and a most attractive smile. Here, we felt, was a natural leader of men'. Big men were who they are, not what they said. For those given to heroic visions, Brown gives a sobering description of one of Sithone's speeches before a group of Alak people:

> He spoke well in circumstances of considerable difficulty. His audience remained impassive and showed no signs of enthusiasm during his speech. There were constant distractions: someone stepping forward to put more wood on the fire, dogs chasing around his feet, children crying, etc. A constant and uninspiring background to his speech was the bubbling of the tribal pipes—bassoon-size bamboo tubes through which tobacco smoke is sucked through water—which are smoked by the whole population, male and female down to quite small children . . . His peroration, accompanied by clumsy gestures, spoke of the necessity for continuous struggle to achieve a united, peaceful, and independent Laos.[34]

These latter references were no doubt too abstract for his audience, while his references to the Boun Oum–Phoumi clique, let alone Chiang Kai-Shek, would have been downright strange. No matter, these were the 'bad guys' identified by the leader they knew. Similar personal and kinship allegiances were drawn upon by Hmong PL leader Faydang Lobliayao, although unlike Sithone, who faced no comparable leader in the southern highlands, Faydang had to compete with the influence of Touby Lyfong's clan. Generally, however, the structure of the Leninist party kept *phu nyai* posturing under control. There were few spoils to be redistributed in PL areas, but once the communists gained power it would be another story.

# The minorities

Perhaps one of the most persistent misunderstandings of recent Lao history is that the PL won their struggle because they were able to mobilise the minorities and the RLG lost because it remained huddled in the larger towns and cities in the lowlands along the Mekong. This view is based on no sustained research and is simply one that has been repeated from one commentator to another, becoming the standard view by default. The minorities played an important role in modern Lao history because of their geographical location, spread out as they were along the Central Vietnamese Cordillera that had for so long acted as a natural frontier between Laos and Vietnam.

In Laos, unlike in Vietnam, Cambodia or Thailand, the dominant ethnic group is not the overwhelming majority. Ethnic Lao make up between 40 and 50 per cent of the population, with the rest (often described as 'hilltribes') divided into many different groups. This general description is misleading in several ways. To begin with, included under the category 'hilltribe' have been the upland, non-Buddhist Tai, the ancestors of the Lao and Thai, whose gradual cultural conversion into Lao and Thai continues today. These groups were organised into *muang* that occasionally grew into petty states and therefore cannot be described as 'tribal'. The Buddhist Tai Lue of northwestern Laos are also sometimes called 'tribal', but are almost indistinguishable from Lao. In the south of Laos, in Khammouan, Savannakhet and Saravan, one finds the Phu Thai, who are non-Buddhist Tai, like the Black and White Tai to the north. Many of these groups are in the process of becoming Lao, and this general process of Lao-isation blurs the boundaries between them. Thus persons of broad Tai ethnicity perhaps make up between 60 and 70 per cent of the population. The degree to which various groups perceive or mark their boundaries has varied from one place to another and over time, tending to vary with the context in which people find themselves.

Beginning in the early 1950s, and based on an earlier French classification, the RLG began officially to refer to the Mon Khmer and Austronesian people as *Lao theung*, a geographical designation which pointed to their tendency to reside in the hills. This was designed to replace the term *kha*, a general term for those of inferior status regardless of ethnicity. (This hierarchical meaning is retained in polite speech, where *kha noi* means 'I' when, for example, a younger person refers to an older person.) From the outset the RLG began a conscious transition from pre-modern social relations to those demanded by modern democracies. Thus, the Constitution of 1947 stated that 'Citizens of Laos are all those individuals belonging to races that are permanently established in the territory of Laos and do not possess already any other nationality', a statement of ethnic equality well in advance of neighbouring Thailand, for example. It was also in front of liberal democracies like Australia, where Aborigines were denied full political rights until 1967, or the USA, where blacks only attained full civil rights in the south in the mid-1960s. This, of course, did not stop commentators from such countries adopting a morally superior attitude concerning Lao prejudices towards minorities.

Individual members of the elite, such as Prince Somsanith, who had distinguished himself as Governor of Hua Khong province (now Luang Nam Tha and Bokeo) in the northwest, took a deep and persistent interest in minority affairs. He was believed to have travelled by foot to all the villages of his minority-inhabited province several times. *Muang Lao*, the magazine he established in 1959, distinguished itself by running articles on and photos of various minorities. Katay's history of the Lao Issara (published in 1948) deliberately carried a photo of Katay with two Ta Oi women from Saravan. Katay had once suggested that Laos rename itself Lan Xang to remove the ethnic implications embedded in the name. Traditional ritual connections between upland minorities and the Lao were reconfirmed annually by the Luang Phrabang court, and by Boun Oum in Champasak, whereby the Lao King and the aristocracy recognised the *kha* as their 'elder brothers', reversing the normal hierarchy because of their assumed prior possession of the land. Indeed, far from being tribal, many minorities were connected not only into wider ritual relationships with lowland states, but were also part of at least regional economies. Khamu from Luang Phrabang, for example, worked on a seasonal basis in the teak logging forests of Chiang Mai, Thailand. Only some of the most remote groups in the rugged high mountains began to approximate what is often implied by the term tribal, and only in some areas did very small groups carry on their lives as hunter-gatherers.

## Hmong highland politics and the RLG

The ethnic groups who stood most clearly apart were those who had in the relatively recent past migrated into Laos from China, or overlapped the Lao-Chinese border. They included the Hmong (Meo), Yao (Iu Mien) and Koh (Akha), among others. These groups were given the geographical designation *Lao sung* because they were generally found high up in the mountains, but the term was relatively uncommon in use before 1975. The Hmong were the largest of these groups, with by 1975 a population of over 300 000 centred on Xiang Khoang and scattered throughout the surrounding northern provinces. They became the majority in Nong Het district, where they had been given administrative control here by the French in the 1920s. This arrangement tended to stabilise what had always been the more volatile cross-clan alliances that were formed through marriage. Even so, enmities could still erupt between the endlessly manoeuvring groups and individuals, and in one case with fatal long-term implications. Chao Saikham, Phuan governor of Xiang Khoang, and descendant of the Phuan principality, explained:

> In Nong Het two Meo families shared power between them: the Lo clan and that of the Ly. The Lo's chief was Blia Yao, the Ly's the father of Touby. An alliance had been sealed between the two families: the father of Touby had married a daughter of Blia Yao. But almost immedi-

ately the daughter returned to her father's home claiming that her husband was mistreating her. Blia Yao insisted that his daughter return to her husband's home, but soon after she fell ill and died. Blia Yao and his sons therefore turned against the Ly clan claiming that his younger daughter had died as a result of mistreatment.[35]

To this would be added a dispute over succession to office in the administration. Touby Lyfoung and his brothers were among the first Hmong to gain a French education. Extraordinarily, their father, using wealth gained from opium, in the 1920s hired a Lao teacher to come to Nong Het to instruct his children. They would later go to study in Xiang Khoang town and in Vientiane, along with Chao Saikham, among others. This access to education would give the Ly clan an edge in the competition for office, and so when Blia Yao died Touby's older brother took his place. A little later competition for the position as head of one *tasseng* occurred between Lo Fay Dang, the son of Blia Yao, and Touby. The educated Touby was favoured, as he explains in his memoirs:

> The Hmong notables and elders met several times but were unable to nominate the new Tasseng of Keng Khuai. In the end, they agreed to suggest me for that position. They told me that I was really young but I was *educated* . . . They also said that I belonged to both the Lo and the Ly families. My father was a Ly and my mother was the daughter of kiatong Lo Blia Yao. Nominating me to that position would probably bring back [inter-clan] peace to the area. The French administration agreed with the Hmong notables . . . my uncle Lo Fay Dang remained unhappy. He developed, thereafter, a deep hatred for the French . . .[36]

The dispute would lead Fay Dang into the ranks of the NLHX, while Touby went on to become one of the main supporters of the RLG.

137

Highland politics were complicated by internal clan rivalries and by the often problematic relationships between ethnic groups. Richer Hmong, for example, could not only afford to hire a Lao teacher or a poor Vietnamese to build them a house, but also employed other minorities, such as Khamu, as labourers on their poppy fields, workers who often became addicts. Similarly, the ethnic hierarchy in the south was not a simple dichotomy between lowland Lao and the highlanders. There, inter-ethnic suspicions dating back to the days of slave trading remained rife well into the 1960s. The Loven, for instance, had preyed on neighbouring groups such as the Nya Heun, treating them with as much arrogance as the old Lao seigneurs. So, when Khommadam led many Loven into the NLHX this fact alone ensured that the Nya Heun would not follow.

*(L–R): Touby Lyfoung, Toulia Lyfoung, Prince Khamman Vongkotrattana, his daughter Princess Khamfong, wife of Toulia, and Tougeu Lyfoung. (Courtesy Prince Khamman's family)*

Xiang Khoang Province and its Plain of Jars was at the strategic centre of northern Laos. This ensured that its population, and in particular its Hmong population, would play a central role in post-World War II Lao history. As the new Lao state took shape so the administrative integration of this important highland population gathered pace. In 1946 Touby, of the Ly clan of the Hmong, became the assistant governor of the province; in 1947 his brother Toulia became one of the province's representatives in the new National Assembly. In the same year Touby received from King Sisavangvong the title of Phaya, coveted by commoners, for his role against the Japanese in World War II and his support of the King against the Lao Issara. Two months later his elder brother Tougeu was appointed to the King's Council. In 1965 Touby himself would become a member of King Sisavang Vatthana's Council. The granting of citizenship in the 1947 constitution was, according to Touby, a momentous occasion:

> At last, for the first time in the Hmong collective memories, the Hmong really had a country like any other people in the world. The wandering life without any specific tie of the Hmong people seemed to come to an end, in Laos . . . The first step towards making the Hmong people be part of the Laotian nation had been achieved, but there was still a long way to go to complete the process.[37]

Touby encouraged Hmong participation in Lao national and annual festivals, and in particular encouraged the learning of Lao language and education. While social and cultural change among the Hmong accelerated in the 1950s, including the influence of Christian missionaries, it was not traumatic. Growing Hmong interaction with lowland Lao demanded adjustment on both sides, and it occurred slowly.

## The rise of Vang Pao

Although Hmong society had been disrupted at times by the war between the Viet Minh and the French, it was the retreat of Lao neutralist forces to the Plain of Jars in 1961 that irrevocably swept them into the vortex of war. In early 1959 US intelligence began to recruit highlanders for long-range reconnaissance patrols into NLHX territory and North Vietnam, and by the end of the year were creating Special Forces teams. Aiding them in their activities was Lieutenant Vang Pao, young and energetic and at that time the only Hmong officer in the Royal Lao Army. He helped to establish village Auto Defence Forces throughout Xiang Khoang, Houaphan and Phongsali provinces. Those with talent were sent off for further training in Thailand. Interestingly, the US presence, both military and Christian, quickly stimulated dormant millennial yearnings among the Hmong, some of whom began to circulate a story of Jesus Christ coming in a jeep wearing American military uniform and handing out weapons with which they could repel their enemies. By the time of the Kong Le coup, Vang Pao had established a solid base among the Hmong in Military Region 2; aligned with the rightists under Phoumi Nosovan, his forces would harass the PL and neutralists after they had retreated to the Plain of Jars.

To supply these irregular forces scattered across the northern mountains the CIA engaged the commercial airline Air America, which also became vital for the thousands of refugees fleeing the fighting that erupted on and around the Plain of Jars. At the end of December 1960 some 70 000 Hmong began relocating themselves to positions determined by Vang Pao around the plain; having deserted their fields they had to be supplied with food from the air, thus beginning a massive air operation that continued until the end of the war. The conditions suffered by these refugees were often appalling. Donald Schanche described the plight of one group of 5000:

> Small children sat quietly in the ochre mud of the hillside, too enervated to seek dryness or comfort, and too weak even to plead for help as their vacant eyes, many caked with the drying pus of conjunctivitus, stared

blankly . . . a Meo man emerged from a bamboo lean-to shelter and fired his flintlock musket into the air . . . From farther up the hill, as if echoing the shots, came three more reports. Another death.[38]

Once relocated, however, many of these Hmong became willing recruits for the irregular army commanded by Vang Pao. The supply of food, medicine and arms to Hmong across the mountains, and deep inside the PL zone, was a major source of contention during and after the Geneva agreement, but given that Vietnamese compliance with these accords could not be monitored, the CIA was not prepared to end its covert support for the Hmong. Now holding a larger fixed territory, the PL were therefore faced with pockets of guerillas in much the same way as they had harassed the RLG, and of course they wished

*Hmong refugees arrive at Sam Thong, Xiang Khoang Province.*
*(Courtesy Joel Halpern archive)*

141

to get rid of them. The intransigence of both sides would finally torpedo the Geneva agreement.

The fighting around the Plain of Jars had by the end of 1962 created 141 500 refugees, most of whom were being fully or partially supported by USAID supplies (88 000 Hmong, 26 500 Lao Theung, 19 000 ethnic Lao, around 6000 Yao and 2000 Tai Lue). Vang Pao's forces grew from around 9000 to around 18 000 men, and became increasingly effective against both PL and North Vietnamese troops in operations directed from his base at Long Cheng on the flank of Phu Bia, Laos's highest mountain in northern Vientiane Province. Vang Pao provided a breakdown of the ethnic composition of the nine Special Forces battalions under his command in the late 1960s—Hmong 48 per cent, Lao 27 per cent, Khamu 22 per cent and Yao 3 per cent—it was not simply a 'Hmong Secret Army' as many accounts have claimed, but an ethnically mixed force. Using Air America's expanded fleet of helicopters and light aircraft, these forces leaped from mountain top to mountain top, deep into Houaphan Province and up to the Vietnamese border. USAID, in conjunction with Air America, flew in supplies to small airstrips hacked out of the jungle. The USA began to train the Lao air force in the use of T-28 aircraft, to both provide air support for these ground forces and make airstrikes against the Ho Chi Minh Trail and other infiltration routes from Vietnam. The war escalated as communist offensives were launched in 1964. America, with Souvanna Phouma's permission, began to fly reconnaissance flights to monitor the communist build-up; inevitably one was shot down. This led to their accompaniment by armed escorts that struck back against ground fire, thus beginning the American air war in Laos. Another crucial escalation at this time was the introduction of Thai mercenaries as pilots and artillerymen under the command of Vang Pao.

In the mid-1960s Vang Pao was promoted to the rank of general and placed in command of the vital Military Region 2. He and his Hmong followers were immensely proud that he had risen to the top of the Lao Army, and he was one of King Sisavang Vatthana's most

*Vang Pao (pointing) directs his troops during a battle in the mid-1960s.*
*(Courtesy Roger Warner)*

loyal generals. He was supposedly in charge of a 'secret army' operating from a 'Secret CIA base' at Long Cheng, 'a rather euphemistic title for such a squalid collection of ramshackle bamboo-and-thatch buildings,' wrote Charles Weldon, a medical doctor with USAID at the time. 'It was one of the most unattractive places in Laos.' The forces under Vang Pao were in fact a mixture of regular and irregular soldiers, and Thai mercenaries. Operational advice was given by a small number of CIA operatives. All was paid for by US aid. The covert support for the irregular soldiers matched the covert support the other 'secret army', the North Vietnamese and Chinese, was giving to the Pathet Lao—all in contravention of the Geneva Accords. The spotlight of critical commentary has to date fallen on the so-called American 'secret army', mainly because more information is available. Allegations have been made of CIA involvement in 'drug running', referring to the fact that Vang Pao and Air America helped to provide transport for the Hmong's most important cash crop, opium.

In the south, US Special Forces 'White Star' teams began recruiting and training people from the various upland minority groups there. By 1962 there were twelve companies, which were used mainly to interdict the Ho Chi Minh Trail and for reconnaissance. In this region the communist forces had begun recruiting much earlier than their opponents, and the role and prestige of the legendary Khommadam was unmatched by any figure on the RLG side. Vietnamese cadres which had been recruiting across the border also searched for recruits among similar groups on the Lao side. These, like the minorities recruited in the north, were sent for training at the Khommadam school for cadres from Laos in northern Vietnam, named after Sithone's father. As the security of this southern region was absolutely vital for the Ho Chi Minh Trail, it was paid special attention in long-term Vietnamese strategy. For both sides, recruiting in the south was difficult because of the relative lack of wider indigenous political structures and popular reluctance to become engaged in 'lowland' politics. In the end the southerners were marginal to the outcome of the war, though they would be ravaged in the process.

While RLG influence and support among the minorities was not as weak as it has been perceived, nevertheless it is true that the NLHX did recruit heavily from among certain minorities, although the latter were mainly foot soldiers. Yet reliance on 'Lao Theung' was seen as a weakness by observers such as Mervyn Brown, as well as the Vietnamese adviser cited earlier who lamented: 'In our unit we had only Lao Theung; no Lao Loum were joining the Pathet Lao. How could we say that the people supported us?' Both sides had limitations in their recruiting bases, and this situation would not change for the duration of the war.

*Left:* These window shutters in Vat Siphutthabat in Luang Phrabang are generally believed to represent the Dutch merchant Gerrit van Wuystoff, the first European to visit Vientiane in 1641. Given that the shutters were made in 1861, it is possible that the figures were copied from a Chinese stamp depicting a foreigner. (Photo Grant Evans)

*Below:* The Black Tai are one of the main so-called 'tribal' Tai groups in the northern mountains of Laos. This Black Tai woman from Houaphan province has the typical coiffure of a married woman. The silver clasps on her vest are also typical. (Photo Grant Evans)

# MAINLAND SOUTHEAST ASIA IN THE 15TH CENTURY

The mandala kingdoms of traditional mainland Southeast Asia were oriented towards sacred centres ruled by a king, not defined by borders. These kingdoms at their extremities waxed and waned, shading off into vassal states and peoples. This is represented here as strong colour focussed on the centres, with the colour fading at the extremities and then shading into the next mandala. Over the course of the next three centuries the kingdoms changed: Sukhotai and Ayudhya disappeared and were replaced by a mandala centred on Bangkok, while Lan Xang split into three small kingdoms centred on Luang Phrabang, Vientiane and Champasak. It was not until the 20th century that national boundaries were fixed and drawn.

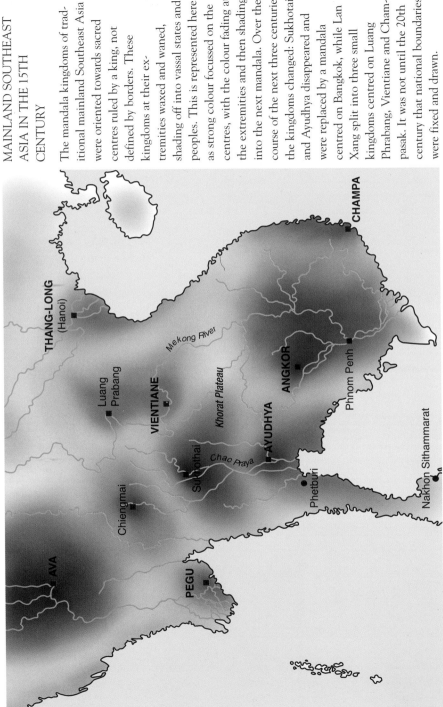

THANG-LONG (Hanoi)

Luang Prabang

VIENTIANE

Chiengmai

Sukhotai

Mekong River

Khorat Plateau

Chao Praya

AVA

PEGU

AYUDHYA

Phetburi

Nakhon Sithammarat

ANGKOR

Phnom Penh

CHAMPA

Some of the propaganda posters produced under the RLG are strikingly similar to those used by the LPDR. Here, in a poster representing ethnic solidarity, Lao males at the front carry the flag of the RLG, followed by a Lao woman, who is then followed by Hmong or 'Lao Soung', who are then followed by 'Lao Theung', presumably Khmu and southern highlanders.

In the 1990s the LPDR turned to traditional culture to bolster its legitimacy following the failures of communism. This billboard reads: 'Together preserve and enhance the beautiful national culture'. (Photo Grant Evans)

A float during National Day 2000 bearing a portrait of President
Khamthay Siphandone. The text on the float reads: 'Leader of the Party
and State'. (Photo Grant Evans)

Hmong in Xieng Khoang province turn bomb casings into herb gardens.
(Photo Grant Evans)

# 4
# WAR, AND THE DESTRUCTION OF THE RLG

War displaced tens of thousands of refugees inside Laos. The highland province Xiang Khoang became a major battleground between Vietnamese and Lao communists on one side, and the RLG and American bombers on the other. A Hmong General, Vang Pao, along with his irregular forces, often bore the brunt of the fierce fighting in the highlands. Meanwhile Lao society was maturing, and the 1960s saw the growth of a thoughtful and critical intelligentsia. They would disappear with the communist victory. Economic crisis in the early 1970s coupled with America's desire to retreat from Indochina had the RLG enter a coalition government in 1973 on unfavourable terms. The communists cleverly undermined the agreement, while the continued presence of North Vietnamese troops and America's withdrawal of financial and military support ensured the collapse of the RLG.

# The war years

In a sense the relative popular support for the two sides in the Lao conflict was irrelevant to the outcome of the war which escalated in intensity from the mid-1960s. As America became deeply embroiled in neighbouring Vietnam, the centre of gravity of US strategic thinking shifted and Laos became a 'sideshow' to the main theatre of war—but this did not mean that the country was spared war's savagery or its fatal consequences.

The war in Laos was conducted behind the façade of the 1963 Geneva agreement which, among other things, banned the use of foreign troops on Lao soil. This façade, which caused the epithet 'secret war' to be applied by sensationalist western journalists to this period, and the 'secretiveness' of the war were, strangely, in the interests of everyone. As the country slid towards war with the collapse of the Geneva agreement, Souvanna Phouma and the RLG increasingly relied on US military support, a support which had to be covert as Souvanna wanted to keep the option of a negotiated settlement on the table. The USA, now preoccupied with Vietnam, did not want to be drawn into a wider Southeast Asian commitment by going public on the situation in Laos. The PL, for their part, relied on North Vietnamese military support and did not want the cover of their 'secret army' blown, while the Vietnamese, whose focus was also on the escalating war in Vietnam, needed a secure Laotian flank, especially for the Ho Chi Minh Trail. Throughout the war the PL and the DRV denied the presence of Vietnamese troops in Laos, despite the RLG parading the occasional captured soldier before journalists in Vientiane. Only after 1975 would the 'solidarity' of the two armies involved in the struggle be openly celebrated inside Laos, in communist propaganda and war memorials to Vietnamese 'volunteers'.

While it is impossible to say when the war actually 'began', its certainty was guaranteed in 1963 once the neutralist army had been forced off the Plain of Jars; Souvanna's military power base had been undermined, and along with it the possibility of a workable neutralism. The galvanising of an army around Vang Pao capable of retaking the plain, and the accompanying escalation of the air war, marched in lockstep towards the charnel-house of war.

The escalation of the war meant the steady marginalisation of both the RLG and the PL in its conduct. United States ambassadors to Laos played a central role in the direction of the war, to the point where people quipped that the Ambassador was the 'second Prime Minister'. While American control of the RLG never approached the day-to-day intricacy of Vietnamese control of the PL, the magnitude of its participation in the war would make up for this. The fatal meridian in this respect was crossed on 1 December 1964, when Souvanna Phouma, now convinced of the total reliance of the PL on the Vietnamese, authorised independent American aerial interdiction in northern Laos, primarily in support of Vang Pao's ground forces. Code-named BARREL ROLL, this operation marked the separation of American from RLG war aims and campaigns. Previously the USA had worked through the RLG forces, but now they began to work almost independently. In March 1965, Operation STEEL TIGER, aimed at the Ho Chi Minh Trail complex in southern Laos, commenced and grew into a massive bombing campaign directed by American generals. In the north, up until 1968 the war see-sawed seasonally. Vang Pao's forces had the tactical advantage of air transport that during the wet season allowed them to strike at will stranded communist forces whose ground communications and supplies from North Vietnam were hindered. During the dry season the communist forces counter-attacked. In early 1968, however, paralleling the huge communist Tet Offensive in southern Vietnam, North Vietnamese troops launched attacks on positions held by Vang Pao's forces throughout Houaphan Province, positions he finally abandoned after bloody attempts to retake them. Casualties were heavy on both sides, and approximately 10 000 Hmong refugees fled the province. The coming of the wet season saw the communists holding forward positions relatively free from guerilla harassment.

The battering suffered by Vang Pao's forces led to an expansion of the use of air power in the northern region. This was facilitated by the October 1968 temporary bombing halt of North Vietnam called for by President Nixon, which freed planes for sorties over Laos. Consequently, in the first half of 1969, in addition to the hundreds of daily bombing runs over southern Laos, the rate of air strikes in northern Laos escalated from 20 per day flown previously by Royal Lao Airforce T-28s, to between 200 and 300 per day, flown mostly by US aircraft based in Thailand. Nevertheless, communist forces pressed forward during the 1969 wet season in an attempt to fully occupy the Plain of Jars. They succeeded temporarily, but aerial bombardment had taken its toll and with their supply lines stretched they were vulnerable to counter-attack by Vang Pao's forces, which re-took the Plain in September. The region was now one big battlefield. The number of refugees dislocated over 1969–70 grew to 150 000. Tens of thousands were gathered in the hills to the south of Long Cheng, others headed west to Xaignabouri. Aware that he was unable to hold the Plain of Jars against a renewed dry season offensive, in February 1970 Vang Pao and USAID had 15 000 people, mainly Tai Phuan, flown to refugee villages in the Mekong lowlands. One refugee recounted:

> They brought us to Vientiane, where it is safe and nothing will harm us and life is healthful. I very much didn't want to come because I miss my former village so. But because of my great fear of the never-ending gunfire, I decided to leave my fields and gardens, the various animals, all my fruit trees, and bring only my body here. But when the plane took off and I looked down at my village, I was immediately so homesick for my village, my birthplace, for the region where I had lived my life day by day.[39]

Thereafter the Plain of Jars became a 'free fire' zone, where B-52s flew their first devastating bombing raids. In contrast to World War II, when it was military policy to bomb and terrorise the civilian population (Hiroshima and Nagasaki being the shocking finale of this policy) in both Vietnam and Laos the policy was to avoid civilian casualties. We who live in an age that follows televised 'smart bombs' to their targets know just how impossible this is even today. Bombing during the Vietnam War used primitive technology by comparison, and the inevitability of civilian casualties was that much higher. The landscape of the Lao mountains is still covered with unexploded ordnance which continues to take civilian lives. As for the indiscriminate carpet bombing of the B-52s, it could only have occurred on the improbable assumption that the areas they bombed were free of civilians. Of course they were not, and those that remained behind and survived lived in holes and tunnels, or in the southern mountains fled into the deep jungle to become almost hunter-gatherers. Aerial terror reigned. The communist leadership dug themselves deep caves for protection in the mountains of Vieng Xai in Houaphan Province—ironically, now a tourist attraction.

A widening war was under way in the south as well. The overthrow of Prince Sihanouk in Cambodia in March 1970 cut off North Vietnamese supply routes through the port of Kompong Som, routes to which Sihanouk had turned a blind eye in a vain attempt to keep Cambodia from becoming embroiled in Vietnam. This made the trails through Laos even more important for the communist military campaign in southern Vietnam, therefore they expanded their control westward in Laos capturing the long-isolated provincial seats of Attapu in April and Saravan in June, and by mid-June 1971 they controlled the Boloven Plateau which hovered over the southern capital of Paksé.

Starting in 1970, Vang Pao's forces were subjected to withering onslaughts by Vietnamese forces, which could afford to sustain much higher casualties than could Vang Pao, whose recruiting pool was steadily diminishing. Estimates are difficult, but between 1960 and

1970 perhaps 20 per cent of the Hmong population had died as a result of the war in the region. The CIA turned increasingly to Thai mercenaries to augment Vang Pao's battlefield strength and by 1973 there were approximately 18 000 of them in Laos, making up around 75 per cent of the irregular forces. The war in Laos had indeed become fully 'internationalised'.

As a result of American negotiations with the North Vietnamese in Paris, a cease-fire was called in early 1973, and a war-weary Laos staggered towards the formation of its third and final coalition government.

# A new society?

While the war raged in the mountains, lowland Lao society was undergoing profound change. Despite the almost grotesque imbalance between military aid and civilian aid, the general inflow of foreign assistance began to have an impact on the country's development. Most visibly, of course, from the late 1950s it had begun to transform the urban landscape of Vientiane as new buildings went up to accommodate the influx of foreigners and newly affluent Lao. During his short stint as Lao strongman, Phoumi Nosovan had attempted to give the city a modern aspect by widening Lan Xang Avenue into a grand boulevard capped by a triumphal arch (a monument to the war dead), the Anousavaly, which according to legend was built with USAID money intended for an aircraft runway. A USAID-sponsored film of the mid-1960s follows a young couple as they wheel around Vientiane on their motorcycle, the still unfinished Anousavaly in the background, presenting a panorama of a city 'on the move' into the modern world—new buildings, high school students in freshly pressed uniforms, the new radio transmitter, and so on. Despite the PL attacks that continually disrupted road traffic, communications throughout the country began to improve as telecommunications links were established between the main provincial centres and air transport expanded. This brought a more immediate sense of the physical expanse of their country to the Lao.

The leadership of the early RLG was made up of a remarkable group with a cosmopolitan outlook and confidence. Formed by French colonialism, they had travelled beyond the boundaries of Laos for their education—but they were a tiny island in a sea of peasants. In the late 1950s they were challenged by the Young Turks of the CDNI, who saw them as old fashioned and too traditionalist, while CDNI followers were thoroughly convinced by American modernising propaganda. The military core of this group soon subverted its original intentions. By the mid-1960s the social structure of Laos became more complex, with the growth of occupations and groups associated with a middle class. A small intelligentsia emerged, newly returned from overseas studies, ready to grapple with the enormously complex problems facing Lao society. At the beginning of 1967 they began publication of *Mittasone*, a periodical which over the next few years would investigate and discuss social, political, economic and cultural problems facing Laos with a degree of frankness not previously seen. The late 1960s and early 1970s saw an unprecedented flourishing of intellectual activity (which was to be stamped out by the revolution). During the 1960s the publishing programme of the Lao Literature Committee, first established in 1948, gained pace and published a wide range of traditional Lao literature that had previously been unavailable to the general public. In 1970 the Committee became the Royal Academy, charged not only with continuing this programme, but also with modernising the Lao language, which meant, among other things, creating lexicons for such disciplines as the law, the economy and science. In 1970 the *Bulletin des Amis du Royaume Laos* began publishing on a wide range of cultural topics, its special issue on Lao Buddhism in 1973 becoming a benchmark on the subject. In June 1972 *Phay Nam*, a literary and historical magazine, began to appear under the tutelage of nationalist historian Sila Viravong, its pages giving voice to a modern Lao literature. This was followed in November 1972 by the appearance of *Nang*, the first women's magazine, which refracted the wider world's interest in feminism into the Lao context. Alongside this was a vibrant daily press willing to discuss the full gamut of the country's problems. In October 1971, the first English language weekly, *Vientiane News*, appeared. Also around this time, the first and only feature films in Lao were released.

## A new sensibility

These changes were largely an urban phenomenon, but no less important for that, because for better or worse it is urban based social groups who ultimately determine not only the political and economic direction of a country, but also its sensibility. Young Lao writers began to produce stories that critically engaged with the pressing social and often political issues of the day. Themes of betrayed love, and unfaithful husbands and their concubines, combine with contrasts between city and country life. In a 1971 collection entitled *The Sea of Life*, short story writers grapple with nationalistic themes, such as the role of the French language, or the easy criticisms of home made by Lao overseas. In another collection in 1973, Duang Champa's story 'Father Still Isn't Dead' dealt directly with the war, and how commanding officers cheated a widow of her husband's pension. Somphavan Inthavong, one of *Mittasone*'s most prolific writers, expressed his concern about the ongoing war in poems such as this, which appeared in March 1969:

'A Man Is Dead . . .'

Put on your most lovely white costume
And smile broadly
It is only a simple burial
The celebration of one who has departed.

A man is dead
And that is not all

Fa Ngum is also dead
And Anou and Pangkham too.

A man is dead
And that is not all
Hate has been inherited
And vengeance hoped for.

A man is dead
Who wished to live one hundred years
The latest victim
Of our Twenty Year War.

A man is dead
And that is not all.[40]

These attempts to reflect on the complexities of social and cultural change found a ready audience among educated Lao.

## Social change and cultural anxiety

The rapid social and cultural changes in the cities, especially Vientiane, were a cause of anxiety to those who saw them eroding traditional norms, and Buddhist monks in particular began to produce texts preaching the need to protect Lao culture. The young people caught up in these changes found them simultaneously a liberation from traditional constraints but also a source of confusion, sentiments which found their outlet in popular columns in the press under such headings as 'Mending a Broken Heart'. One peculiar cultural manifestation of change was the appearance of 'cowboyism' among some younger men in the cities. They broke starkly with traditional attire by dressing in tight blue jeans or black pants, wearing sunglasses and cowboy hats. Some even outfitted themselves with holsters and pistols. Their slick language, their drinking and in a sense their narcissism set them at odds with traditional standards. Many 'cowboys' were newly mobile, either

*Caberet in Vientiane in the 1960s. (Courtesy Phouvong Phimmasone)*

occupationally or as refugees, and their cowboyism was an attempt to fabricate a new identity in the rapidly changing world around them. Given the American influence in Laos at the time, it was not surprising that they drew on American cultural themes that would set them apart from the Francophile elite. The 'cowboys' were for a time a highly visible marker of cultural change, but by 1975, as a wave of radical nationalism spread through the country, they had all but disappeared. Another highly visible group that also threatened traditional values was the bar girls and prostitutes. (One of the stories in the *Sea of Life*, 'The Daughter I Lost', is about a peasant girl who elopes to the city with her boyfriend, is abandoned, and becomes a prostitute.) One of the side effects of wars is that they collect together large groups of unattached men with money in their pockets. In conditions where poorer women have few job outlets, either because their family cannot sustain them or they are refugees, many may be drawn into prostitution. This happened in Laos, with many poor girls from the Thai northeast also being drawn across the Mekong into the bars. In Vientiane there were a few high-profile cabarets and bars, with names like the White Rose or Lulu's, catering mainly to foreigners, where women worked freelance for reasonable rewards. Most of them worked in seedy, cheap, back-street brothels catering to a Lao clientele. A study by two anthropologists in 1970 estimated that there were about 1000 women involved in prostitution in Vientiane. Although the numbers were not exceptionally high, from the late 1960s onwards the Lao Women's Association, led by wives of the elite, some of whom would go on to found *Nang*, campaigned for a clampdown on prostitution. Restrictions were placed on bars before Buddhist festivals such as the That Luang festival, and some of the more seedy places were closed in the early 1970s. Soon after, the revolution would close them all down.

In the late 1960s a kind of radical nationalist mood gathered pace among intellectuals, but few of them became pro-communist. The convoluted influences from both inside and outside that they were attempting to negotiate and mediate were probably best and most humorously captured by Somphavan Inthavong in his 1968 essay, 'Hippies and the Rain'. Drawn by the easy availability of marijuana and opium, a small colony of hippies had established itself in Vientiane, their *raison d'être* being the rejection of 'western materialism' in favour of the 'simplicity' and 'spontaneity' of rural life supposedly embodied in the Lao. Somphavan writes of their participation in the Rocket Festival, a ribald fertility festival to call the rains, as their discovery of Eden. But, he says, we Lao want development, not this misrecognised rural idyll:

> Those who wish to be like us, we Lao Loum, Lao Theung, Lao Soung, they will not be able to realize their dream here. Because, their problem is that our dream is to no

longer be hippies as we have always been up to now. We are going in exactly the opposite direction to you, my brother Hippies.[41]

Lao leaders at the time had also begun to speak of the bad effects these foreign drop-outs might have on the morals of their youth, and several times moves were made to expel all hippies from Laos. Only the revolution, however, would bring a complete clamp down on such 'decadent' foreign influences.

## Facing the dilemmas of development

The intellectuals grouped around *Mittasone* showed an acute awareness of the paradoxes of underdevelopment in Laos, including the fact that their own higher education was one of the fruits of foreign aid. Almost all of their writing in one way or another despairs of the 'backward mentality' of Laos, or as Somphavan wrote, 'the immense mismatch between the ideas that we have for our society and the facts and upheavals which surround us at present'. Writing on 'Nationalism and Development', he commented on how foreigners had mis-recognised Lao distrust of outsiders as nationalism, when in fact it was the distrust expressed by a society wedded to traditional ways:

> We have however been forced to recognize our economic weaknesses, our unfavourable geographical location for international commerce. Like someone who lacks confidence, Laos is suspicious towards all offers of friendship. It is this distrust or this reserve that our friends confound with nationalism. But Lao nationalism, if that is what it is, still lacks the maturity which would produce actions that are profound and positive.[42]

At the back of all these debates was an awareness of the country's heavy dependence on foreign aid. While no one could deny that for the foreseeable future this was inevitable, it did at times stimulate anti-foreign sentiments. Profound critiques of the use of foreign aid were produced by the intellectuals around *Mittasone*, in particular by Khamchong Luangphasert in a book-length study of foreign aid published in 1973, where he proposed that one way around the waste of aid and corruption was to develop methods of delivering aid directly to the villages rather than through the bureaucracy. This was in keeping with the 'bottom up' ideas of the delivery of aid emerging in the aid community by that time.

The *Mittasone* group also attempted to see Laos's problems as typical of those faced by developing countries, which had difficulties in creating a modern, uncorrupt state administration and economy. By the late 1960s corruption had become a matter of public debate and the government had established a Bureau of Public Opinion to both gather and disseminate information on the problem. B. Somhack, writing in *Mittasone* in late 1969, applauded this move and called for an anti-corruption commission. Unlike many foreign commentators he was sensitive to the fact that corruption would persist for as long as low-level functionaries received low pay and therefore sought 'commissions' from members of the public who approached them. Corruption also flowed from the *phu nyai* cultural complex, under which favouritism was widely practised and expected, and from foreign sources: 'Exemplary sanctions should be taken against those who are at the origin of corruption: dubious merchants and foreigners, who we have mostly welcomed with open arms but who conduct themselves as if they are in a conquered land, having several highly placed persons in their pay.' The focus on foreign sources of corruption, particularly by Chinese, would intensify in the run-up to 1975. Writers like Somhack saw the problem as one shared by all developing countries, and he repulsed some of the conceited moralism of western commentators by pointing out that financial scandals are also commonplace in highly developed countries such as the USA.

These themes were taken up by the press, which also vigorously explored the notion of freedom of the press. Phone Chantala, the editor of *Xat Lao Daily*, saw his role as tackling corruption and reporting fearlessly on political events, for which the paper occasionally suffered a 'mild form of censorship', as he put it, including at one time being closed for a month. In mid-1974, after the formation of the coalition government, the paper continued to criticise the presence of Vietnamese troops in the country and its editor received threats from the left. In 1975 *Xat Lao*, along with other independent newspapers, was closed down by the new regime.

## Corruption and familism

The scale of corruption in the late 1960s, however, was not as uncontrolled or anarchic as during the late 1950s. Among other things, this was because the USA, burnt by the earlier experience, now monitored the flow of aid more closely. But corruption had also become more institutionalised, as it was in Thailand, although less secure. In Thailand the formation of state-owned companies controlled by the elite, plus an alliance between the military and Chinese businessmen, provided a secure base for a corrupt elite. In Laos, partly because of the war, there was no industrial or financial base. Corruption fed off foreign aid and the few minor monopolies that the elite could carve out. Some became wealthy by Lao standards, but the pickings were not large. Prince Boun Oum was known as 'the biggest small businessman in Laos', a reference to his corpulence in old age and his wealth. In some respects Boun Oum and the far-flung and influential members of his Na Champasak family most closely resembled the Thai elite in its operations. They combined aristocratic legitimacy (photos of the prince could be found in ordinary households throughout the south as he was considered *saksit*, magically powerful) with an alliance with elements of both the military and Chinese businessmen. The Chinese established semi-legal casinos in Paksé and Savannakhet, from which Boun Oum received a share of the profits, and they invested heavily in Lao Airlines, an enterprise backed by the southern elite. A cousin of Boun Oum, Chao Ieng, controlled trade between Laos and Thailand along Route 10, using thugs to enforce his monopoly. Members of the Na Champasak family, with elements of the military, also engaged in smuggling and illegal logging. A secret US report in 1970 claimed, however: 'Although the Na Champasaks may be collectively the wealthiest clan in Laos, the family is now so divided, principally over economic matters, that it represents a series of competing fortunes, probably varying greatly in size, rather than a single unified economic interest group.' Between them they controlled about US$400 000 per year in 1970, which once divided up was small by Thai standards but substantial in Laos. Prince Boun Oum by then had diverted a large amount of the family fortune into building a large and ostentatious palace in Paksé. Still unfinished in 1975, it languished until taken over by a Sino-Thai businessman in 1995 and turned into a luxury hotel. Prince Boun Oum and his family were natural targets for the left, not only because of their wealth but also because of their consistent support for the political right. The Sananikhone family in Vientiane came in for similar treatment. In a familiar pattern for the region as a whole, the exercise of political power was the means to economic wealth in conjunction with Chinese businesses. Thus the politicians or bureaucrats would gain tax concessions or monopolies for businesses in return for shares or payments. For example, the tobacco company 555, whose board included members of the Sananikhone family, was able to secure tax forfeits. There were other such deals, resembling insider trading, whereby local elite companies would get aid contracts. Favouritism would be expressed by, for example, Minister of Public Works Ngon Sananikhone, ensuring that roads were built in the area of a candidate he supported. Such manipulation or even vote buying did not always work, as Oun Sananikhone found in the 1972 elections when he was outvoted despite spreading around 500-kip notes and travelling along the Mekong in a barge filled with World Vision goodies which he passed out to the villages. Besides redistributing wealth to their entourages, the Lao elite largely spent its money on building big houses in the city, buying expensive cars and sending their children overseas to study. Few made enough to set up Swiss bank accounts, and most would flee Laos in 1975 with little money in their pockets. When I interviewed Ngon Sananikhone in 1998, for example, he lived with his daughter and her husband in a simple worker's flat on the outskirts of Paris, a shadow of his former self economically, but intellectually uncowed. The practices of the RLG elite were little different from those found throughout Southeast Asia at the time, and indeed persist today. Increasingly, younger members of the elite were seeking ways around the more deleterious forms of corruption and making serious attempts to seek out ways that would carry the country forward. One of the main achievements of the RLG, perhaps even by default, was that it allowed relatively open debate about social and political issues, and in this respect was almost unique in the region at that time.

## Opium politics

In the early 1970s sensationalist claims were made by an ambitious young American academic, Al McCoy, in *The Politics of Heroin in Southeast Asia* (1972), about the Lao elite's involvement in drug smuggling. Opium, under the French and afterwards, had long been an important part of the Lao economy. Following the introduction of American aid in the 1950s the State withdrew from involvement in the opium trade, except briefly in the early 1960s when Phoumi Nosovan tried to circumvent the US aid embargo to pay his troops and followers. Trade in opium was legal up until mid-1971, and Phoumi's actions, from a Lao point of view, were acceptable. In 1969, when Lao revenue from the gold trade dried up as a result of competition from Singapore, thoughts quickly turned, as they had in the past, to opium. McCoy indignantly cites Finance Minister Sisouk Na Champasak's statement to a BBC reporter in 1970: 'The only export we can develop here is opium, and we should increase our production and export it.' This option was quickly squashed by the USA, however. General Ouan Rathikhoun was in charge of Phoumi's opium administration in the early 1960s for which, as he once complained, he only received $200 a month. Once Phoumi fled Laos this operation collapsed, although McCoy, without producing any hard evidence, alleges that Ouan continued to control it. Ouan was not only quite frank about his earlier involvement, but showed an understanding of the problems of opium not exhibited by McCoy or other outsiders. He told a hostile and apparently uncomprehending McCoy of Interpol visits to him in 1967 and 1968:

> I told them there would be commerce as long as the opium was grown in the hills. They should pay the tribesmen to stop growing opium . . . I told Interpol to buy tractors so we could clear the trees off the plains. Then we could move the montagnards out of the mountains onto the plains. It is too warm there and there would be no more opium growing. In the mountains the people work ten months a year to grow 100,000 kip worth of opium and rice. And if the weather is bad, or the insects come, or the rain is wrong they will have nothing. But on the plains the people can have irrigated rice fields, grow vegetables, and make handicrafts. On the plain in five months of work they can make 700,000 kip a year.[43]

Opium continued to be traded in Laos, long after it was banned, because for many highlanders it remained an important cash crop. But by the late 1960s the war, and the resulting massive disruption of Hmong society, had caused a huge drop in production. Some of it was certainly traded out through Air America, but as straight highland commerce rather than some CIA commercial conspiracy. Rebutting McCoy in October 1972, Ouan said: 'There was no "big man" trader, no "King" in the trade who used Air America planes. They had no cause to, because these people were international traders who all had their own aircraft.' The Lao, at most, played a small role alongside these international syndicates, but by the early seventies a fatigued America and a morally pure anti-war movement was outraged to think that US aid could be in any way involved with 'drug running', and sensationalist reporting made the most of it. Although there is little clear evidence that any of the Lao elite became seriously rich as a result of the drug trade, the charge that they were 'drug runners' has stuck. Ouan unquestionably was a *phu nyai* who used the proceeds of opium to consolidate his status. It is alleged, for example, that when his troops crushed a 1967 attempt by Burma's Shan State warlord Khun Sa to establish a foothold in northern Laos they confiscated almost 16 tons of raw opium. The spoils were shared among the troops of the 2nd Paratroop Battalion who were involved in the operation, with each man receiving enough money to build a simple house for his family. While Ouan's wealth was often gained through corrupt or semi-legal means, it was a fortune only by Lao standards and even then he shared it with his followers.

## The royal family

The most important family in the country was the Luang Phrabang royal family, yet they were probably among the least wealthy members of the elite. The Palace was supported out of the state budget, but members of the royal family showed little interest in commercial activity and were content to live relatively humble lives. King Savang Vatthana had come to the throne during one of the most turbulent periods of the RLG. Cautious and conservative, he resisted attempts throughout the crisis in the early 1960s to pressure him into taking over the prime ministership and forming a national government. His overarching concern was to protect the constitutional monarchy, which he felt would be jeopardised if he became openly involved in politics. His cautious public statements and actions led many to believe that he was inactive, but US archives reveal the key political role he played. The domineering American Ambassador, William H. Sullivan, even found him beyond reach, and commented on the King soon after taking the post in late 1964: 'Whenever I attempted to pin him down to take certain actions he faded into a vast Cheshire cat's grin and retreated into the sanctity of his monarchy. In short, he is a highly intelligent, rapidly evasive, personally charming person who will doubtless frustrate me in precisely the same measure as he has my predecessor.' While the monarchy had begun to modernise during the 1950s, in particular by making it more visible through the King's presence at key public events, King Sisavangvong's age and illness had meant that many of these tasks fell to Savang Vatthana, the Crown Prince. In the first years of his accession to the throne King Savang Vatthana was preoccupied with managing the country's political stability, and there was no deliberate attempt by the State to promote a monarchical cult, as the military did in Thailand at the time. Indeed, the young Thai monarch was initially a captive of his country's military rulers and was only gradually able to reassert the Crown's power. In Laos, by contrast, the Crown's consent was needed by any prospective military ruler, and that was never forthcoming. Thus did King Savang Vatthana ensure that Laos before 1975 never degenerated into military dictatorship.

Attempts were made by the RLG to popularise the monarchy through the production of pictures of the King for general distribution, calendars with the King and Queen, and through magazine and radio coverage. As the mass media was relatively undeveloped, and this was a pre-TV age, the promotion of the monarchy progressed slowly and unevenly. The King, his daughter Princess Savivan and the Crown Prince, Vong Savang, were active in many social and cultural events, and when they could they toured minority areas. The King and Prince Souvanna Phouma visited Sam Thong for the Hmong New Year in 1968, and the King visited Long Cheng the year after. The security situation would, however, restrict the King's movements and the Crown Prince took on the visits to Long Cheng and other remote places in later years. When the Boloven Plateau fell to North Vietnamese troops in mid-1971, however, the King insisted on touring the southern

*As fighting grew more intense, Crown Prince Vong Savang (left) took over more duties*
*from his father, in particular visiting minority areas. Here he visits Koh people at Ban*
*Houayxay, north Laos, who are giving him offerings of flowers as a mark of respect.*
*(Courtesy Joel Halpern archive)*

provinces in person to raise morale. The King was at the centre of all key lowland Lao Buddhist rituals and in this way had a secure place in Lao culture. In response to suggestions that he relocate his main palace to Vientiane for greater safety, the King explained his reluctance to move to the US Ambassador Winthrop Brown in March 1961:

> I asked him what he would do if Luang Phrabang should be attacked. He said that of course he would stay in Luang Phrabang. This was the symbolic importance of Luang Phrabang and as the royal capital and religious center, the presence of the King there was extremely important for

> the Lao people . . . Vientiane had a reputation as the
> capital of trouble. Every king who had made his head-
> quarters in Vientiane had come to a violent end sooner or
> later. He was not particularly superstitious but people
> believed this. In any event, Vientiane did not have the
> religious symbolism of Luang Phrabang.[44]

Despite his well-known anti-communism the King had maintained
a low political profile in order to be able, when necessary, to act as a
mediator between the contending sides. As a prelude to the 1973
negotiations for a coalition government, Prince Souphanouvong in
November 1972 had appealed to his impartiality: 'The NLHX is firmly
convinced that His Majesty the King will exercise his royal privileges
and great influence to compel the Vientiane side to extricate itself
from being a US puppet . . .' And right up until 2 December 1975, the
NLHX declared its support for the throne. King Savang Vatthana had
deliberately delayed his formal coronation, initially mooted for 1967,
until after national reconciliation had been achieved, so that the coronation could also be its crowning moment. In March 1975, perhaps as
a last desperate manoeuvre by the Royalists, an announcement was
made that the King's coronation would take place in December 1976.
It was never held.

# The final coalition

Not only was the RLG vulnerable militarily, but its dependence on
foreign aid placed it at the mercy of its donors and the international
economy. From 1968 to 1973 the Lao economy was delivered several
solid blows that triggered discontent and feelings of despair. The
RLG usually could only raise about 45 per cent of its budget revenue,
the rest coming from foreign aid. A major source of RLG revenue
since the kip exchange-rate reform of 1958 had been taxes raised on

the import of gold—40 per cent of revenue in 1967. During the 1960s Laos became one of the major legal importers of gold in the Far East, although approximately two-thirds of that gold was then smuggled into South Vietnam. The communist Tet Offensive in 1968 disrupted this trade severely, and in that same year, the first inklings of a reform in the international financial system in which the US dollar had been 'as good as gold' came through, separating the official from the free-market price of gold, thus reducing speculative demand. In 1969 Singapore established itself as a gold entrepôt, finishing off the Lao market and destroying gold as a source of revenue. The 'crisis of the dollar', which in 1971 would tear apart the Bretton Woods Agreement on which the international system had rested since 1948, was also bearing down on the tiny Lao economy. The Lao budget had been buoyed up by the Foreign Exchange Operations Fund (FEOF), established in 1964, which within agreed limits made foreign exchange available to the government. The USA was the main donor (60 per cent), along with Japan, the UK, France and Australia. Faced with a dramatic fall in tax revenue in 1970, either the FEOF would have to cover the shortfall or the kip would have to be devalued. This was finally done in November 1971. The government also attempted to introduce exchange controls but this simply created a black market for dollars. The financial crisis not only increased the RLG's dependence on foreign aid for any development plans, but the inflation caused by the devaluation strained the already low salaries of state employees. The 1973 global oil crisis put further pressure on prices, only partially offset by the proceeds from the Ngam Ngum hydrolectricity dam opened in late 1971. It was against this background of economic crisis that the negotiations for the third coalition government began.

The RLG and the NLHX followed the lead of their respective patrons in negotiating a cease-fire and a political agreement. On 10 October 1972, a draft peace agreement was signed between North Vietnam and the USA. Within days the NLHX had dropped their main condition for entering into negotiations with the RLG, the cessation of US bombing, and talks began. The Paris Agreement on Vietnam was signed on 27 January 1973, and in early February a caravan of US politicians visited Vientiane—Vice-President Spiro Agnew, Secretary of State Henry Kissinger and former US Ambassador William Sullivan—to pressure the RLG into an agreement. As Ngon Sananikhone, one of the RLG's chief negotiators, told me, 'What could we do when Kissinger told us to come to an agreement as quickly as possible? America underwrote our army!' But Kissinger had been tricked by Le Duc Tho, one of the most ruthless men in the Vietnamese Communist Party, into thinking that a cease-fire agreement in Laos would mean a withdrawal of North Vietnamese troops. When he travelled on to Hanoi from Vientiane, he soon discovered that the DRV had no such intention.

A Lao cease-fire agreement was signed on 21 February. It called for the formation of a Provisional Government of National Union, but for another seven months the two sides would wrangle over the protocol for this government. During this time there were continual cease-fire violations on both sides, but relatively little heavy fighting. The NLHX were negotiating from a position of strength, given the determination of the North Vietnamese to stay and the desire of the Americans to leave. The RLG negotiators, although weakened, were generally only levered into concessions by Souvanna himself, who appeared to be genuinely convinced that the other side sought reconciliation. The meeting between President Nixon and Mao Zedong the previous year seemed to have raised hopes among some people in Vientiane that China could play a key role in restraining the Vietnamese, although Beijing, in fact, had no influence in Hanoi. A major initial concession by the RLG side was Souvanna Phouma's agreement that the Provisional Government would be known as the 'Government of Vientiane', thus conceding equal status for the two sides and sidelining the National Assembly's claim to represent the country. Many members of the military were unhappy with

*Henry Kissinger (left) in Vientiane with Souvanna Phouma, Sisouk Na Champasak and Leum Insisiengmai, where he assured them that the North Vietnamese would honour the Paris peace agreements. (Courtesy Prince Mangkra Souvanna Phouma)*

Souvanna's concessions and rumours of a coup circulated in Vientiane. But Souvanna was now more than ever America's man, the one who would ensure that the USA could get out of the war, and this kept the military in check. The attempted coup, when it came, was launched by Lao exiles in Thailand on 20 August. Former airforce General Thao Ma, who had fled with Phoumi Nosovan, led a group of 60 rebels in a quixotic assault on Vattai Airport, hoping thereby to provoke a general uprising. Ma himself commandeered a T-28 and bombed the army headquarters on the outskirts of Vientiane, killing two soldiers. But the attempt quickly floundered, and Ma's T-28 crash-landed, whereupon he was arrested and summarily executed. This desperate and unexpected action put paid to any thoughts of a military coup from within Laos. However, it provided a propaganda coup for the NLHX, who lambasted 'rightists' and all those who were against 'peace and reconciliation'.

## Subverting the RLG from within

The protocol activating the Vientiane Agreement was signed soon after, on 14 September. The key provisions were the neutralisation of Vientiane and Luang Phrabang, the composition of a new National Political Consultative Council, and a sharing out of Cabinet positions on an equal basis. Each Minister had a Vice-Minister from the opposite side who had the right of veto. In effect, this meant that the NLHX could paralyse the administrative machinery whenever it liked,

*Joint RLG and PL police patrol in Vientiane, September 1973.*
*(Courtesy Joel Halpern archive)*

169

and thus the Czechoslovakian scenario, prematurely feared by America in the late 1950s, came into effect, and the PL slowly subverted the government from within. Significantly, Souphanouvong did not join the Cabinet and instead took control of a Consultative Council, which he based in Luang Phrabang, that soon eclipsed the National Assembly. Most significantly, PL troops would move into Luang Phrabang and Vientiane to form a joint police force, but there was no reciprocal movement of RLA troops into the other side's territory. Once these cities were secured, the PL leaders and Souphanouvong flew to Vientiane on 6 April to a tumultuous welcome. As one journalist for the *Far Eastern Economic Review* described Souphanouvong's arrival at the time:

> Possessing a degree of vitality that was unusual in a Lao politician, he drew enthusiastic and demonstrative crowds wherever he went. He seemed at ease in any company, a veritable 'people's prince' whose rapport with the populace was reminiscent of the Prince Sihanouk of Cambodia, though Souphanouvong was more reserved and he had a sense of mission. He had come to restore Laos' faith in itself. He was the hero of the Lao student movement. He had presence, if not charisma, and this rubbed off on the men who came down with him from Sam Neua.[45]

A Lao friend who was a student at the time in Luang Phrabang described the reaction there when the two brother princes visited soon after: 'People saw it as a family reconciliation. Souphanouvong and Souvanna Phouma like Laos had been divided, but now they had come back together. From now on everything would be peaceful and happy.' This nostalgic family idiom combined with the aristocratic aura of the two main protagonists worked its magic, and the whole of Laos heaved a huge sigh of relief that the war was finally over. The PL, spearheaded by Souphanouvong, took the initiative in presenting themselves as the party of peace and branded anyone who opposed them as warmongers. Confrontations between the two sides in Cabinet and the administration soon became commonplace, however. Alongside the younger Souphanouvong, the 72-year-old Souvanna Phouma looked the aged and tired politician that he really was. Indeed, the two men appeared to embody two principles, the dynamism of the new order and the exhaustion of the old. On 12 July, Souvanna suffered a heart attack, and on 25 July he flew to France to recuperate. Only Sisouk Na Champasak could fill his shoes, but as he would have been strongly opposed by the PL as one of their longtime adversaries, at this crucial time the 'Vientiane side' was left rudderless.

The NLHX quickly capitalised on this weakness. They used their infiltration of labour organisations in the capital to launch a rash of strikes over July and August, playing on discontent over pay in the deteriorating economic conditions. They also used the strikes to demand the removal of officials they deemed corrupt. Demonstrations by students in Paksé against rising prices and against the operation of casinos had already occurred in January, partly inspired by the 1973 success of the student movement in Thailand in toppling the military dictatorship in 1973. Significantly, these southern demonstrations whipped up anti-Chinese feelings, with the students demanding that the government close the Chinese schools in Paksé.

In accordance with the protocol for the Provisional Government of National Union, foreign troops were to be withdrawn from Laos within 60 days of its formation. By 4 June American and Thai military personnel had been withdrawn, and air strikes and reconnaissance flights halted. There was never any attempt at verification of the withdrawal of Vietnamese troops, the 'secret army' whose existence had never been officially acknowledged. The suspension of US bombing made movements down the Ho Chi Minh Trail easier, as the communists prepared for their final offensive in southern Vietnam. In August 1974 the PL pressed their growing military advantage by

171

pushing beyond the ill-defined cease-fire line, and launching assaults against Vang Pao's diminished forces. In December 1974 Yao special forces units in Ban Houayxai rebelled, demanding peace but also a repeal of the laws prohibiting the growing of opium. The economy had continued to deteriorate over the year and there was growing pressure to devalue the kip again. The NLHX feared that this would be unpopular and opted instead for statist restrictions on the movement of money. An increasingly demoralised and paralysed RLG had entered the new year when Souvanna Phouma returned on 24 February from convalescence, weakened physically and politically, and virtually conceded leadership of the country to Souphanouvong.

The collapse of US military support had caused demoralisation in the army, although some commanders fought on, in particular Vang Pao. In April 1975, a major battle took place between his forces and the PL for Sala Phu Khoun, a major junction north of Vientiane—it ended in the retreat of Vang Pao's forces with the road left open to the capital. In Cambodia, Phnom Penh fell to the Khmer Rouge on 17 April, then Saigon fell to the NVA on 30 April. In the face of these neighbouring upheavals, the King's Council finally relented to PL pressure and King Savang Vatthana signed a decree on 13 April dissolving the National Assembly, with no guarantee that elections would be held. Following the victories in Cambodia and Vietnam, the communists' march towards complete power in Laos intensified. Anti-American demonstrations were organised throughout the country, and on 9 May a large crowd converged on the US Embassy, its leaders demanding the resignation of 'rightist' ministers from the government. Among those who resigned and promptly went into exile was the Minister of Defence, Sisouk Na Champasak, who was replaced by the PL General Kham Ouan Boupha, who set about dismantling what was left of RLG control of the armed forces. In this rapidly deteriorating situation Vang Pao also fled. The King was on a tour of Houaphan Province at the time of these events. Guided by Souphanouvong and treated with dissembling respect by the PL, the long-time anti-communist King was feted with

*Souphanouvong (left) conducts the King and Queen on their visit to Vieng Xai, Houaphan Province, May 1975. Pathet Lao cadres simulate subserviance to the King.*

revolutionary songs, something he bore stoically. By the time he returned to Luang Phrabang the virtual coup in Vientiane was over. On 19 May PL forces began to enter the Mekong towns of Paksé, Savannakhet and Thakhek. The flames of anti-American feeling were fanned across the country, and demonstrators occupied USAID headquarters in Vientiane and Luang Phrabang, demanding an end to the organisation's activities. American personnel began leaving immediately and by June, after 20 years, USAID in Laos had closed shop. These 'popular uprisings', spearheaded by small but powerful groups of PL, with each assault or denunciation of 'reactionaries' or 'corrupt rightists' slowly removed opponents from the administration and replaced them with their own appointees. The crowds that gathered to witness the sacking of administrative buildings mostly watched passively, and no police

173

intervened. The mixed police forces were dissolved at the end of July and PL troops assumed their role. In August a new 'revolutionary administrative committee' took power in Luang Phrabang, and on 23 August the PL declared to a large demonstration that the city of Vientiane had been 'completely liberated'.

## A slow takeover

What is most intriguing about the communist takeover of Laos in 1975 is the slow pace at which it was executed. Victory by their allies in Vietnam did not lead to a sudden military assault on the Mekong towns in Laos by the PL. This could only have been done with the help of Vietnamese troops, an option that was unacceptable as it could have provoked reaction by the Thais. The slowness of the takeover was also partly due to the fact that the PL's support was weak among the two-thirds of the population living in the RLG-controlled zone. To grab for power too early and abolish the monarchy risked an anti-PL uprising. Thus, using the legitimacy of the coalition government and proclaiming their desire for reconciliation and their support of the monarchy, they slowly whittled away the opposition's power base, Souphanouvong's role in this process was absolutely crucial—his declarations of support for the monarchy convinced many doubters, especially in the army, that the PL side really desired peace and re-conciliation. Only this explains the meekness and willingness with which generals and hundreds of other army officers went off to the interior for 're-education'. They and their wives were told they would be gone for only a few months. For many it was ten or fifteen years, and others never returned. The implacable attitude of the communists towards their opponents was revealed in September, when a 'people's court' announced that the 'rightist' Ministers who had fled had been sentenced to death in absentia, and another 25 former leaders were sentenced to 25-year prison terms. This slow decapitation of the RLG set the stage for the final takeover.

On 26 November another orchestrated demonstration demanded

*PL tank in Savannakhet. The slogan reads, in part, 'down with the imperialists and reactionaries'. (Courtesy Joel Halpern archive)*

the dissolution of the coalition government and the abolition of the monarchy. Souvanna Phouma and Souphanouvong flew to Luang Phrabang where they gained a letter of abdication from the King. On 1–2 December, a secretly convened Congress of People's Representatives was held in the gymnasium of the former US school in Vientiane where the Crown Prince, Vong Savang, read out his father's letter of abdication. The establishment of the Lao People's Democratic Republic was then proposed, with Souphanouvong as President and Kaysone Phomvihan as Prime Minister. All other members elected to the new government were members of the NLHX. The one-party state had arrived in Laos.

# 5
# THE LAO PEOPLE'S DEMOCRATIC REPUBLIC

The harsh regime that came to power in late 1975 caused many Lao to flee their country. Hmong fought on for several years after the RLG's collapse, but were savagely crushed in 1977. The LPDR put in place all the usual trappings of a tightly controlled communist society. However, its attempts at radical economic change, such as agricultural collectivisation, were a failure and thus in the 1980s market-style reforms began. The 1990s saw considerable relaxation of state control of everyday life, with bars opening and young people beginning to dress in modern styles. The state, however, kept tight control over the mass media and political activity, although by the late 1990s there were some signs that this control was slipping.

# Exodus

If the beginning of the Royal Lao Government in the late 1940s had seen the fleeing of the Vietnamese and a Lao-isation of the cities, the first years of the Lao People's Democratic Republic (LPDR) saw the fleeing of Chinese merchants and most educated Lao. The composition of the cities changed again as many upland Tai and various minorities came into town with the revolutionaries. In some respects the countryside reclaimed the cities, and indeed city residents often referred to the PL as *khon pa*, 'jungle men', with all the connotations of ignorant country hicks. It is a term one sometimes still hears today to explain one policy failure or another by the LPDR. The shutters came down on most businesses in the cities, cars disappeared from the roads as fuel prices shot up with the collapse of the economy, and bicycles reappeared on the streets in large numbers. Lipstick and make-up faded from women's faces, little jewellery was visible, and simple austere clothing became the unspoken rule. It was as if Vientiane had been suddenly propelled backwards into the 1950s, except for the sombre mood that had settled on the populace as the reality of the revolution dawned upon them.

Suddenly the figures who so dominated the political scene over 1975 had either disappeared or taken a back seat, as with Souphanouvong, to the revolutionary leaders who had come down from Vieng Xai for the December proclamation of the LPDR. Kaysone Phomvihan, General Secretary of the Lao People's Revolutionary Party (LPRP), and now Prime Minister of the LPDR, emerged as the country's strongman. People from the former RLG areas knew almost nothing about him because his power had always been disguised by NLHX frontman Souphanouvong. In these early years Kaysone and his party remained aloof and secretive, and from this they derived their power to intimidate the population. Political indoctrination sessions were held at all levels to instruct people in the party line, not to ask their opinion.

Their voices were only required to either praise the leadership or to denounce 'imperialists' and 'traitors'.

Many individuals quickly found life under communism intolerable, and the scale of the ensuing exodus after 1975 was unprecedented. Perhaps it is only comparable to the depopulation of the lowlands by the Siamese following Chao Anou's revolt in the early nineteenth century. The raw refugee figures disguise the disproportionate number of people with skills and education who fled. The exodus of the old elite had begun as a trickle before the final communist takeover, and turned into a flood over the following years as remnants of the elite and the country's small, educated population left. Soon they were joined by peasants voting with their feet against the regime's agricultural policies. By 1980, 10 per cent of Laos's total population had fled, and more would follow, enfeebling the country's development in the late twentieth century.

*Revolutionary billboards in Vientiane in the early 1980s. (Photo Grant Evans)*

The first imperative of the burgeoning totalitarian state was the enforcement of order, which was achieved by sending off to labour camps the military and political personnel of the old regime, and the outlawing of all organisations, including newspapers, magazines and journals, that claimed any autonomy from the state. The key mechanism for the swallowing up of Lao civil society was the NLHX, in 1979 renamed the Neo Lao Sang Xat (NLSX), the Lao Front for National Construction. This was the umbrella organisation for all potentially autonomous forms of social organisation, such as the Buddhist *sangha*, businessmen, minorities, workers' unions, youth and women's organisations, and so on. In the villages that made up the cities, and in the rural villages, committees comprising the heads of the various Front organisations took control, and where possible Communist Party members became village headmen. From late 1975 they organised mass meetings of villagers to study the party line. These seemingly endless meetings, although initially greeted with enthusiasm by some, soon became stultifying. Demonstrations of 'spontaneous' mass enthusiasm for the revolution were compulsory, however. Political cadres took charge of the few technically competent bureaucrats who remained behind, and politics was placed in command. The LPRP set out to create society anew and to give birth to 'the new socialist man'.

As part of the 'cultural revolution', wayward youths were forced to conform to styles dictated by the party, in what can only be described as a puritanical backlash. As journalist John Everingham described in early 1976:

> Western-influenced youths were taken to task for their dress; girls, too, were criticized. Youths were dragged in for haircuts and women admonished not to wear any make-up. To listen to Thai radio stations was to risk being labeled 'reactionary', as with playing western music. Both the pursuit of pleasure or profit was denounced as being unpatriotic while the task of re-building the country remained. For this people were urged to go to bed early.[46]

Those who failed to comply or were deemed prostitutes were sent off to camps situated on islands in the middle of the Ngam Ngum Dam north of Vientiane.

## Prison camps

From mid-1975 officers, soldiers, police and high officials of the RLG were packed off to the countryside to attend 'seminar', the euphemism used for the prison camps. By 1975 many Lao had become war-weary, and they believed Pathet Lao propaganda that little would change with the coming of peace except that 'the foreign imperialists' would be expelled. When the President of the NLHX, Souphanouvong, told the people confidently that the monarchy would be preserved, and that Laos would soon rediscover its traditional culture, unsullied by foreign influence, they wanted to believe him, and initially many trudged off to the camps voluntarily. After December many others were rounded up and sent there. Rather than staying a few months as they were promised, however, these people spent years in the prison camps in the mountains of northern Laos, in Xiang Khoang or Houaphan provinces and in Attapu in southern Laos. The LPRP did not carry out large-scale massacres of the former leadership like their Khmer Rouge 'comrades' in Cambodia (they remained 'comrades' until 1979), nor did the Vietnamese. Nevertheless, many people did not return from the camps, and to this day relatives have never been informed officially of what happened to fathers, sons or loved ones. Of those who did return many quickly fled as refugees. Whatever the imperfections of the old RLG, it never attempted political repression on this huge and vengeful scale.

Compared with Vietnam, and certainly with Cambodia, relatively little attention has ever been paid to the establishment and the effects of this vast prison system in Laos. There has never been any systematic study made of it, nor are there any reliable estimates of how many were interned. Suggested numbers have ranged from 10 000 to 40 000. The higher figure probably represents the number of ordinary soldiers and officials who underwent a short period of 're-education' of several months. Somewhere between 10 000 and 15 000, however, endured periods of up to fifteen years. Others were summarily executed or imprisoned until they died. None of these people was ever charged legally, thus in this huge extra-legal prison system those interned had no rights. Many accounts by Vietnamese interned in camps in their country have been published internationally, as have accounts by Cambodians who endured the horrific repression of the Khmer Rouge. Few Lao, however, have written about their lives in the camps.

One of the few accounts is by Thongthip Rathanavilai. *Man in the Region of Death: Passing Through the Five Stages of Hell*, published in Lao in America, tells a story which is depressingly familiar to anyone who has read about internment in China or Vietnam. In July 1975 he and other officers and RLG officials were flown to Xiang Khoang, where they believed they would stay for three months. In fact, he spent nine years in the camps. They were soon flown on to Vieng Xai, the war-time headquarters of the NLHX, from where they were marched to Camp Number 6. Their guards told them they were there to protect them from the wrath of the local people, and that if they passed any locals they were not to look them in the eye, just as the locals were instructed to ignore them. It was the first sign that they had disappeared from social sight. Camp 6 was near the Vietnamese border and was simply a forest when they arrived. Their first task, therefore, was to build their own prison. As the hard work of felling trees and building houses began, a climate of fear and suspicion descended on the inmates. 'Re-education' began with daily study of party policy, then self-criticism and denunciations. At first it was new, but the same message repeated day in, day out became boringly oppressive.

> We had to repeat strictly according to the words of those on high, the head of our group would speak first, 'all

praise', 'all praise', 'all praise', three times, and then we would repeat it. The Party and Government's intelligence is clear and bright: all praise, all praise, all praise. We must be on our guard against the American imperialists and the traitors: all praise, all praise, all praise. From here on they are our enemies: all praise, all praise, all praise. The Party leads the people to be masters: all praise, all praise, all praise. We said it until we were stuffed full. All praise, all praise, all praise, like that everyday.[47]

Interestingly, Thongthip and the other inmates who had never experienced life under the PL quickly identified the regime of oppressive hard work, poor food and monotonous diatribes as being 'non-Lao' and really 'Vietnamese'; in a sense they were right, because it was a system that had been pioneered by the Chinese and Vietnamese and taught to their Lao apprentice. In 1976 they were visited by Central Committee member Sithone Khommadam, who told them:

You have been brought here for your own good. If this was Cambodia you would have already disappeared. You have been brought here to be cured and cleansed and to become new men. All of you here have been leaders, but you are really ignorant. But whoever listens to us and reforms will be able to return home and become a good citizen.[48]

Following his visit a pall of depression fell on the camp as its inmates realised that they were there indefinitely. Some became withdrawn, would not even eat, and just lay on their beds after a day's work. Some attempted escape, were caught, badly beaten, paraded before the inmates and either shot or sent to an even higher security camp.

By 1978, however, the camp regime began to relax. The new government realised that skills were going to waste in the camps and so engineers or mechanics or drivers were put to work on various projects.

The camp inmates were also put to road building and maintenance, and in this way the camps were transformed into prison labour camps. Inmates could also work for local farmers and enter into exchanges with them, and so some established close relations with the people and gained better food. Clearly with an eye to relocating the inmates in the mountains permanently, after 1978 wives and children were allowed to join their husbands. A few did so, but returned home after a year or so as conditions were usually too tough. The absence of good medicines was an important reason for deaths in the camps, and a good reason for wives not to stay. Small numbers began to be released from the camps in the early 1980s. Thongthip returned to Vientiane in 1984, and the city appeared to him a shadow of its former self. Like many other returnees, he soon fled to Thailand.

The purpose of the camps had been to break the will of the members of the 'old regime' and instil in them fear of the new regime. The threat of internment also hung over the heads of the rest of the population. Many men returned broken and withdrawn, and wives confronted with husbands who had grown remote separated from them, sometimes deciding to become refugees. Others, quietly unbowed, still joke about how they were sent for 'further studies' at the 'university of Vieng Xai' but were 'too ignorant' and so did not graduate. By 1986 the government claimed that all the camps had been closed down, but some people remained confined to the boundaries of the provinces in which they were imprisoned until 1989. Others who had been imprisoned in the infamous Camp 05 were never released. King Savang Vatthana, the Queen, the Crown Prince, and one other son, Prince Savang, were incarcerated there in 1977 following allegations that they were involved with 'reactionaries'. None of them survived, the King believed to have died around 1980. The LPDR have never given any details of their deaths. Others who disappeared into the camps and never returned included Bong Souvannavong, Touby Lyfong, Ouan Rathikhoun, Général Bounpone Makthéparak, and there were many others.

# The Hmong resistance

Although no major torture and death camps were established in Laos, there were massacres of Hmong in the aftermath of the revolution. To those in the refugee camps that received the exhausted survivors it sometimes seemed that the LPDR was intent on annihilating them. Had it been current back then the term 'ethnic cleansing', born from the horrors of Yugoslavia in the 1990s, would no doubt have been used for Laos.

The war in the northern mountains had been bitterly fought, and as often as not it had been Hmong soldiers pitted against Vietnamese. While latent ethnic tensions were mostly kept under control before 1975, they burst forth in the campaigns against the Hmong afterwards. Even during the war, Hmong civilians had been caught many times in the crossfire as they were forced to flee their homes. Sometimes this had degenerated into mass killings. Charles Weldon reports one occasion in 1965:

> They had stopped to spend the night in a small, bowl-shaped depression on the side of a mountain. While they slept, they were surrounded by Pathet Lao and Vietnamese. At dawn's first light, the enemy fired a few shots into the air and shouted to them that they were surrounded and would be killed if they resisted . . . Everyone panicked and began a mad flight down the trail to the east they'd been following. The enemy began firing at random into the mass of terrified people with automatic weapons and mortars.[49]

Stories of such killings spread like wildfire among the Hmong, leading to fears of extermination if the communists ever took over.

By the time the NLHX began to assert final control over Laos in mid-1975, the upland economy was in crisis, unable to sustain the

Hmong population which had previously been supported by USAID. The thousands of Hmong spread through the mountains to the south of Long Cheng needed to move on, for their upland fields were already depleted. For many in fear of the communists, a natural move was to Thailand, where Vang Pao and other leaders had already fled. His departure in itself had caused a panic, and thousands of Hmong began to surge down Route 13 in late May 1975. Touby, emissary of Souvanna Phouma, tried to calm them. 'Vang Pao has gone,' he said, 'because he was too involved in the war. But you have committed no crimes, so why are you leaving the country?' But the crowds were not satisfied and surged on to Hin Heup where, on 29 May, their way was barred at a bridge by PL troops. By this time their numbers had apparently swelled to somewhere between 20 000 and 30 000 people. The soldiers told them to return to their villages, but the crowd rushed the bridge, whereupon the troops opened fire, killing five people and wounding around 30 others. A Thai photographer, Anant Chomcheun, who was on the scene the following day, reported seeing PL troops herding groups of Hmong back to the hills at gunpoint, while others melted into the countryside off the highway to continue their trek towards Thailand. 'I want to stay with my father Vang Pao,' one Hmong told the photographer. By the end of 1975 the Hmong refugee population in Thailand had reached around 34 000. News of the killings at Hin Heup quickly spread, confirming the Hmong's worst fears. At Long Cheng, Hmong soldiers and officers had been rounded up and sent off to 'seminar', and when they did not return their families were convinced they had been executed.

Accounts of continuing sporadic fighting in the mountains emerged in early 1976, and in July there were reports of the use of napalm against resistance strongholds. While soldiers loyal to Vang Pao made up part of this resistance, another group came to prominence, the Chao Fa, perhaps best rendered as 'Soldiers of God'. This was a nativistic millenarian movement that had emerged in the early 1960s, a result of the disruption of Hmong culture and society. Its

185

leader Yong Shong Lue promoted his own messianic script for the Hmong, believed in the coming of a Hmong king and that he could protect his followers from enemy bullets. There had always been some overlap between Vang Pao's men and the Chao Fa, although Vang Pao had tried to suppress the Chao Fa's influence. In the chaos that followed the fleeing of Vang Pao the influence of the Chao Fa grew dramatically, fuelling Hmong resistance to the new regime. These forces, however, had little ammunition and could only harass the new government.

Opposition was intolerable to the new leaders in Vientiane, and in 1977 they decided on a showdown with the Hmong resistance. This coincided with a treaty drawn up with Vietnam which legitimised the use of Vietnamese forces against the resistance; perhaps upwards of 30 000 NVA troops were used in the large-scale operation launched against the Hmong in 1977. The fighting by all accounts was ferocious and included shelling, aerial bombing with napalm, and perhaps even the use of chemical agents. The Hmong resistance fighters lived with their families and therefore operations against them entailed indiscriminate civilian casualties, leading to charges of genocide when the survivors staggered into the camps in Thailand and told their stories. Some stories were so horrific that they billowed into charges that the communists were using a hitherto unknown chemical weapon, known as 'yellow rain'. These claims, promoted by hawks in the USA, were never substantiated. That the Hmong were fighting against overwhelming odds is clear from the account given, for example, by an officer in December 1977: 'My group of 30 fighters got separated from the others a month ago. We had only 50 rounds of ammunition per man, no food and no medicine.' The fighting further disrupted the Hmong economy, and many who took flight through the forests arrived in Thailand emaciated.

It is clear that the campaign against the Hmong at times degenerated into the savagery associated with 'ethnic cleansing'. Even though the LPDR and its ally Vietnam broke the back of the resistance by 1978, they had killed and mistreated so many people in the process that resentment still festers today, finding sporadic expression in outbreaks of fighting against the government.

# National security

During the first years of the LPDR geopolitical pressures and internal policies were tightly interlocked. For example, the closing of the border by Thailand in November 1975 due to clashes with the Pathet Lao probably dictated the exact timing of the December declaration of the LPDR. The virtual collapse of the urban economy following the withdrawal of USAID, the flight of entrepreneurs and capital, combined with government restrictions on trade and commerce and the first nationalisations of businesses, naturally caused discontent with the LPDR, and heightened concern with security. Although trade with Thailand began again in early 1976, it was on a limited scale because of restrictions on the Thai side and depressed activity on the Lao side. Thai–Lao relations took another turn for the worse in October 1976 when a coup brought a right wing government to power in Bangkok. This not only led to further trading restrictions, but promised active Thai support for the resistance both inside and outside Laos.

Alongside the depressed urban economy, the rural economy suffered a mild drought in 1976, and severe floods in 1977. Only foreign food aid staved off famine in some areas. While leftists had criticised the RLG for its dependence on foreign support, this became equally true of the LPDR, whose budget deficit over the years has been covered by foreign aid. The new government had taken over the RLG's membership in various multilateral organisations, and without the support of the IMF, the most important aid donor in these early years, the nation would have been bankrupt. This leaves out of account military aid from the USSR and Vietnam (the exact amount has never been disclosed). The Lao People's Army was no less dependent on foreign donors for its maintenance than was the previous government's army on the USA.

It was thus not surprising that in July 1977 Laos signed a 20-year Treaty of Friendship and Cooperation with the Socialist Republic of Vietnam (as the country was renamed after official reunification in 1976). Both insecure economically, and surrounded by an increasingly problematic international environment, the two moved to shore up their long-standing alliance. Geopolitically, the Vietnamese communists played a crucial role in supporting this new state because its existence conformed to Hanoi's foreign policy aim of being surrounded by friendly socialist states. They were also in Laos to shore up the regime as relations between Vietnam and China soured over Hanoi's conflict with Pol Pot's Kampuchea. As Vietnam's main ally in the region, Laos was inevitably embroiled in this conflict, over which it had no control. Thus did international imperatives continue to impinge on Laos.

## Vietnam's mission civilatrice

The Lao communist movement had been dependent on Vietnamese advice and support from the very beginning. Indeed, the relationship seemed a natural one for the Lao leadership who had worked with the Vietnamese for so long and spoke their language easily. This was even more so for leaders like Kaysone, whose early enculturation was Vietnamese and remained bi-cultural throughout his life, or indeed for Souphanouvong, who had married a Vietnamese. Others among the leadership were also Lao-Vietnamese or had taken Vietnamese wives. The broader Lao leadership had all been schooled in the Vietnamese version of Marxism-Leninism, cadre schools were overseen by Vietnamese instructors; texts for pupils in these schools were Vietnamese ones, many of them translated into Lao. Translation of Vietnamese political tracts into Lao, with minimal modification, has continued up to today. Vietnamese advisers were placed at all key levels in the new administration and worked closely with the LPRP cadres who took control of the state apparatus. The long-standing dependence on Vietnam is reflected in the culturally anomalous celebration each year of the birth of Ho Chi Minh, which acclaims his support for the Lao revolution. This was jarring for Lao who had grown up under the RLG and been exposed to intense anti-Vietnamese propaganda, and to those leftist nationalists who had joined the NLHX to shake off 'foreign domination'. The major role played by the Vietnamese communists at key levels of the state appeared to contradict LPRP claims to have fought against the RLG for 'true independence', against the 'new colonialism' it said the old government was part of. To many Lao the new regime seemed equally part of a 'new colonial' system, especially following the signing of the 20-year treaty between the two countries. It was probably among these disaffected people that the several attempts made on Kaysone's life in the early years of the regime originated. Although the internal everyday policing of the Lao population had been gradually taken over from the army by a regular police force formed in 1976, in late 1978 a secret police organisation was set up under Vietnamese supervision. This organisation was deemed necessary to control dissent within the ranks of the LPRP and the army, as well as among civil servants.

Even if Vietnam was somehow considered the exemplary revolutionary model, its *mission civilatrice* in Laos stumbled on the fact that Laos too was an underdeveloped agrarian-based economy and society, not a model of 'advanced industrial socialism'. That role was fulfilled by the Soviet Union. By 1979 the USSR, along with communist Eastern Europe, was providing Laos with 60 per cent of its external assistance, as well as substantial military aid. Proportionally it was not much different from the US role before 1975, except that roubles did not have the buying power of dollars. Furthermore, the products of Soviet industrialisation compared badly with those from the capitalist world, and the Soviets were never a pole of cultural attraction. By 1976 there

189

*Souphanouvong greets Vietnamese Communist Party leader, Le Duan.*
*Khaysone Phomvihan is on the left. (Courtesy K.P.L.)*

were already around 1500 Soviet experts at work at all levels in Laos—
economic advisers, professors, doctors and mechanics. With Eastern
Europeans and a number of Cubans, the adviser population would later
swell to 4000. They took over some of the compounds evacuated by
American personnel, and where there had once been a 'Little America'
was now a 'Little Moscow'. While many Americans had either volunteered or chosen to go to Laos, the Soviets and Eastern Europeans were
largely assigned there, and fulfilled their aid role begrudgingly, with
little sympathy for or knowledge of the local culture. There were excep-
tions, of course. The newcomers came from societies now jaded and
cynical about the claims of socialism, and Laos was more of a backwater
to them than it had ever been for the French or the Americans. There

was one compensation, however—they had access to cheap foreign commodities from Thailand that were unavailable back home.

Many young Lao, a large proportion of them children of party members, were packed off to the lands of 'advanced socialism' for higher education, and many others went to Vietnam. It was hoped that the thousands sent away for training could replace the few technically competent bureaucrats left from the old regime with new bureaucrats loyal to the LPDR. The outcome, however, was mixed, and they often returned with skills unsuited to Laos, and fluent in a babel of languages. For some it remained an eye-opening experience, full of pleasant interactions with Russians or Bulgarians. This appreciation was expressed by one returnee who called his child 'Leninakone'. For others the experience was disillusioning.

Although the Chinese had for a long time provided the PL with support and had thousands of workers in the north building a road south from Oudomxai to Luang Phrabang, they had been frozen out of establishing closer relations with the Lao by the Vietnamese. The Chinese welcomed the Lao revolution and continued to supply aid, but the conflict over Cambodia brought aid to a halt in 1978 when, in line with the Vietnamese, Kaysone denounced Beijing as 'international reactionaries'. Very few Lao had ever studied in China and only a few of them defected to China as a result of the conflict. Those that remained were for a time under a cloud of suspicion. Relations with China would only begin to change radically for the better after the settlement of the dispute over Cambodia, and the collapse of communism elsewhere thrust the remaining communist states of Asia into each other's arms.

# Collectivisation

In the worsening security context of the late 1970s the Lao communists attempted one other radical reform—agricultural collectivisation. They did this for two main reasons, one being a search for internally generated economic surpluses with which to finance the state and development. The subsistence peasants in Laos had not been taxed by the RLG and agricultural productivity was low. Communist orthodoxy claimed that the productivity of agriculture could only be raised through economies of scale (by analogy with an industrial model), and this could only be achieved by collective ownership of the means of production. Cooperatives, they argued, could maximise the use of modern inputs into agriculture. The second main reason was political. Although the LPRP had immediately set about recruiting members and sympathisers at the village and district levels in the former RLG zone, and established them in positions of leadership there, the degree of control was still deemed insufficient. By drawing

*Threshing rice at a cooperative farm in Xiang Khoang Province in the early 1980s.*
*(Photo Grant Evans)*

peasants into cooperatives they would lose their 'individualistic' ('capitalistic') economic base of resistance to the new regime and the cooperatives could slowly come to be not only an economic form of organisation in the rural areas, but also a key political structure. Just as importantly, through these political-economic structures surpluses could be transferred without resistance from the peasants to the state.

Besides the party and state officials, the various front organisations that were part of the NLHX, and later NLSX, were reproduced at all levels. Thus villages had more-or-less active branches of the Lao Women's Union, the Lao Peoples' Revolutionary Youth, the Lao United Buddhists' Union, and perhaps others, depending on the locality. These sent representatives to the district level, which sent representatives to the province level, which in turn sent representatives to the national level. These representatives, along with officialdom, kept an eye on the population and ensured that there were no open expressions of hostility towards the policies of the regime.

From the very beginning the LPRP had encouraged collective forms of economic organisation in the countryside, but it was only in the deteriorating economic and political situation of 1978 that it decided to launch a collectivisation campaign mid-year. No sooner was the campaign launched than the southern parts of the country experienced serious floods. This did not stop the campaign, although reports of resistance began to flow in as the number of newly formed cooperatives slowly mounted. Problems encountered in their formation were ascribed to inept cadres and the General Secretary of the Party, Kaysone, called for intensified training. In November a troubleshooting committee was set up under the direction of the head of State Planning, Sali Vongkhamsao, to try to straighten out the situation. In February 1979 Kaysone continued to maintain that the cooperatives were the only way peasant agriculture could overcome natural calamities and achieve food self-sufficiency. In April the first National Congress of Agricultural Cooperatives was held and new targets were proclaimed.

Yet two and a half months later, when the number of co-operatives in the country was said to stand at 2500, the Central Committee of the LPRP stopped the campaign. A statement on 14 July said: 'Efforts to mobilize farmers to join agricultural coopera- tives or set up new ones during the current production season should be immediately and strictly suspended while the people are engaging in production in order rapidly and effectively to increase production.' The overriding reason for the suspension was that it had become obvious to the party that collectivisation was seriously disrupting production. It realised that the country could not afford another year of disastrous results this time brought on by man-made factors. Cadres, according to the statement, had simply concentrated on the numerical growth of cooperatives without ensuring an increase in production. Cooperatives had been rushed together without ade- quate preparation; peasants had been forced to join and means of production such as cows and buffaloes had been expropriated or peas- ants offered minimal compensation for them. This created serious tensions in the countryside that not only threatened the economic basis of the campaign, but also its intended security benefits. The Central Committee statement went on to say that 'enemies' had taken advantage of the campaign's weaknesses

> . . . to infiltrate into cooperatives to create confusion among the people and sabotage the party and state line, thus disturbing the peaceful situation in the country. Because of this, the people, including the peasants, have become discouraged and unhappy, thus seriously affecting and delaying production. Some people have abandoned their farms, turned to other occupations, sold or secretly slaughtered their animals or fled to other countries. This has now become an urgent problem which will create an immediate and long-term danger if it is not quickly, effec- tively and skilfully resolved. It will become not only an

economic danger affecting production and the people's living conditions, but also a political danger.[50]

The Central Committee emphasised the voluntary nature of the programme and insisted that 'those who have already joined cooperatives should be allowed to leave when they wish'. In short, the aims of the campaign were threatening to backfire on the communist government. The danger had become most apparent in the fact that it was no longer the members of the old elite, or people from the urban areas, streaming across the Mekong into refugee camps in Thailand, but the supposed backbone of the LPRP, the peasants.

It was this that forced the government to retreat from its pursuit of an orthodox communist programme, and in December 1979 Kaysone announced the first steps towards a form of market socialism. Restrictions on some forms of small private enterprise were lifted, and there was a shift towards a greater use of market prices in the trading of goods. The aim of establishing agricultural cooperatives was not given up, only the pace of change adjusted, for the LPRP remained convinced that cooperatives would ensure the establishment of socialism in Laos. They began to realise, however, the importance of modern inputs into agriculture, of relatively efficient marketing mechanisms for both the procurement and sale of agricultural produce, and the provision of commodities and other supplies to the peasantry. To this end, a greater emphasis began to be placed on the formation of trading cooperatives that would be linked on favourable terms with the state trading services. Later, for a short time, trading cooperatives would be seen as the first step towards the formation of producers' cooperatives. In fact this never came to pass. As the LPRP in the mid-1980s moved towards an even more market-inclined economy, so the imperative to form cooperatives declined. As Kaysone told me during an interview in late 1988: 'Our previous cooperative policy was in the old style practiced by other socialist countries. After some investigations into the actual situation in Laos, we decided to change direction and start from the family.' In fact, from then on agriculture started from and stopped with the peasant family. By 1990 the cooperatives had all but disappeared from the rural landscape of the LPDR.

# Stabilisation

While relations with China deteriorated sharply in 1979 following Vietnam's invasion of Cambodia, relations with Thailand improved temporarily under the government of General Kriangsak in Bangkok. Laos was able to withdraw its support from the pro-China Communist Party of Thailand, hoping that in return the Thai would reciprocate by not encouraging or supporting the Lao resistance based in Thailand. In early 1979 the two governments signed a communiqué 'ushering in a new era in Lao–Thai relations of friendship', and some Thai restrictions on trade with Laos were eased. Yet Thai–Lao relations would fluctuate, sometimes wildly, throughout the 1980s. Always victim to Laos's strong alignment with Vietnam over Cambodia, they would only stabilise in the 1990s following Vietnam's withdrawal of its forces from both Cambodia and Laos.

By 1980 the resistance forces inside Laos had been largely crushed, and while incursions from Thailand could create havoc on a local scale, they presented no serious threat to the Lao armed forces and their Vietnamese allies. The stage was thus set for a degree of social relaxation alongside the economic changes in direction signalled by Kaysone the previous December. With the revival of some small-scale commerce, everyday consumer items began to reappear in the markets, and the increased availability of money saw some of it flow in the direction of the temples and family celebrations. Some colour flowed back into civil society.

Over the first half of the 1980s three important international shifts had begun to weigh heavily in the calculations of the LPRP leadership. The first had been the intra-Communist crisis caused by the outbreak of war between the 'Red Brotherhood' of Vietnam and China and Democratic Kampuchea. Dreams of a communist international were hard to sustain in the face of this kind of antagonism. The second was the recognition of a growing crisis in the heartlands of European communism, reflected in the declining aid from Comecon sources over the 1980s, and their total collapse by 1989. The third was the startling economic boom in neighbouring Thailand and Southeast Asia, a boom presided over by more or less authoritarian governments. It was at this time we began to hear talk of how 'Asian values' were inimical to liberal democracy. Hard work and strong leadership were all that was needed for economic success. The leaders of Laos, Vietnam and China saw that the key to their legitimacy and long-term viability lay in economic growth. It was this that led Kaysone in the late 1980s to talk increasingly of 'state capitalism' as the road to socialism, for it was hoped that these economic forces could be hitched to the party's original aims.

At the crucial 1986 Party Congress, resolutions were passed which would begin the dismantling of recognisably socialist economic structures. While there was trepidation about this among some of the politically more hidebound members of the party, those whose attention was on the long-term maintenance of state power by the new elite through the elaboration of realistic policies won out. The reasons why are fairly straightforward. Unlike socialist regimes elsewhere, the state industrial sector of the economy was minuscule, even compared to Vietnam, and there were few deeply entrenched, powerful interests able to obstruct the 'new economic mechanism' announced at the Congress. The old ideas had manifestly not worked, and new ones were required if the regime was to survive. In his Political Report to the Congress Kaysone criticised the old line: 'Our main shortcomings lie in subjectivism and haste, in our inclination to abolish the non-socialist economic sectors promptly . . . We are bent on egalitarianism. Consequently we did not encourage good workers with high labour productivity. There was no relationship between responsibility, rights, obligations, and interests.'[51] In elaborating the new economic mechanism Kaysone talked of the need for 'socialist economic accounting', a rhetorical device used to placate the party faithful while proclaiming a severing of the state enterprises from the state budget and placing them on an autonomous footing—in other words, the dismantling of central planning and a shift to market accountability for these enterprises.

## Reorientation towards the world market

The most radical shifts in economic direction occurred in 1988 as the consequences of Gorbachev's policies in the USSR became apparent. At February and April sessions of the Supreme People's Assembly, Kaysone announced fundamental reorientations of the economy with respect to the world market. A foreign investment code was adopted in April, aimed at bringing foreign capital and expertise into the ailing Lao economy. Joint ventures were encouraged in all sectors, including tourism. In order to facilitate this, moves were made towards a unified exchange rate for the kip instead of the multiple exchange rates that had prevailed over the previous ten years. People have commented on the swiftness of the Lao economic reforms in the mid-1980s compared with other communist countries. Alongside the dismantling of internal constraints noted above, the other crucial factor was the leadership's acute understanding of the Lao state's dependence on outside sources of funding for its viability. In 1986 official exports were US$55 million or 8.6 per cent of GDP, whereas imports amounted to US$186 million or 29 per cent of GDP. A large amount of unofficial trade along the Thai–Lao border was not recorded, and thus the true payments position of the country was understated. Laos's trade deficit of US$130.7 million was 20.5 per cent of GDP. Consequently, capital inflow in the form of economic aid was vital to plug the current account deficit, which in 1986 was US$90 million or 14.1 per cent of GDP. Growing instability in the communist bloc, which now supplied some 70 per cent of foreign assistance, set off alarm bells in the Lao leadership. It acted swiftly before the dramatic collapse of

Comecon-supplied aid to the tune of US$1 milllion in 1989, down from US$52 million in 1988, to zero in 1990. The coincidence of a drought and a shift in terms of trade for electricity (a major export item) in 1988, also threatened the fragile Lao economy. The new policies promised to offset these problems by an inflow of private capital, growing customs receipts, and attracting greater inflows of aid from the west.

Clearly a more outward-oriented strategy had been in the wind for several years. No doubt with an eye to encouraging international investor confidence in the 'rule of law', thousands of detainees from the old regime were released in December 1986. There was recognition that the LPDR no longer faced a serious threat from the resistance, and that there was growing social stability. This message was reinforced by the withdrawal of the remaining 45 000 Vietnamese combat troops from Laos over 1988–89. Part of the intention behind the new foreign investment laws was to encourage overseas Lao refugees to invest in the Lao economy, and for this they needed political reassurance. The economic reforms and the release of political prisoners led quickly to a more politically relaxed atmosphere, and people were encouraged by the announcement of the first national elections since before 1975, to be held at the end of 1988 and in early 1989. The elections were strictly controlled by the LPRP—of the 79 deputies elected, 65 were party members while the other fourteen were vetted by the party. Nevertheless, the populace began to feel some sense of participation in the political process, and some were hopeful that it would be a step towards greater democratisation. The winds of change blowing through other communist societies were beginning to be felt in Laos, and there was revived talk of a constitution, which the LPRP had ruled without since 1975. By 1989 people from different walks of life were openly talking about the need for a constitution. They spoke of it as a minimal prerequisite for the provision of a basic legal framework to define the citizenry's fundamental rights and obligations and to safeguard them against arbitrary governmental or party action. The new openness of the government was also shown by the fact that in 1988 scholars from outside the communist bloc were given much greater access to Laos through the Committee for Social Sciences, first set up in 1985.

## Only one party

While the demise of communism in Europe and the USSR was one factor propelling Laos into taking a more open stance towards the world, the turmoil associated with it also drove the LPRP to re-affirm its ties with the remaining communist countries in the Asian region, China in particular. Like Deng Xiaoping, Kaysone saw reform occurring under the aegis of the party, and as if to underscore this he became the first foreign leader to visit Beijing after the Tienanmen Massacre of June 1989. Dissent, he signalled, would not be tolerated. Continuing debate over a constitution led in early 1990 to a group of some 40 Lao intellectuals, the 'Social Democrat Club', beginning to meet and criticise the country's one-party system. Similar criticisms were voiced by students studying abroad. Party member and Vice-Minister for Science and Technology, Thongsouk Saisangkhi, submitted an open letter of resignation to Kaysone in which he labelled the LPDR a 'communist monarchy' and a 'dynasty of the Politburo' (a reference to the growing influence of the children of the leaders). He declared that 'Laos should change to a multi-party system in order to bring democracy, freedom and prosperity to the people'. This followed publication of the draft constitution on 4 June in the party paper *Pasason*, in which the opening article declared that the LPDR was 'a people's democratic state under the leadership of the Lao People's Revolutionary Party'. Three leading figures in this group of critics—Thongsouk, Latsami Khamphoui, Vice-Minister of Economics and Planning, and Pheng Sakchittaphong from the Justice Ministry— were imprisoned in October 1990 and finally tried in November 1992 on charges of libel and of disseminating propaganda 'against the country'.

They were each sentenced to fourteen years' imprisonment, and confined to a camp in Houaphan Province. Thongsouk died in prison in early 1998 due to poor medical facilities at the camp, while the other two continue to languish in harsh conditions, but remain unrepentant.

A final draft of the constitution was adopted by the Supreme People's Assembly (SPA) in August 1991, by which time it had undergone some important modifications, suggesting that the actions of the dissidents may not have been entirely in vain. The controversial first article of earlier drafts had been dropped. However, the role of the Party was reintroduced in article 3, where it is described as the 'leading nucleus' of the political system, and the LPDR is defined as a 'People's Democratic State' (article 2), all of whose organisations 'function in accordance with the principle of democratic centralism'. Socialism is not mentioned at all. It was, however, the guiding principle in the resolutions passed at the Party's Fifth Congress in March 1991, and has remained so in subsequent resolutions. Perhaps the most important development to emerge from this general process of change was the establishment of a judiciary and the evolution of a body of law, at least relating to the economy, one of the main reasons for the original legal reforms. The National Assembly Standing Committee (dominated by the LPRP) remains the final interpreter of the law, rather than the courts, and has the power to remove judges. Such a provision ensures that the Party gets its way in politically contentious trials, and makes a mockery of the constitution's claim to respect individual political and religious rights and freedoms. In economic disputes the law is increasingly seen to act impartially and this in itself provides some cultural reinforcement of at least the principle of the rule of law.

Khamthai Siphandone, who took control of the LPRP after Kaysone's death in 1992, left his audience in no doubt about the continuing supremacy of the Party. Speaking in 1995 he said, 'The Party is also the sole Party whom the people trust. All slanders and attempts designed to undermine the leadership role of the Party are regarded as contradictory to historical reality and the national interest.'

# Culture and society

The flight of the small middle and merchant class from Laos, and the political decapitation of the old elite after 1975, simplified Lao social structure. The state monopolised the non-rural sphere, and social status was directly tied to the state and its bureaucracy. The 80 to 90 per cent of the population who were peasants remained peasants, despite the cooperatives. The main effect of the revolution was to disengage them even further from market transactions and, ironically, to reinforce the natural subsistence economy. Restrictions on movement also heightened their isolation from the rapid changes taking place in the region, ensuring that many customary cultural practices would be preserved despite the regime's political commitment to change.

The impact of the revolution on Buddhism was probably the most widely felt modification of traditional practices. In line with communism's secularism, Buddhism was no longer the official religion of the state, and the Sangha became simply one organisation among others in the National Front. Attempts were made to reinterpret Buddhist doctrine in ways that were compatible with the claims of socialism, and to suppress beliefs and practices associated with 'feudal superstition'. At the local level there was a great deal of confusion about how to interpret 'superstition', as many of the officials in charge of policing the instructions were implicated in the self-same deeply rooted cultural practices. Their suppression was therefore uneven. One popular solution was to interpret beliefs and practices as 'national custom', which protected them from restrictions. Practices that clearly fell outside the boundaries of Buddhism, however, such as those associated with spirit mediums, were more easily suppressed. Annual festivals such as the Boun Bang Fai, where an overlap between the worship of territorial spirits and Buddhism occurred, were problematic and attracted inconsistent restrictions.

Theravada Buddhism rests on the reciprocal relationship between the Sangha and the laity, with the latter supporting the

Sangha through offerings and the monks transforming this support into merit for laymen. In the early years of the revolution both economic collapse and political restrictions served to weaken this relationship. The economic collapse meant that there was less wealth available to support the monks and to rebuild and refurbish temples. The channelling of economic resources towards the temples for the purposes of merit-making was interpreted as economically wasteful by the new regime, which wished to capture all economic surpluses for the purpose of building socialism. 'Extravagant' offerings and festivals were frowned upon. An important source of merit for parents and for a young man is for the latter to enter the temple as a novice, even briefly. After the revolution, however, permission had to be sought from local officials for a young man to enter the 'unproductive' temples, and the practice was often obstructed. Such restrictions caused considerable popular resentment among lowland Lao, and consequently some refugees reported that Buddhism was being suppressed. Restrictions on Buddhist practice, and the new ideological interpretation of Buddhism, began to relax along with more general tendencies towards relaxation in the 1980s. Certainly in the countryside, no new socialist structure was able to ensure cohesion, or indeed answer the perennial need for humans to celebrate and regulate life and death, as Buddhism could. Thus by the 1990s attempts to change the society's relationship with Buddhism had all but disappeared.

## Revival of tradition

In fact, by the beginning of the 1990s the LPDR had begun to elevate Buddhism to somewhere near its former status under the RLG. The reason was that the collapse of communism in its original heartlands, and the general failure of socialism economically, demanded an ideological reconfiguration so that the regime could continue to claim political legitimacy. Party leaders therefore participated more visibly in the main Buddhist rituals and, like the *phu nyai* of old, began to sponsor the casting of Buddha images and the sustenance of temples.

*A procession to the temple. Buddhism, despite early restrictions, has remained central to lowland Lao culture. (Courtesy EFEO)*

There was no *saksit* King acting at the centre of these Buddhist rituals, although their very structure often subliminally signalled his absence. The revival of tradition risked calling into question the reasons for the revolution in the first place, for in a sense it was a cultural revival of the old regime. One of the most visible signs of this reversion came in 1991 when, along with declaration of the new constitution, the That Luang, or Grand Stupa, in Vientiane replaced the hammer and sickle as the centrepiece of the national symbol, which adorns each ministry and all official documents, including money and stamps. From the beginning the state expended energy on promoting its own National Day on 2 December, but this occasion rarely attracted any spontaneous enthusiasm, compared with the That Luang Festival which occurs some weeks beforehand. The festival has long acted as a kind of national celebration of cultural communion, and so the Grand Stupa's adoption as the official national symbol was an attempt to yoke a potent symbol to state-sponsored nationalism.

Such cultural revivals occurred across the spectrum. After the revolution deferential forms of speech were denounced as 'feudal' and the use of *sahai*, 'comrade', became ubiquitous. Beginning in the late 1980s the honorific *than*, 'sir', began to make a comeback, and by the 1990s *sahai* had retreated from the public sphere to the inner circles of Party meetings, replaced by almost the full range of traditional hierarchical forms of speech. For instance, the more neutral *pathan*, 'president', which the regime had promoted for key official positions, was overtaken by the traditional form of address, *chao*, with its connotations of 'lord'. Deferential bodily practices, such as the *nop*, clasping the palms of one's hands together in a prayerful motion in greeting, had been discouraged in favour of the egalitarian handshake—which involved problematic cross-sex body contact. This too has been abandoned, and children are now instructed to *nop* teachers and adults. These reversions in both formal and everyday ritual illustrate the failure of the new regime to construct culturally convincing new forms. Over the 1990s, as the whole society gravitated back to the old forms, the government's cultural apparatus indulged in almost xenophobic claims of having defended and protected 'traditional and beautiful Lao culture'. The xenophobia arose from the fact that the revolution had weakened Lao culture's ability to respond to the rapid changes that were taking place in the outside world to which the regime was now opening its doors, a weakening that was partly a result of the enfeebling of its cultural intelligentsia.

The flight of the middle class after the revolution, along with the suppression of the freedom of expression, crippled the fledgling intelligentsia that had emerged in the late 1960s. Independent exploration of social and cultural problems was overtaken by party orthodoxy. Literature was produced in the wooden style typical of socialist realism, where war heroes and heroines fell in pure patriotic love on the battlefield. On the radio, love tunes were replaced by patriotic songs or songs which extolled socialist construction. Thai radio was listened to only secretly. Few people had a television set, and access to newspapers and magazines from the west was prohibited. Contact with foreigners was strictly policed, and those who worked for them as maids or secretaries were closely monitored. The western expatriate community was tiny, its social centre the Australian Club situated on the Mekong River, for there were few other places to go now that restaurants and hotels were state owned. Only in the mid-1980s did this situation begin to change, signalled by the opening of the Nam Phu restaurant in central Vientiane. The few sexual liaisons that occurred were kept secret, and visits to Lao homes were difficult because the local security forces would always quiz the hosts about any foreign visitors. Staying with Lao was virtually impossible for outsiders.

## The new 'old' society

One outcome of the country's opening to the capitalist world was the rapid growth in the 1990s of the expatriate community in Vientiane. Previously largely confined to the capital, expatriates also moved to provincial centres. The augmentation of this community was associated with increased formal aid commitments, a rapid growth in overseas non-government aid organisations, an influx of small business, and a growing number of tourists. These factors all contributed to the transformation of social life, particularly in Vientiane, as commercial venues such as bars and discos proliferated throughout the capital, and then the provinces. An almost hedonistic mood settled on Vientiane in the early 1990s as more cash began to wash around the urban economy; with it appeared a craving for outside fashions in music and clothing and a disdain for socialist austerity. A sense of civil society began to re-emerge. The appearance in 1994 of the first English-language weekly paper since 1975, the *Vientiane Times*, to cater to the influx of foreigners at first suggested a possible forum for new ideas. Any tendencies in this direction, however, were quickly curbed.

The influx of foreigners was a bonanza for property owners in Vientiane, some of them members of the old elite who had sat tight for fifteen years, joined now by the new elite who had confiscated properties of the old elite and made them their own. A form of rentier capitalism flourished. The newly rich went on a building spree of gaudy mansions, drove around in brand-new cars, and draped themselves in gold and jewels. A form of decadence had arrived, but this newly affluent elite became alarmed when their sons and daughters began to race through the streets of Vientiane in motorcycle packs and bop to the sounds of Thai pop in the capital's discos, some high on drugs. A moral panic set in among them and among party stalwarts who attributed their wildness to foreign influence. Thus there have been occasional crackdowns and attempts to enforce moral codes associated with dress and music. Thus, even as the regime liberalised, many of the structures of the totalitarian state remained intact; in crackdowns on 'spiritually polluting' material, cadres continued to respond to latent political reflexes. The regulations still reflect a desire to control large swathes of social life. For example, in 1994 the mayor of Vientiane issued a set of instructions to enforce 'Lao culture', which state, under etiquette and dress for persons in places of entertainment: 'Men should wear international suits, or national, ethnic or some other appropriate outfit. Women should wear Lao traditional skirts [sinh] and wear their hair in a bun or in some other proper and appropriate manner.' Similar instructions are issued for traditional festivals and other ceremonies. For example, 'foreign songs are prohibited at marriage ceremonies except for marriage ceremonies of foreign persons'. As for discos and bars: 'International songs may be sung or danced to, however, they must be specifically selected and inspected by, and registered with, the Department of Culture and Information of the Vientiane Municipality.' And so on. Thus in Laos we find an ongoing 'civil' war between ordinary Lao who seek to break through these state-drawn boundaries and the authorities with their sudden arbitrary crackdowns. The degree to which state rules are or are not enforced is a source of graft for street-level police and highly placed officials. Prostitution has once again become visible. The lurid bars that catered to foreigners had already been under attack under the RLG, and these have not come back, but pick-up joints catering to foreigners abound, as do cheap brothels for Lao men. Here the revolution can claim only one achievement, and that is to have 'nationalised' prostitution, for the women who work in these places are exclusively Lao. To make money young Lao girls try to get jobs in bars in Thailand, and the cross-border flesh trade is thriving.

## The Kaysone cult

In an attempt to compensate for both the global collapse of communism and the weakness of the new state's rituals the LPRP party has, since the death of Kaysone Phomvihan in November 1992, tried to promote a personality cult around him not unlike that of Ho Chi Minh in Vietnam. The ceremony surrounding Kaysone's funeral was a dramatic demonstration of the reintegration of Buddhist rituals into those of the state. Chanting Buddhist monks were prominent, and the new President, Nouhak Phoumsavan, while urging those at the memorial service to 'remember the comrade's teachings', ended with an extraordinary exhortation for a long-time Marxist-Leninist: 'Comrade President Kaysone Phomvihan's cause remains with us forever. Comrade, we wish your soul may reach paradise and the state of bliss.' Since then the cult of Kaysone has been promoted through the establishment of memorial museums, the erection of memorial busts and statues, and by endless articles and speeches. The hundreds of busts and statues of Kaysone that have been installed throughout the country at great expense since 1995 have been made by North Korea, a country expert in personality cults. The larger statues and busts in the main centres, the smaller ones across the nation, are a clear attempt to symbolise the unity of national space. The largest statue of Kaysone stands outside the Kaysone Memorial Museum, built at a cost of US$8 million and opened on the anniversary of his birthday, 13 December 2000. It is a huge white and gold building that blends communist style with Buddhist decorative motifs, containing the rather uninspiring bric-a-brac of Kaysone's life. The cult has never really taken off, despite the Party's efforts, in part because the cultural wellsprings of ancestor cults of East Asia that work for a Mao or a Ho do not work in Laos. Cults may exist around figures considered to be *saksit*, such as Prince Phetsarath, but they arise from the historically close relationship between royalty and Buddhism; any full-blown secular, political cult of personality drifts dangerously into the space formerly occupied by the overthrown monarch and is spontaneously aborted. Enthusiasm is muted. Some complain, 'Did Kaysone make the revolution on his own? There is not a single statue of Prince Souphanouvong in the whole of Laos.' Many did not welcome the new museum. 'I think it's crazy,' a young Vientiane resident said. 'This leadership thinks it has money to waste like that on another statue, when our country so desperately needs schools, hospitals and roads.' As in other communist countries, a cynical humour has grown up around the claims of the regime and the 'great leader', exemplified by the following joke I was told:

One day *Than* Kaysone had the opportunity to visit a zip factory to discuss production in the factory with the manager and the workers. Following the report he opened the meeting for opinions and questions from the floor. Immediately *Thao* [Mr] Kidaeng who was sitting right at the front wished to speak. On the platform in front of him were the leaders, including the factory manager who called on the workers:
*Manager:* Valued comrades, all of you who are patriotic and wish that the country will advance and become rich,

you should have opinions to express. Oh! Kidaeng, sitting just in front of us, what would you like to say?

*Kidaeng:* Oh . . . Ah . . . It seems that the z–z–z–z– has fallen down, sir!

*Manager:* What's that? Could you speak up and throw your voice so that others can hear. We on the stage can hardly hear too.

*Kidaeng:* Er . . . The z–z–z–z– it's fallen down, sir!

*Manager* (angrily): Kidaeng! This is an order! Speak up so that everyone can hear!

*Kidaeng:* YRZR 370822 of *Than* Kaysone has fallen down, sir!

This gentle spoof is cousin to a line of jokes found the world over concerning the pretensions of those in power and their hangers-on ('The emperor with no clothes'), and through Kidaeng's resort to the production number of the zip it alludes not only to the ubiquitous bureaucratic nomenclature, but also to the elliptical language of the system itself. It suggests that the LPRP has some way to go before it convinces the populace of the gravitas of Kaysone.

## Education

As for education, there is no question that the LPDR inherited a weak system from the RLG—but initially they further enfeebled it. Although the French had introduced modern education to Laos, it remained tied to an Indochina-wide system for higher education rather than being developed within the country. The RLG was the first to bear the brunt of French failure to prepare the country to run an independent state. Under the RLG education steadily improved, with annual enrolment growth rates over a 20-year period of 10 per cent. By the 1970s literacy rates among young men had climbed to around 75 per cent, for women around 30 per cent. Rates were lower in rural areas, particularly among remote minorities. Traditional forms of literacy were important among some groups—Vang Pao, for example, had insisted that his troops be literate, and rates among Hmong were relatively high. (The role of armies in promoting literacy is often overlooked by educationalists.) At the secondary level French aid, and therefore French language, had remained pervasive into the late 1960s, and the textbooks and the language of higher education were French. By the 1970s, Lao language was beginning to gain ground, as American aid boosted education, and financed the opening of the Fa Ngum Lao-language secondary schools. Students travelling overseas to university began to go to America and Australia as much as to France, and the English language gained influence. The various colleges established by the RLG were amalgamated into the Sisavangvong University in the early 1970s. In the PL zone, by contrast, higher education was mostly in Vietnamese, and very often in Vietnam itself.

Education is a vital part of the modern state's legitimacy because not only does schooling introduce pupils to 'the nation', it prepares them for the active citizenship which is presumed to be the foundation of democracy. In other words, schooling plays a strong political role, regardless of its purely educational function. From the beginning the LPDR made extravagant claims for its success in education, and strong efforts were made to draw pupils into the system. By the early 1980s it claimed to have eliminated illiteracy. Given the enormous exodus of teachers after 1975, the claims for expansion in schools and literacy were really propaganda, responding to demands for expansion from above. Even the most sympathetic writers on Lao education acknowledge that the quality of the new system was low and that its primary function was political. By the early 1990s the weakness of the system had to be acknowledged, with the rate of illiteracy of people aged between fifteen and 40 standing at 40 per cent. In other words, little had changed. Higher education remained as dependent on foreign input as ever, except that instructors now spoke Russian, which had to be simultaneously translated. University students pursued their studies in Moscow, Prague or Hanoi. The Sisavangvong University was dismantled after 1975. A National University reestablished only in 1996, but the educational level is low by international standards, and the curriculum politically controlled. The LPDR has turned to western aid to support its system of higher education. A growing number of students in the 1990s headed off to the USA, Australia and Thailand to study, but the impact of this reorientation in higher education has yet to be felt.

# Minorities

Many of the claims about the differences between the RLG and the LPDR with respect to minorities were exaggerated. This became apparent after the revolution, when the top leadership of the LPDR remained as lowland Lao-dominated as it had ever been—and remains so. Indeed, as the new regime has entrenched itself in the lowland towns and cities it has become less dependent on minority support, and less responsive to minority demands. The LPDR's pervasive propaganda claims to represent Lao minorities has ironically produced its own problems, because it has made the minorities more aware of their ethnic differences while simultaneously raising their expectations about social advancement. Under the RLG the various ritual forms centred on royalty partially accommodated ethnic differences as hierarchical ones, thereby muting potential conflict, whereas the modern secular state simply trumpets ethnic equality—but it is clear to everyone, especially to the minorities themselves, that they are not equal citizens. The truth is that the relaxation of political correctness in everyday life has seen the re-emergence of an older, derogatory nomenclature and a proliferation of ethnic jokes at minority expense, especially of the Hmong. Since the days of the RLG 'ethnicity' has become a much more potent idea throughout the world, and is a guiding idea in the policies of aid agencies. LPDR rhetoric is in line with this 'politics of ethnicity', but reality is another thing.

Rising expectations have been one source of disgruntlement with the new regime, especially among the few minority individuals who have managed to get into secondary or tertiary education. While most minorities live in the remote mountainous areas of Laos and government is largely marginal to their lives, it does impinge on them when cadres appear in the villages to demand that they relocate to the lowlands. In many instances in the immediate aftermath of the revolution this was done at the point of a gun. These days, under the watchful eyes of foreign aid donors, more subtle persuasion is used. Relocation aims not only at increasing the state's political control of its population, but also at delivering better social services. It is also concerned with the ecological impact of upland farming. The policy of relocation was first recommended to the RLG by Prince Somsanith in the early 1960s, and Ouan Rathikhoun saw it as a solution to the problem of opium growing. The issues involved, everyone agrees, are complex. Under the LPDR, however, they have been simplified by the imperatives of politics and thus Party commands for relocation have too often been executed without proper preparation so that the minorities have ended up more impoverished than before. This has been a potent source of resentment.

The more relaxed policy on movement in the 1990s has also fed discontent, particularly among the Hmong. Allowed to visit relatives in America, and have those relatives visit Laos, debates among the Hmong over their past and future, which are vigorous overseas, have made their way back into communities in Laos, setting up a discourse parallel to the one promoted by the NLSX. Hmong desires for autonomy have been hardened by exposure in America to the politics of ethnicity, but it is unclear what impact these ideas have when they reach Laos. Less visible but equally important minorities such as the Khamu are also quietly voicing their discontent. They were an important part of the PL army and some of their members rose through the ranks, but few hold high positions outside the army. One influential Khamu spoke to me in 2000 of his unhappiness: 'During the revolution it was all about how the Party supported the people, now it is the people must support the Party. Look around Vientiane, the Lao people are rich, but go to the countryside, the Khamu there are poor. They can't get into the university, unless of course their father is a colonel who can get them through the back door. It is not right.' It is unlikely that such rumblings will go away in the near future.

## New economic contradictions

The shift to the new economic mechanism made state enterprises more accountable to the market, while the provinces became increasingly responsible for raising revenue for the various services they provided, such as health and schooling. Central government investment in health and education has always been low, never exceeding 4–5 per cent of budget expenditures, but the new orientation ensured that resource-poor areas were even worse off than before. (The World Bank estimated that in 1993 per capita income ranged from 88 000 kip, or roughly US$100, in Houaphan Province to 230 000 kip in the Vientiane municipality, or around US$255). Growth in expenditure in these areas is dependent on outside assistance, and the continued lack of central government expenditure appears to have been a calculated strategy, given the propensity of overseas donors to channel aid in these directions. By 2000, however, the government made a commitment to raising educational outlays.

The new policies have exaggerated regional income differences, and differences between the main cities and the countryside. Vientiane acquires a great deal of foreign income from the renting of premises to foreign organisations and companies, and from the facilities that service them. Some people have speculated that this growing difference could lead to political unrest in the provinces. The devolution of responsibility for raising revenue to the provinces encouraged local level corruption involving deals with foreign companies (sometimes these were annulled or overridden by Vientiane), as well as forms of 'insider trading' where, for example, knowledge about a future development would lead to the purchase of land from local farmers at low prices in order to sell it to developers at higher prices later. Whether this has caused the emergence of local mafia-style strongmen, equivalent to the provincial *chao pho* in Thailand, is unclear.

The short-term aims of the government, set out in broad brush-strokes by Prime Minister Khamthai at the Party Congress in March 1996, were to achieve a growth rate of over 8 per cent between 1996 and 2000, and to increase per capita income to US$500 by the millennium. How was this to be accomplished? Revenue continued to flow in from familiar sources, with timber exports making up around 50 per

*The old national laurel with the hammer and sickle lies discarded in a Vientiane street.*
*(Photo Grant Evans)*

cent, followed by sales of hydropower and garment exports from foreign firms (established in Laos since the early 1990s to take advantage of import quotas in their own countries). The government was essentially looking to the expansion of hydro-electricity potential, and in particular of the coming onstream of income from the Nam-Theun Hinboun Dam in 1998 and other dam projects, to expand its export revenue. The actual long-term economic impact of such projects is questionable, as they have few backward linkages into the Lao economy and are dependent on foreign financing and hence subject to the repatriation of profits. It also appears that the actual profitability of at least some of the dams has been greatly over-estimated. Furthermore, unrestrained dam development has been challenged by the growing number of foreign NGOs in Laos, which object to the forceful resettlement of highland ethnic groups from the watersheds, have demanded environmental investigations, and object to military logging companies moving into the watersheds in anticipation of dam building. In an unprecedented move, the government has had to respond to these challenges in print and through consultations and conferences. Given that indigenous Lao NGOs are not permitted by the government, these foreign NGOs have become a kind of proxy Lao civil society. Pressure from NGOs outside Laos against the dams has also been significant.

Government hopes for revenue from these dams reflect the narrow interests of the state in regard to development. The strong urban bias of much other development is most apparent when attention is turned to the main drag on the Lao economy, the relative stagnation of rural production. Since the collapse of the cooperatives programme, and the sudden availability of outside sources of wealth, the rural economy, in which most Lao citizens live and work, has been neglected and starved of investment. A large-scale investment programme of state-financed irrigation projects, begun in 1998, may ultimately help some diversification of agriculture, but in the short term has contributed to serious inflation. It is also unlikely to achieve the government's stated aim of rice self-sufficiency, and regional terms of trade in rice do not favour rice grown in Laos.

It is perhaps ironic that it was the largely subsistence-level rural sector that was least affected by the economic crash which began in Thailand in mid-1997 and spread across Asia. As Thailand was both Laos's main source of imports and exports, and its main foreign investor, the effects of the crash on the Lao economy were immediate. By the end of 1997 the currency had fallen from 900 kip to the US dollar to 2700 kip per dollar. As the crisis deepened, the kip fell further, trading between 3200 and 4200 to the dollar in early June 1998, while the government railed against 'speculators'. On 28 May the central bank officially devalued the kip, pegging it at 3120 to the dollar, but it continued to skyrocket upwards, to over 10 000 to the dollar in 1999, subsequently stabilising at around 8000. In another ironic twist, at around the same time as the devaluation of the kip the government released new 2000 and 5000 kip banknotes, emblazoned with portraits of the late communist leader, Kaysone. Their value halved even before they entered the market. The collapse of the kip hit government workers and urban dwellers hard and the mood of the populace became one of sullen helplessness. The extent to which companies and elite families became indebted through borrowing 'easy money' from Thailand is unknown because of the lack of transparency in the financial system.

In 1998, work on all projects in the Mekong sub-region was suspended as the Asian Development Bank moved to contribute to loan packages to bail out cash-strapped countries. In Laos itself, foreign investment projects were either suspended or cancelled, and trade slumped. In other words, the sources Khamthai had been banking on to lift Lao incomes evaporated, and to avert bankruptcy the LPDR was once again thrown back on the generosity of international donors. The fundamentals in Laos had changed little in 25 years. Attempts to expand the internal revenue base through improved taxation had largely failed in the face of stagnant rural incomes; even where massive profits had been made they often went untaxed because the people making this money were linked directly or indirectly to the elite and not interested in contributing to the general welfare.

## Public graft and corruption

What proliferated in the 1990s more swiftly than many people anticipated was public graft and corruption, but a different kind of corruption to that practised during the 'high communist' period. Then, high party officials all had access to foreign goods denied to ordinary citizens, through diplomatic stores and special procurement apparatuses, power giving direct access to privileges in a range of areas. The communist elite has been no less immune to the perks of power than the leaders of the RLG. The main difference was that elite privileges under communism were even more exclusive. The new policies, however, diversified the sources of corruption. The rapid growth in businesses being established by Lao and foreigners, both separately and jointly, quickly overloaded an unprepared and cumbersome bureaucratic apparatus. Businesspeople required permits for exporting and importing, trade licences, travel documents, timber concessions, and so on. For many situations there were no clear directives, and graft quickly short-circuited bottlenecks and hold-ups, so that payment for 'services rendered' became expected at all levels. At the higher levels these payments were by no means small. One foreign businessman I spoke with in Vientiane in the mid-1990s said his company had paid US$30 000 into the overseas bank account of one high government official. Others have reported kickbacks running into the hundreds of thousands—while the monthly salary of an ordinary government worker at the time was less than US$50 per month.

Corruption was also evident in the policy of privatising state-owned industries, announced in 1988. Initially privatisation proceeded slowly, as few investors wished to purchase these enterprises, and from 1990 the emphasis shifted towards leasing them, despite the attendant problems this has for long-term capital formation. By 1994 most of the major state enterprises had been privatised, and at the end of the year ministries and provincial governments were given powers to close non-profitable enterprises and sell their equipment. Privatisation was not carried out by public bidding, however, but by direct contact with interested parties. This left the whole process open to corruption, and further consolidated the holdings of a new capitalist class.

Graft and corruption remain endemic in the LPRP and the government, and many people outside the Party realise that being part of the Party means having access to the financial perks, high or low, that go with office. This is probably the main reason why people continue to join the Party. In one sense the Party is a mega-*phu nyai* that presides over a system in which the Leninist ethos keeps the factionalism of multi-party *phu nyai* politics in check, not only by rigid discipline but also by rewarding its entourage with state-financed perks, such as fine houses and cars in the upper echelons and protection for the often-shady business dealings of wives and relatives.

In China the term 'Red Princes' has been coined to describe the children of the communist elite who engage in financial wheeling and dealing. This term has a special irony in Laos because in November 2000 the eldest son of the 'Red Prince' Souphanouvong, Khamsai Souphanouvong, Minister in charge of state enterprises attached to the PM's office, was granted asylum in New Zealand. Since his father's death in 1995 Khamsai had begun to lose out in the *phu nyai* politics of the Party. Leaving behind considerable property, a large house and expensive cars, he is rumoured to have absconded with millions of dollars for a secret arms deal which he was conducting at the behest of the PM. No one in Laos has been forthcoming with facts on the case.

# One step forward, two steps backward

The collapse of Comecon aid was disastrous for the armed forces of Laos, as it had been their main source of modern equipment. Because there were no obvious replacement overseas supporters (although the

Chinese, latterly, have stepped in), other means had to be found to raise the money required to support them. Thus, as part of the new economic mechanism, the generals went into business. Besides hydro-electricity, forestry exports have been one of Laos's main earners of hard cash. The easing of restrictions on the export of timber and forest products saw a rapid expansion of the forestry sector in the first half of the 1990s, mainly benefiting military enterprises. Rights to large swathes of Lao forests are held by the army company DAFI in the south, Phathana Khet Phoudoi in the centre and Phathana Kasikam Hob Dane in the north. The extent of illegal logging by these companies, or their involvement in illegal deals with neighbouring Vietnam or Cambodia, is unknown. In 1998, Global Witness, an environmental NGO, claimed: 'Laos is deliberately flouting its commitment to prevent illegal log imports from Cambodia, and both Cambodia and Laos will try to dupe Thailand into believing the logs are from Laos.' In other areas it is claimed Vietnamese companies are allowed into Lao forests under the protection of the Lao army. The most notorious figure so far associated with this entrepreneurialisation of the army has been General Cheng Sayavong, who led the Phathana Khet Phoudoi from his base in Lak Sao, Khammouan Province, until his dismissal in early 1998. The company had accumulated a fleet of huge Russian helicopters for lifting rare timber out of remote areas for sale to Japan, and also owns three freighters that ferry lumber from Vinh and Danang in Vietnam to Japan. The control of the region by his soldiers led to sustained rumours that he was involved in the drug trade, an always tempting source of wealth in Laos. Cheng's relocation to head the Lao Tourism Authority in early 1998, amid rumours of corruption in the company, was apparently related to Party fears that he was becoming too autonomous. The importance of former generals in the Lao government in the 1990s, most prominently Khamthai as Prime Minister, and President from early 1998, and replaced as Prime Minister by another former general, Sisavat Keobounphan, underlines the growing interpenetration of the armed forces, the Party and the state.

Some commentators have speculated about the convergence of the political systems of the military dictatorship in Myanmar and the Party dictatorship in Laos, especially given the warm relations that developed between the two regimes in the late 1990s. Today, however, the LPDR looks remarkably like the Thai 'bureaucratic polity' that developed in the 1950s and 1960s rather than the Myanmar state. Laos has stepped back in time in its attempt to move forward. The main feature of such a move is the concentration of key decisions in the bureaucracy—the administration, the army, the police—and the relative unimportance of extra-bureaucratic forces. Unlike the Stalinist state, the bureaucratic polity does not require total control of the material foundations of society, such as peasant agriculture or private businesses. It simply needs to extract from them sufficient resources to finance its essential functions. The main difference between Laos and Thailand is that in Thailand the Chinese capitalists were always more wealthy and powerful, and military strongmen were vulnerable to coups. In Laos, on the other hand, the Party welds together the military and administrative wings, and retains its totalitarian reflex. Nevertheless, surveying the political scene in Laos at the twentieth century's close, one cannot help but think that the one-time military strongman, Phoumi Nosovan, would have felt quite at home.

## Unprecedented protests

The regime's control is not absolute, however. In October 1999 an unprecedented event took place when a small group was arrested in Vientiane for planning a demonstration calling for the restoration of democracy. Up to 20 people were rounded up before the demonstration, planned for the end of Buddhist Lent on 6 October, got off the ground. There were no reports about the incident in Laos itself, but government denials of the arrests became implausible after several participants in the movement arrived in Thailand and gave interviews to journalists there. They have since gone to the USA. Oddly, the Lao government came under little foreign pressure to discuss the incident.

Then early in 2000 a mystery bombing campaign began. Small bombs were detonated at various locations around the capital, with only a few casualties, but were enough to signal that the Lao state was no longer omnipotent. In July 2000 there was a quixotic incursion from the Thai town of Chong Mek into the opposite Lao border post, involving about 60 'resistance' soldiers who seemed to think they could provoke a general uprising. They had obviously misread the signs coming from inside Laos. Their naivete was revealed most dramatically when they agreed with the Lao army to release the hostages they were holding, after being given assurances of safe passage. These assurances were broken immediately and five of the raiders were killed as they retreated. The raid was a godsend for the Lao regime—finally, after the October demonstration and the mysterious bombings, the LPDR had an identifiable enemy. All the old slogans about defending the country were dusted off, along with patriotic and revolutionary songs, to fill the airwaves and squash any internal dissension or doubts inside Laos itself. The LPDR also tried to implicate Thailand in the raid, and launched a good old fashioned anti-Thai campaign.

Concern with potential dissent had arisen a couple of years earlier, leading to a crackdown on Christian groups throughout the country. On 30 January 1998, for example, 44 people were arrested during a Bible meeting held at the evangelical Church of Christ in Vientiane. Foreigners arrested at the meeting were immediately expelled from Laos, while ten Lao were sentenced for periods of one to three years' imprisonment for allegedly creating 'a disturbance which poses a danger to society . . .'—that is, they refused to bring their activities under the umbrella of the NLSX. Surveillance of Christian groups continues.

Government military action against the Hmong had left a pool of bitterness, and sporadic conflict with agents of the state has never ceased. In early 2000, however, resentment erupted in Xiang Khoang, over land disputes and other problems between Hmong and ethnic Lao, and over resettlement programmes. The tensions of several years suddenly boiled over into intense and extensive fighting, and it was reported that Vietnamese troops had been called back into the country for the first time since the late 1980s to help quell the insurgents. AFP journalist Steve Kirby reported from Muang Khun, Xiang Khoang, in August:

> Residents say five people were killed, two of them children, and 14 wounded the night the rebels came. Ashes are all that remain of the 17 homes that once faced the central market . . . 'Around 20 of them came into town firing their guns in the air and shouting,' said Chai, 18, as she tended a makeshift tea stall in the charred remains of her home. 'We all just ran out and hid while they ransacked and burned our homes,' said Chai. 'It was a real shock—nothing like this had ever happened in our town until this year,' said Thit Bounphan, who runs the town's biggest cafe. 'There are two army garrisons near the town, but they didn't stop the attack. Now we've got our own armed guards but people are still too scared to leave their homes at night.'[52]

The government denied that there was a serious problem and tried to blame 'bandits'.

This sudden upsurge of dissent and resistance from within the country represented no great threat to the state. Unlike Thailand, where economic development produced a relatively large and politically conscious middle class that demanded democracy, in Laos the middle class is very small and urban based, and the army is recruited from poor country lads who can be marched into the cities at any time to crush upstart protesters. Independent forms of political or social organisation remain outlawed and coordination of dissent is almost impossible. It would seem that Laos is condemned to the long march through authoritarian rule of the kind some politicians and thinkers believe is necessary, if not inevitable, for developing countries.

No doubt RLG leaders such as Prince Souvanna Phouma and King Savang Vatthana, who wished to establish a constitutional democracy, would be pained to see in Laos today what looks very much like the regime they sought to avoid in the early 1960s, a country which seems to have moved only in a circle over the past 40 years. Yet important changes may be on the horizon. The population of Laos is small relative to any of the states that surround it, where social, cultural, economic and political transformations are occurring, sometimes at breathtaking pace. The larger international forces bearing down on Laos may compel it to change in the future at a pace none of us now can anticipate.

# 6
# LAOS IN THE MODERN WORLD

In the 1980s an economic boom gathered pace in Asia, and in Thailand in particular. Laos was drawn into the region economically and politically when it joined ASEAN in 1997. These outside influences are levers for change within the country. The tens of thousands of Lao who fled the country to make new lives in the west have, in time, become a force for social and economic change back in Laos. Few of their children, however, see a future in Laos. The coalition government of 1973 was supposed to be a vehicle for reconciliation, instead the communist victory divided Laos radically. Reconciliation remains an aim for the future.

# The region

Globalisation is in the process of transforming Laos's relations with the world at large. The most immediate and visible effects of this are regional, and the geopolitical and economic realities in play since the late 1980s have caused economic and cultural contacts with Thailand to flourish. Thailand's economic influence over Laos is partly the outcome of the country's rapid growth during the halcyon days of the Asian boom, while Laos was still 'building socialism'. This has led to concern in Lao circles about Thai 'economic domination' and, yoked to the demands of nationalism, has diverted discussion from exploring the possibility of more formal economic cooperation between the two countries. Some arrangement along the lines of some kind of economic union sometime in the future seems unavoidable, however.

Equally worrying for the LPRP has been the rapid democratisation of Thai society throughout the 1990s. The growth of a large and confident Thai middle class as a result of Thailand's economic transformation not only produced clear demands for democracy, but also gave rise to sophisticated discourses on culture and society, and on Thai history. These are not only changing Thai perceptions of themselves, but also their perceptions of the region and of Laos. As the Thai grapple with the consequences of many years of authoritarian rule and rapid capitalist development, with all the social and cultural dislocations and problems these have caused, they are inclined to look nostalgically towards a Laos whose cultural practices seem to embody a world they have lost. Thai tourists now make pilgrimages to this 'lost world' in search of solace. Other Thai, awash with aggressive modernisation, see the Lao as backward country hicks, the butt of jokes (to which, naturally, the Lao are hyper-sensitive).

The Lao are equally ambivalent about the Thai. On the one hand they admire their modernity and sophistication, which since the late 1980s they have avidly followed via Thai TV. On the other hand, via this same medium, they are exposed daily to all of the most unattractive and frightening consequences of Thailand's rapid economic ascent—which the Lao characterise as typically Thai, whether they be problems of drug addiction, gangsterism, prostitution, corruption or marital breakdown. Lao leaders seem to think that authoritarian rule is the way to protect Laos from these dire consequences, but it is no more likely to be successful than was authoritarian rule in Thailand. Authoritarian rule prevents frank and open discussion of such social problems, and in communist systems the discouragement of voluntary associations to deal with social problems means that they are usually dealt with even less adequately than elsewhere.

The close historical, social and cultural links between Thailand and Laos will ensure that ambivalence marks their relationship for

*The Thai King presents robes to monks at That Luang during his 1994 visit. Behind him stand the Queen and Princess Sirindhorn. (Courtesy K.P.L.)*

many years to come. Lao nationalism has always had to distinguish itself primarily from the Thai, and the existence of a distinct monarchy during the period of the RLG provided a clear cultural anchor point. The intellectuals and politicians who created Lao nationalism in the 1940s were supremely confident in their dealings with the Thai, and the intelligentsia of the 1960s could engage the Thai on equal terms. When the communist revolution destroyed these particular supports, it did not matter much initially, in that Lao nationalism became closely tied to the socialist project, and the boundary between Thailand and Laos was sharply marked by political differences. Once the Lao state began to 're-traditionalise', the boundary blurred again. In the absence of a monarchy, many Lao have taken a deep interest in the goings-on of the Thai monarchy, and the visit of the Thai King to Laos in April 1994, and the regular visits of his daughter Princess Sirindhorn, have been a source of delight. It is not that Lao somehow confuse Thai royalty as Lao royalty, but the very structures of their culture draw their eyes towards them, making Thai royalty a proxy for an absent Lao royalty.

In the 1990s, as young Lao started to travel to the west for higher education, a group of intellectuals who could hold their own with the Thai began to form. It is a very small group, which still has to operate in a context in which intellectual freedom is restricted, and thus more sophisticated grounds for Thai–Lao relations cannot yet be explored. Having, albeit unwittingly, weakened Laos's ability to deal with the outside world, the LPDR has fallen back on often crude, chauvinistic and dogmatic assertions as a basis for nationalism, encouraging an almost paranoid obsession with distinguishing Lao culture from Thai. Only the growth of intellectual confidence inside Laos will mute this dogmatism.

Back in 1947 Katay, contemplating the country's economic vulnerability while at the same time asserting its place as a new nation, looked forward to a time when Lao 'could dream of much later, following the example of Switzerland and the United States of

America [one would add the EU today], a confederation of states of Southeast Asia (Siam, Burma, Malaysia, Cambodia, Laos, Vietnam, etc.).' This prescient idea would come to pass in 1997 with the entry of Laos into ASEAN. It was a watershed event, drawing the country into a wider regional orbit that will help balance the obviously unequal relationship between the Thai and the Lao. Here too the Lao found themselves intellectually unprepared, and ASEAN stepped in to help with training for their new tasks. Laos entered ASEAN just as the regional body had diversified in its political views and was confronted by complex political and economic questions that it had not anticipated. Paralleling the political structure of ASEAN are ambitious plans to crisscross mainland Southeast Asia with a system of road and rail links, indeed a road system that runs from Kunming in Yunnan to Singapore. The Asian economic crisis stalled some of these projects, but only temporarily. The Lao government began to talk of the country as 'land-linked' rather than 'land-locked', and hopes to benefit economically from the growth of the regional economy. Besides bringing fundamental changes to Laos in the coming decade, such developments will place further strains on centralisation as provinces engage directly in regional trade. This will present one more challenge to the durability of authoritarian rule.

The modern Lao state has always been economically weak and dependent on outside support. Multilateral and bilateral aid is fundamental to its survival and will remain so for the foreseeable future. Foreign organisations have an important say over the future direction of Lao development, although they try to be discreet. In this sense the nationalist utopia of pure sovereignty is remote in Laos, and its vulnerability to outside forces occasionally produces knee-jerk reactions against 'foreign interference'. Unlike the RLG period, the states surrounding Laos today are committed to its stability and therefore to its survival. Stability has allowed the government, with the help of foreign aid, to engage in a vigorous programme of road building vital to the country's integration. This and other aid programmes have

229

*Future roads and railways for mainland Southeast Asia. The planned expansion of road and rail links across the region in the coming decades is likely to have a profound effect on Laos internally and externally.*

gradually strengthened the hold of the central government, while stability and then some prosperity in the 1990s has reinforced its legitimacy. Other influences flowing in from the outside challenge the hegemony of the LPRP, while it remains to be seen whether the ethnic divisions will erupt in political confrontation. Here the activities of 'long distance' ethnic nationalists abroad may prove crucial.

# The diaspora

The haemorrhage of people from Laos following the revolution was only comparable with the forced deportations of the Chao Anou period, although then the furthest people were transported was to the southern isthmus of Thailand. By contrast, the destinations of the refugees who left Laos during and after 1975 were the advanced capitalist countries of the world: the US, France, Australia, Sweden, New Zealand and so on. There was one exception; a colony of Hmong was established in Guyana. International travel had previously been confined mainly to the elite, but now Lao from all walks of life found themselves in faraway lands about which they knew very little. Here they began to build their lives anew and to create a global sense of 'Laoness'.

Refugee camps are dispiriting anywhere, yet most felt they were better than staying on in Laos and few volunteered to be repatriated. Many Lao spent years in the camps waiting for resettlement, and only those who already had kin abroad were processed quickly. In the camps they began their first experiments in setting up new communities, centred around Buddhist monks for the Lao and Hmong shamans. Marriages were contracted, babies born, and death rituals carried out for those who would travel no further. Foreign aid workers prepared them for their destinations by teaching English, while others proselytised. In general, the former elite headed for France, while many members of the army, officers and soldiers alike, went to the USA. America was also the main destination for the Hmong, because it was here that Vang Pao established himself. Ultimately close to 50 000 went to France and 225 000 to the USA. Smaller refugee populations in Australia and New Zealand tended to be drawn from the ranks of ordinary Lao. Approximately two-thirds of those who left were lowland Lao, the others from upland groups.

The establishment of a new Lao community in a foreign land was easier where there were larger conglomerations of refugees who could raise the money to establish a temple whose ritual round provided a sense of familiarity and stability. Among the Hmong, clan and lineage networks provided the social ballast for their lives. Some Lao who already had relatives abroad before 1975, those who were educated and others who could capitalise on former military connections were often able to gain for themselves reasonably respectable middle-class jobs. Most of the refugees, even those who had educational qualifications, would find themselves doing menial jobs, and many relied on state welfare for years. Compared with their compatriots at home they lived well, and the flow of medicines and money back to kin in the homeland began. This repatriation of funds played a significant part in the house building and small business boom that began in Laos as the economy liberalised.

In everyday life, Lao from all social strata were equal citizens of whatever country they resided in, but in the associations that they began to form for purposes of cultural cohesion, whether they were women's associations or cultural ones, or groups planning the reconquest of their homeland, they recreated the hierarchical structures familiar to them. Men or women who held ordinary day jobs could become *phu nyai* once again at night during gatherings of these associations, in the ritual and theatre of exile recreating their lost world. The Hmong established separate associations, but in exile they found themselves on the same level as the Lao in every respect and have been compelled to identify Laos as their homeland, for all refugees must have one. Thus these two communities are driven together, but the fact that they meet on equal terms has been difficult for some Lao at least.

While those who fled Laos in their late teens or as adults were fully socialised in a Lao context and held fond and nostalgic memories of their native places, this was not true for the children who grew up bicultural and bilingual in France or America, or somewhere else. Many Lao who went into exile may have thought that it was only temporary, but the gradual integration of their children into the host society as they grew up made their exile permanent. Pressures on the young to assimilate were influenced by internal and external factors. Among the Hmong the internal pressures to maintain their identity were stronger than among the Lao. This, however, has not stopped young Hmong from becoming very successful in their host societies, especially educationally, which has created some tension with the Lao who have on the whole done less well. In France the republican tradition strongly encourages refugees to become French, an expectation negotiated with relative ease by the large numbers of the old elite who relocated there. In the USA, however, the pervasive politics of ethnicity compels young Lao to parade their ethnic heritage, and for many this creates psychological confusion. Forced by the broader culture to identify themselves as Lao–American, these young people have turned their attention to Laos, the fabled homeland. In the 1990s especially, many have made a pilgrimage back to meet relatives and to visit their parents' villages, only to find the culture strange and, for many, the language difficult. For them it is easier to be Lao in America, and in particular on the Internet. The blossoming of the Internet in the 1990s has been a boon for the Lao diaspora and websites, both collective and personal, have proliferated. These have enabled easy contact between dispersed relatives and friends abroad, and increasingly inside Laos too, thereby creating the sense of a global Lao culture. Yet the content of most websites rarely goes beyond touristic information, and some of the chat rooms are frankly depressing in their displays of ignorance of Laos itself.

Yet the traffic between the Lao overseas and the Lao inside Laos is increasingly important not only economically, but also socially and culturally, if not politically. It is a traffic in ideas and in people, and it travels both ways. Lao and Hmong men return to Laos to find wives, for women in the diaspora can marry up and out of refugee society.

Laos can also provide the material accoutrements for the continuation of Lao traditions elsewhere, especially the trade in marriage costumes, and more generally Lao textiles for women. Some offspring of the diaspora have decided to try to make their way in Laos, bringing with them a thoroughly modern outlook, and their adaptation to traditional culture and society has sometimes been difficult.

Initially, many Lao in exile saw themselves as bearers and preservers of traditional Lao culture, especially during the years of high communism when traditional ideas were under challenge and Laos appeared to them to be a Vietnamese colony. The members of the Lao royal family who went into exile formed a ritual centre around which the RLG was recreated through its annual festivals. The escape of the eldest son of the Crown Prince to France in 1979 also gave the diaspora a legitimate pretender to the throne, Prince Soulivong Savang. The movement around him is weak, however, and while Soulivong's activities are a source of interest inside Laos, few are deeply committed to him. With the 're-traditionalising' of the Lao state the *raison d'être* of those concerned with preserving Lao culture has lost much of its force, especially because the Lao government controls the key sacred spaces, such as That Luang and the Palace in Luang Phrabang, to which rituals overseas can only refer. Nevertheless, the diaspora remains an important pool of historical counter-memory to that being promoted by the LPDR. By its very nature, the diaspora must refer back to Laos itself, and in this respect it has become a new and important part of long-term change inside the country.

## History and nation

At the end of 2000 the LPDR celebrated 25 years in power, having been in government for almost as long as the RLG. In this time seismic demographic shifts occurred. The population almost doubled to over 5 million, with 62 per cent born since 1975. The LPDR is all they have known. This could be said of another 10 per cent, who were infants under the old regime. In other words, more than 70 per cent of the population has grown up with no immediate knowledge of the recent past. In the aftermath of the revolution older people were wary of talking openly, even within their families, about the RLG period. Publicly, discussion was reduced to clichés about 'neo-colonialism' and 'traitors'. A huge silence had fallen over the RLG period, almost as if it had never existed. When the political situation relaxed in the 1990s and people began to speak privately about the past, their stories were episodic and fragmented, for there was no public framework for placing this past. Even those who remained sympathetic to the RLG sometimes used words from the new regime to describe it, such as the 'imperialist regime'. School textbooks, the main mechanism for transmitting national history, contain little detail about the RLG, basically present-ing a narrative of the inevitable and triumphant rise of the LPRP. Many young Lao are uncomfortably aware that they once had a king, but know little about him or about his demise. School textbooks in many countries are notorious for their biased, nationalist representation of history, but the need in Laos to place the Communist Party at the centre of its history produces a further distortion. If to this is added the central role of one individual, as with the Kaysone personality cult, another distortion is added, blotting out, for example, the central pre-1975 role of Souphanouvong. These multiple distortions of history produce strange ellipses and silences in the various narratives and discourses found within Laos today. To the extent that there is a debate within Laos about history, it is almost all about pre-modern history— about Chao Anou, for example, or the origins of the Lao—in other words, it is safely distant from the contentiousness of modern history over which the Party still claims a strict monopoly of interpretation.

All history, even recent history, is subject to interpretation. Different historians offer varying perspectives on the past, sometimes due to different political persuasions or theoretical approaches. The rule for historians in liberal democracies is that everything we know about the past is potentially open for discussion, and no facts should be suppressed. Historians may differ about the relevant facts, or the weight given to them, but they agree on their open and free discussion. Absence of political *diktat* allows the growth of an intellectual culture where people can disagree, for example about national history, without feeling their world fall apart. And perhaps this is a sign of a mature nationalism. Recall Somphavan Inthavong's words, writing of Lao lack of confidence in dealing with the outside world: 'It is this distrust or this reserve that our friends confound with nationalism. But Lao nationalism, if that is what it is, still lacks the maturity which would produce actions that are profound and positive.' One might say that only when Lao can look back at their past in all its complexity, and debate its meaning without restraint, will nationalism have achieved the maturity Somphavan was yearning for. Hopefully this book will help Lao in this necessary process of looking back in order to look forward more clearly and confidently.

But history is more than intellectual contemplation, it is equally a set of social and cultural practices. The missed opportunity for reconciliation in 1975 awaits its final ritual resolution. We will know that this has occurred when the bones of King Sisavang Vatthana are exhumed from their secret resting place in the mountains and returned to Luang Phrabang. The chants of the monks echoing through the temples of the ancient capital, sending the *vinyan* ('soul') of the King on its way, will heal the deep rift in the Lao nation caused by the revolution.

# NOTES

1. Cited by Charles Archaimbault, 'La naissance du monde selon les traditions Lao: Le mythe de Khun Bulom', in Charles Archaimbault, *Structures Religieuses Lao*, Editions Vithagna, Vientiane, 1973, p. 100.
2. Cited in 'Two Accounts of Travels in Laos in the 17th Century', prefaced and annotated by Paul Lévy, in *Kingdom of Laos*, edited by René de Berval, France-Asie, Saigon, 1959, p. 55.
3. Cited in Sila Viravong, *History of Laos*, Paragon Press, New York, 1964, pp. 125–6.
4. Cited from an annotated translation of *Leup Pha Sun* by Peter Koret, yet to be published.
5. Cited in Snit Smuckarn and Kennon Breazeale, *A Culture in Search of Survival: The Phuan of Thailand and Laos*, Monograph Series 31/ Yale University Southeast Asian Studies, New Haven, 1988, p. 25.
6. James McCarthy, *Surveying and exploring in Siam: With descriptions of Lao Dependencies and of battles against the Chinese Haws*, introduction by Walter E.J. Tips, White Lotus, Bangkok, 1994, (c1900), p. 51.
7. Cited in Patrick Tuck, *The French Wolf and the Siamese Lamb: The French Threat to Siamese Independence 1858–1907*, White Lotus, Bangkok, 1995, p. 195.
8. S.P. Nginn, *Nostalgie du Passé: Les mémoires du Professeur Somchine P. Nginn*, Fondation Somchine Nginn (Vientiane), 1971, p. 20. The original title of this text, which was writtin in Lao, is *Aditanuson (kithortbeunglang)*.
9. Cited in Yang Dao, *Les Difficultés du Developpement Économique et Social des Populations Hmong du Laos*, Thèse de Doctorat de 3ᵉ Cycle, Université de Paris, Avril 1972, p. 73.

10. Cited in Jean Lartéguy avec le collaboration de Yang Dao, *La Fabuleuse Aventure du Peuple de l'Opium*, Presses de la Cité, 1979, p. 94.

11. Louis-Charles Royer, *Kham: la Laotienne*, Editions Kailash, Paris, 1997 (originally published by Éditions de Paris, 1935), p. 261.

12. Katay D. Sasorith, *Souvenirs d'un Ancien Écolier de Paksé*, Éditions Lao Sédone, 1958, pp. 22–3.

13. S.P. Nginn, 'Comment j'ai vu la France', *Kinnary: revue de culture franco-lao*, No. 3, Octobre 1943.

14. Letter: 'Sa Majesté Sisavang-Vong, Roi de Luang-Phrabang a Madame Auguste Pavie à Paris, le 18 Octobre, 1927', held in the Centre des Archives d'Outre-Mer, Aîx en Provence, France.

15. Gaston Strarbach and Antonin Baudenne, *Sao Tiampa, épouse lao-tienne*, Éditions Kailash, Paris, France, 1997 (originally published by Éditions Grasset, Paris, 1912), pp. 106–7.

16. André Escoffier, *Dans le Laos au Chant des Khènes*, Imprimerie d'Extrême Orient, Hanoi, 1942, p. 192.

17. Jeanne Cuisinier, 'La grande pitié des Buddhas au Laos', *Revue Indochinoise Illustrée*, nouvelle série, Numéro 25, Juillet 1925, p. 6.

18. Cited in A. Raquez, *Pages Laotiennes*, F.H. Schneider, Imprimeur-Éditeur, Hanoi, 1902, pp. 102–3.

19. Cited in Eric Pietrantoni, 'Le Problème Politique du Laos', unpublished report, Vientiane, 1943, p. 101.

20. Charles Rochet, *Pays Lao: Le Laos dans le Tourmente 1939–1945*, Jean Vigneau, Éditeur, Paris, 1946, pp. 74–5.

21. Thao Katay, *Contribution à l'Histoire du Mouvement d'Independence Nationale Lao*, Éditions Lao-Issara, Bangkok, 1948, p. 77.

22. Houmpanh Saignasith, 'Essai de Contribution à l'Histoire Politique Contemporaine du Laos. Souvernirs personnels pendant la 2è Guerre Mondiale (période de 1941 à 1945) et Le Mouvement Lao Issara (de 1945 à Mai 1946)', Paris, 1991. (roneo)

23. Graham Greene, *Ways of Escape*, The Bodley Head, London, 1980, pp. 170–3.

24. Oden Meeker, *The Little World of Laos*, Charles Scribner's Sons, New York, 1959, p. 32.

25. Cited in Joel Halpern, 'Economic Development and American Aid in Laos', *Practical Anthropology*, Vol. 6, No. 4, 1959, p. 158.

26. ibid., pp. 159–60.

27. Quoted by Haynes Miller, 'A Bulwark Built on Sand', *The Reporter*, November 13, 1958, p. 11.

28. Hugh Toye, *Laos: Buffer State or Battleground*, Oxford University Press, London, 1968, p. 147.

29. Cited in Arthur J. Dommen, *Conflict in Laos: The Politics of Neutralization*, Revised edition, Praeger Publishers, New York, 1971, p. 182.

30. Report from Ambassador Young, US Embassy Bangkok to the State Department, May 5, 1962. (National Archives, Maryland, Washington DC.)

31. Cited in Georges Chapelier and Josyane Van Malderghem, 'Plain of Jars: Social Changes Under Five Years of Pathet Lao Administration', *Asia Quarterly*, Vol. 1, 1971, p. 74.

32. Cited in Paul F. Langer and Joseph J. Zasloff, *North Vietnam and the Pathet Lao: Partners in the Struggle for Laos*, Harvard University Press, Cambridge, Massachusetts, 1970, p. 127.

33. ibid., pp. 144–5.

34. Mervyn Brown, 'An Involuntary Tour of Southern Laos', July 2, 1962. One of two reports submitted to the US embassy in Vientiane, acknowledged in their dispatch to the State Department on July 14, 1962. (National Archives, Maryland, Washington DC.)

35. 'Biographie deČàu Sai K'àm, chef de province de S'ieng Khwang', Appendice, Charles Archaimbault, 'Les Annales de l'Ancien Royaume de S'ieng Khwang', *Bulletin de l'École Française d'Éxtrême Orient*, Vol. 53, 1966–67, p. 660.

36. *Touby Lyfoung: An authentic account of the life of a Hmong man in the troubled land of Laos*, an autobiography by Touby Lyfoung, edited by Dr Touxa Lyfoung, Burgess Publishing, United States, 1996, p. 138.

37. ibid., pp. 143–4.
38. Don A. Schanche, *Mister Pop: The adventures of a peaceful man in a small war*, David McKay Company, Inc., New York, 1970, pp. 88–9.
39. Cited in *Voices From the Plain of Jars: Life under an Air War*, compiled with an Introduction and Preface by Fred Branfman, Harper Colophon Books, New York, 1972, pp. 112–13.
40. Somphavan Inthavong, 'Un homme est mort', *Lao Comme Liberté, Impressions 1965–1970*, Vientiane, 1972, p. 10.
41. Somphavan Inthavong, 'Les Hippies et la pluie', *Lao Comme Liberté, Impressions 1965–1970*, Vientiane, 1972, p. 36.
42. Somphavan Inthavong, 'Nationalisme et developpment', *Lao Comme Liberté, Impressions 1965–1970*, Vientiane, 1972, p. 27.
43. Alfred W. McCoy with Cathleen B. Reed and Leonard P. Adams II, *The Politics of Heroin in Southeast Asia*, Harper Colophon Books, New York, 1972, p. 344.
44. Ambassador's Audience with King Savang, March 24, 1961. Despatch to the State Department March 30, 1961. (National Archives, Maryland, Washington DC.)
45. 'Laos', *Far Eastern Economic Review Asia 1975 Yearbook*, p. 208.
46. John Everingham, 'A Struggle in Microcosm', *Far Eastern Economic Review*, 9 April 1976, p. 26.
47. Thongthip Rathanavilai, *Man in the Region of Death: Passing through the five stages of hell*, Lao Press, Fresno, California (n.d.), p. 13. The original title of this text, which was written in Lao, is *Manut Pak Tay Phaan 5 Khum Nalok*.
48. ibid., pp. 23–4.
49. Charles Weldon, *Tragedy in Paradise: A country doctor at war in Laos*, Asia Books, Bangkok, 1999, p. 128.
50. Cited in Grant Evans, *Lao Peasants Under Socialism*, Yale University Press, New Haven, 1990, p. 54.
51. ibid., p. 61.
52. Steve Kirby, 'Laos' hidden rebellion in the mountains', 4 August 2000, (AFP).

# SELECTED FURTHER READING

Laos has a smaller secondary literature to draw on than almost any other country in Asia. There are a disproportionate number of books on the war in the 1960s and 1970s, but these usually have a very narrow focus. This has meant that I have had to go back to primary sources more than is usual in a short history, referring to primary Lao texts, French archives and US archives. Generally, if the source in the text is clear I have not repeated it below. Martin Stuart-Fox's *History of Laos* (Cambridge University Press) is recommended for those who wish to read more. I have only included English language texts below.

## Chapter 1: Before Laos

For the Tai see Georges Condominas, *From Lawa to Mon, from Saa' to Thai* (Research School of Pacific and Asian Studies, Australian National University, Canberra, 1990). Martin Stuart-Fox, *The Lao Kingdom of Lan Xang: Rise and Decline* (White Lotus, Bangkok, 1998) is the most recent and comprehensive account of this early period, although the author tends to read the past through the lens of the present. David K. Wyatt, *Thailand: A Short History* (Silkworm Books, Chiang Mai, 1984) is indispensable for understanding the broader historical context. See also his articles, 'Southeast Asia "Inside Out", 1300–1800: a perspective from the interior', *Modern Asian Studies*, Vol. 31, No. 3, 1997, and 'Relics, oaths and politics in thirteenth-century Siam', *Journal of Southeast Asian Studies*, Vol. 32, No. 1, 2001. For a Lao perspective on the Chao Anou revolt, see Mayoury and Pheuiphanh Ngaosyvathn, *Paths to Conflagration: Fifty Years of Diplomacy and Warfare in Laos, Thailand, and Vietnam, 1778–1828* (Southeast Asia Program Publications, Cornell University, Ithaca,

1998). Snit Smuckarn and Kennon Breazeale, A *Culture in Search of Survival: The Phuan of Thailand and Laos* (Yale University Southeast Asian Studies, New Haven, 1988) through its analysis of the fate of one group provides a guide to developments in Laos and Thailand in the late nineteenth century.

## Chapter 2: Le Laos Français

There is no dedicated study of the French in Laos, but see Virginia Thompson, *French Indochina* (George Allen and Unwin, London, 1937). Thongchai Winichakul, *Siam Mapped: A History of the Geo-body of a Nation* (Silkworm Books, Chiang Mai, 1994), helps understand how modern Thailand demarcated itself from Laos. Eugen Weber, *Peasants into Frenchmen: The Modernization of Rural France 1870–1914* (Chatto and Windus, London, 1977) is a useful comparison with Laos at the time of colonisation. Alice L. Conklin, *A Mission to Civilize: The Republican Idea of Empire in France and West Africa, 1895–1930* (Stanford University Press, California, 1997) also allows some comparison. On early Lao nationalism see Soren Ivarsson, 'Towards a New Laos: *Lao Nhay* and the Campaign for National "Re-awakening" in Laos, 1941–45', in *Laos: Culture and Society*, edited by Grant Evans (Silkworm Books University of Washington Press, 1999). Martin Shipway's *The Road To War: France and Vietnam, 1944–47* (Berghahn Books, Oxford, 1996) outlines the complex debates preceding the French return to Indochina.

## Chapter 3: The RLG and Chapter 4: War, and the destruction of the RLG

On US foreign policy and aid, see the early but excellent study by Charles A. Stevenson, *The End of Nowhere: American Policy Toward Laos Since 1954* (Beacon Press, Boston, 1972); and Timothy N. Castle, *At War in the Shadow of Vietnam: U.S. Military Aid to the Royal Lao Government, 1955–1975* (Columbia University Press, New York, 1993). Because of the almost obsessive interest in the war there is unfortunately no substantial study of US civilian aid. Two early and still excellent discussions of Lao politics are: Arthur J. Dommen, *Conflict in Laos: The Politics of Neutralization* (Praeger Publishers, New York, 1971), and Hugh Toye, *Laos: Buffer State or Battleground* (Oxford University Press, London, 1968). For an early Lao overview of events, see Sisouk Na Champasak, *Storm Over Laos: A Contemporary History* (Praeger Publishers, New York, 1961). On the communist movement, see Paul F. Langer and Joseph J. Zasloff, *North Vietnam and the Pathet Lao: Partners for the Struggle in Laos* (Harvard University Press, Mass., 1970); and MacAlister Brown and Joseph J. Zasloff, *Apprentice Revolutionaries: The Communist Movement in Laos, 1930–1985* (Hoover Institution Press, Stanford, 1986). On the Hmong, see Yang Dao, *Hmong at the Turning Point* (World Bridge Associates, Minn., 1993); and Roger Warner, *Shooting at the Moon: The Story of America's Clandestine War in Laos* (Steer Forth Press, Vermont, 1996). Donald A. Schanche's *Mister Pop: The Adventures of a Peaceful Man in a Small War* (David McKay Company Inc, New York, 1970) provides an insightful account of USAID and the Hmong. For a very early study of the Lao elite see Joel M. Halpern, *Government, Politics, and Social Structure in Laos: A Study of Tradition and Innovation* (Southeast Asia Studies, Yale University, 1964); there is, however, no study of the elite, and social and cultural changes in the 1960s and 1970s.

## Chapter 5: The Lao People's Democratic Republic

The best overview of Laos 1975–85 is Martin Stuart-Fox's *Laos: Politics, Economy and Society* (Frances Pinter, London, 1986). The other important text by Stuart-Fox is his collection of essays, *Buddhist Kingdom, Marxist State: The Making of Modern Laos* (White Lotus, Bangkok, 1996). Another book that provides a comprehensive discussion of policies in Laos 1975–85 is MacAlister Brown and Joseph J. Zasloff, *Apprentice Revolutionaries: The Communist Movement in Laos, 1930–1985* (Hoover Institution Press, Stanford, 1986). It also gives the best discussion of the role of the Vietnamese in Laos. In 1995 the

*Area Handbook for Laos*, last published in 1971 by the US Department of the Army, appeared in an entirely new edition as *Laos: A Country Study*, edited by Andrea Matlas Savada (Department of the Army, Washington, 1995). A more focused text is Grant Evans, *Lao Peasants Under Socialism* (Yale University Press, New Haven, 1990) which is the one comprehensive discussion of the failed attempt to collectivise agriculture in Laos. Grant Evans, *The Politics of Ritual and Remembrance: Laos Since 1975* (Silkworm Books/University of Hawaii Press, 1998) is a political anthropology of the regime and an analysis of cultural change. *Laos: Culture and Society*, edited by Grant Evans (Silkworm Books/University of Washington Press, 1999) contains a range of essays from language to minorities. The most comprehensive economic survey is by Yves Bourdet, *The Economics of Transition in Laos* (Edward Elgar, Cheltenham, UK, 2000). See also *Laos' Dilemmas and Options: The Challenge of Economic Transition in the 1990s*, edited by Mya Than and Joseph L.H. Tan (ISEAS, Singapore, 1997). The reference to the 'bureaucratic polity' follows J.L.S. Girling, *The Bureaucratic Polity in Modernizing Societies* (ISEAS, Singapore, 1981).

## Chapter 6: Laos in the modern world

For an overview, see Martin Stuart-Fox, 'Laos: towards subregional integration', in *Southeast Asian Affairs 1995* (ISEAS, Singapore, 1985), but also Yves Bourdet, *The Economics of Transition in Laos* (Edward Elgar, Cheltenham, UK, 2000). Andrew Walker provides an illuminating ethnographic account of regional relations in *The Legend of the Golden Boat: Regulation, Trade and Traders in the Borderlands of Laos, Thailand, China and Burma* (Curzon, London, 1999). On refugees, see Penny Van Esterik, *Taking Refuge: Lao Buddhist in North America* (Monographs in Southeast Asian Studies, Arizona State University, 1992), and Lili Sisombat Souvannavong, 'Elites in exile: transnational Lao culture', in *Laos: Culture and Society*, edited by Grant Evans (Silkworm Books, Chiang Mai, 1999). On Hmong refugees see Lynellyn D. Long, *Ban Vinai: The Refugee Camp* (Columbia University Press, New York, 1993).

# INDEX